Just Interests

ELGAR STUDIES IN LAW AND SOCIETY

Elgar Studies in Law and Society brings together critical and thought-provoking works by scholars from around the globe, on the most pressing topics and issues within the field of Law and Society. The books in this series reflect original, cutting-edge scholarship on aspects of the Law's role in modern society and its intersection with social structures and institutions, such as politics, gender, race, religion and ethics.

The U.S. Supreme Court and Racial Minorities
Two Centuries of Judicial Review on Trial
Leslie F. Goldstein

Just Interests
Victims, Citizens and the Potential for Justice
Robyn Holder

Just Interests

Victims, Citizens and the Potential for Justice

Robyn Holder

Griffith University, Australia

ELGAR STUDIES IN LAW AND SOCIETY

Edward Elgar PUBLISHING

Cheltenham, UK • Northampton, MA, USA

Published by
Edward Elgar Publishing Limited
The Lypiatts
15 Lansdown Road
Cheltenham
Glos GL50 2JA
UK

Edward Elgar Publishing, Inc.
William Pratt House
9 Dewey Court
Northampton
Massachusetts 01060
USA

A catalogue record for this book
is available from the British Library

Library of Congress Control Number: 2018931711

This book is available electronically in the **Elgar**online
Law subject collection
DOI 10.4337/9781786434036

MIX
Paper from responsible sources
FSC® C013056

ISBN 978 1 78643 402 9 (cased)
ISBN 978 1 78643 403 6 (eBook)

Typeset by Columns Design XML Ltd, Reading
Printed and bound in Great Britain by TJ International Ltd, Padstow, Cornwall

For John and Annette Holder

Contents

Figures

Tables

Preface

DAVID: CITIZEN, VICTIM AND HIS POTENTIAL FOR JUSTICE

David[1] was one of the people interviewed for this book. His is a story difficult to classify. If the system does prefer 'ideal' victims then David is not one of them. He would not see himself as a victim. He said he was able to look after himself. He articulated a number of motivations in turning to the law following an incident of violence against him, and expressed preferences for what he wanted to see happen. To these he gave reasons and context.

Over the course of three interviews, David used his experiences with the justice entities he encountered to reflect on the idea of justice and how it applied to people like him. It is David's own references to his membership of the community that inspired the radical re-positioning of victims as citizens in this book.

I first met David after a neighbour had threatened him with a knife and after police had charged that person with an offence. David was living in a small, public-sector apartment in the city. Though it was a bright day, the curtains were drawn, the air was smoky and David was sleepy. Asked why he turned to the law after the incident, he said he wanted to make the person go away and this seemed the easiest way. But he also said he 'was raised not to "dog" and not go to the cops. But now I haven't offended for four years or more and am trying to work and was worried about my girlfriend'. When I asked about his idea of justice prior to the incident he said it was about 'police and the court system'. Perhaps these images were to the forefront of his mind in part because David also had a prior history of non-violent offending (fraud, drugs). He thought 'cops' understood crime but that magistrates were 'too soft'. He wanted his neighbour to 'do as much time as possible' for the offence against him. 'Punishment' was the principle he prioritized. On this occasion, I was struck by his frankness about his past and about himself.

---

[1] All names used in this book for the lay participants are pseudonyms.

The second time I interviewed David, some ten months later, he was staying temporarily with his mother. I could not ignore the fresh injuries to his face from another assault. Perhaps it was this alongside what he said on this occasion that made me more aware of how articulate he was. By that stage the earlier case had finished and I asked him about both the prosecution and the court. He had given evidence and the person had been acquitted. He said, 'I'll never call the cops again. It was a waste of time and effort.' He went on to say that:

> I wanted to change my life and I went to the police but its left a bad taste. They did their best but there wasn't enough evidence. We all waited around, I gave evidence but they brought up my old mental health history and that I wasn't a competent witness.

He said that, when he had been offending, 'they treated me well and kept me out of prison'. This time, he felt he had been discriminated against and treated 'unfairly'. He reckoned 'if it had been a little old lady threatened, it would have been different ... they would have put a more experienced lawyer on it'. The young prosecutor, David said, did not respond to the attacks on him. As an offender, he said he had barristers defending him. This time, 'because I was an ex-offender, live in public housing and am a young man there was no effort in it'.

On the third occasion, at our final interview a further six months later (and some 16 months since the actual incident), David and his girlfriend had been allocated a new house by the Housing Department in a new suburb. It was far away from his old life but he reiterated he would not call for help again except 'if it was someone else then maybe'. Again he said:

> if it was an old lady they would have done something. Maybe they think because of my history. It's much harder as a victim. I guarantee you that ... I wouldn't call or help them. I've never really felt like a member of the community really. Living in refuges etcetera you feel like a piece of shit. You get looked at. I'd deal with it myself next time.

Reflecting on being a participant in the process David said:

> I was always there. I did what I was required to do and testify and meet the prosecutor in advance. I wanted to change who I was and didn't want to hurt others ... I see it's not like the movies or TV. It's based on money and circumstances.

Asked if he thought 'justice had been done', David said, 'if they try its sort of being done. They invest money and time but the way they treat the victim isn't justified. You get torn to pieces on the stand. It's ridiculous.' His final comments were that:

> Before I thought I had a choice to be a responsible citizen but now I see it's also how they see you. Is it about the past or the circumstances of the past? I can understand it to want to help an old lady rather than me. Unless we design a computer program, we can never be objective or completely fair to everyone. There are definitely differences between rich and poor. It's hypocritical.

A person such as David (or any of the 33 lay people interviewed) is generally not allowed the luxury of self-representation, and almost certainly not in the public space of criminal justice. As a citizen-victim his capacity for reflexive and contextualized thinking is untapped. There is no room provided for thinking such as David's that unfolds; nor for thinking that connects with different objects of value or different principles important in his life. The capacity, capability and embeddedness of a person such as David is rich in potential for justice.

In the rigid and scripted confines of criminal justice, socially and politically situated reflections such as David's are routinely ignored. Whether he is an 'ideal victim' or a 'good citizen' or neither of these, David is simply a *thing* in the institutional space.

David is a critical thinker about his world where a focusing event – and process – has served to shift generalized opinion to something specific. Arguably both justice and democracy require just such critical thinkers. David is also explicit in drawing attention to his social and political status. These senses of himself exist prior, during and after his engagement with justice as a victim: 'it's how they see you', he says. So this story is also then about a relationship with 'they' – power-holders who represent the state.

Acknowledgements

I am fortunate to have a long list of acknowledgements to make. Without the men and women who gave so openly of their time and their views as participants in both the criminal justice process and in the research on which this book is based, it would not have been written. I am deeply grateful. None of you are in any way ordinary. The prosecutors I interviewed in Australia and the UK were very generous with their time and thoughtful reflection. Prosecution is an enormously difficult job. Thankfully it attracts great minds and committed practitioners who think deeply on the public interest.

At Griffith University, Queensland, I have had the benefit of thoughtful critique and encouragement over a sustained period from Professors Kathleen Daly and Susanne Karstedt. I could not ask for better guides. Professor Kristina (Tina) Murphy patiently guided me through her dataset and my many questions. The Griffith Criminology Institute (GCI) has provided me with scholarly and practical support over a number of years. Colleagues in the GCI, the School of Criminology and Criminal Justice, and at Griffith Law School were always ready with insightful and critical comment. I am grateful to have been awarded a Griffith University Postdoctoral Fellowship which enabled me to finish the book.

At The Australian National University (ANU) in Canberra I owe a great debt to Professor Peter Grabosky. Peter has a particular skill in drawing one's attention to fields of enquiry that, on first blush, appear unrelated but, when read, are anything but. Encouraging thinking 'outside the box' is also an attribute of Professors Valerie Braithwaite and John Braithwaite; they are ever stimulating. Val's work on the micro-foundations of Australian democracy is a model research programme. She was hugely helpful in discussing what mattered between citizens and authorities and allowing me to use her dataset. Professor Sally Engle Merry, as an Honorary Professor at ANU's Regulatory Institutions Network (RegNet), helped my thinking about the representation of research subjects in longitudinal research. Brigitte Bouhours and Lisa Stewart gave invaluable statistical assistance. I thank Professors Rod Broadhurst and Geraldine Mackenzie for access to their national sentencing dataset, and Thierry Bouhours for helping with the analysis. Thanks also to RegNet colleagues Steve Chon, Seung-hun Hong, Romina Paskotic, Kristina Simion, and Christoph Sperfeldt. Dr Sally Knowles was a wonderful teacher of academic writing.

Professor Julie Stubbs at the University of New South Wales encouraged my turn to political theory. Professor John Dryzek, then at ANU, provided enormous early help in talking through with me the difference between participation and deliberation, provided with me a prepublication version of his engagement with Amartya Sen's book, *The Idea of Justice*; and put me on to Jane Mansbridge's work. Dr Elaine Fishwick (University of Sydney), and Professors Jonathan Doak (University of Nottingham) and Meg Garvin (Lewis and Clark Law School) were insightful critical readers.

I am grateful for permissions to reproduce some materials. An earlier and more expansive version of Chapter 7, including the figures, appeared in Robyn Holder, 'Satisfied? Exploring Victims' Justice Judgements' (2015) in the edited collection from Dean Wilson and Stuart Ross, *Crime, Victims and Policy: International Contexts, Local Experiences* reproduced with permission by Palgrave Macmillan. Figure 6.1 and aspects of the methodology described in the Appendix appeared in Robyn Holder, 'Untangling the Meanings of Justice: A Longitudinal Mixed Methods Study' (2016), *Journal of Mixed Methods Research* (online), a Sage journal. Portions of Chapter 3 appeared in Robyn Holder, 'Victims, Legal Consciousness, and Legal Mobilisation' (2017) in the edited collection from Antje Deckert and Rick Sarre, *The Palgrave Handbook of Australian and New Zealand Criminology, Crime, and Justice* reproduced with permission by Palgrave Macmillan. Aspects of Chapters 6 and 8 appeared in Robyn Holder and Kathleen Daly, 'Sequencing Justice: A Longitudinal Study of Justice Goals of Domestic Violence Victims' (2017), *British Journal of Criminology*, Oxford University Press (online).

The research could not have been done without the trust and support provided to me by the staff at the ACT Domestic Violence Crisis Service and the Victim Liaison Officers in ACT Policing. Also in Canberra, over many years, I enjoyed wonderful collaborators who taught me breadth and depth across criminal justice and beyond. Thank you to Jane Caruana, Dennise Simpson, Nicole Mayo, Ken Archer, Chris Lines, Richard Refshague, Sue Anderson and Karen Fryar.

My son, Liam, grew up with my abiding quest to understand justice – through the professional years, the research, and then into academia. His interest now is in justice for the natural world. *Bon courage.* To the rest of my family – Mum, Dad, Jo, Christina, Phillip, John, Ciara and Leila – I am ever grateful for your love, encouragement, endless political argument, and good humour.

Abbreviations

ABS	Australian Bureau of Statistics
ACT	Australian Capital Territory
AFP	Australian Federal Police
CPS	Crown Prosecution Service (England and Wales)
DPP	Director of Public Prosecutions
DVCS	Domestic Violence Crisis Service (ACT)
GBB	Good Behaviour Bond
HRC	Human Rights Commission (ACT)
UK	United Kingdom
US	United States
VIS	Victim Impact Statement
VoCC	Victims of Crime Coordinator

1. Ideas of justice

> 'It belongs in utopia', said Imogene. This was our third and last conversation. It had been over three years since the assault on her. My final question to her was 'after everything, what now is your idea of justice?' She said (in part), 'I'd have to say it's an ideal. It belongs in utopia. It shouldn't but it does. If it does exist it is more a lottery. It's not what I believe but it's what happens in practice.' (Imogene, 2013)

> In a different place and time, during an interview with an ex-Director of Public Prosecutions, I asked a slightly different question – though I was trying to get at a similar concern. I asked, 'What was the conception of justice you carried in your working life as a prosecutor?' The reflection was (in part), 'the requirements of justice point in different ways which makes it difficult to define it in any comprehensive way. (P3, 2011)

This book sits in an extended conversation about the idea of justice, who has it, who does not and what it means in the everyday setting of criminal justice. It challenges the usual representation of people victimized by violence only as victims, and challenges conventional legal approaches that contain their aspirations for justice. The argument of this book is for inclusion of those with directly affected interests as a first principle of institutions in a democratic society. While the book focuses on people as victims of violence and their involvement with criminal justice, it argues that deliberation with victims and offenders is indispensable to an approach that centralizes the realization of *justice* as a core value in their lives. What is the nature of this hoped-for justice is considered in the following chapters.

From 1996 to 2011 I worked as an independent statutory advocate for victims' rights.[1] Reflections about justice such as those introducing this

[1] Pursuant to Victims of Crime Act 1994, s.14 as the Victims of Crime Coordinator (VoCC) for the Australian Capital Territory (ACT). The position was an appointment of the Attorney General. As an independent statutory position the VoCC combined the promotion of victims' rights and investigation of breaches of rights. I was appointed in 1996 and served with successive appointments until 2011. I was instrumental in two major reforms to the legislation. Briefly, the first reform brought services for victims under the responsibility of the VoCC, and the second saw the position (and its powers) changed to that of a Victims of Crime

chapter were commonplace. My daily interactions with victims of all types of offences involved in various justice processes revealed their bewilderment with a system they thought they would know. Equally, innumerable discussions and debates with judicial officers, prosecutors, police, victim advocates, probation and correctional officers, policy makers and law reformers about the role and rights of victims served to emphasize as many perspectives as there were operational areas to justice. Justice was clearly important to everyone but were we all talking about the same thing?

I came to realize that people victimized by violence who engage with the criminal justice system talked in complex ways about the idea of justice. Listening to their many voices suggested to me that justice was about a whole host of things, just as their identity was more than that of victim. Much of this, however, was hidden from view by the way people as victims were excluded, ignored or diverted. This seemed to me to be a loss. As a 'victim' they were seen as a problem for law to manage and contain. This created other types of loss. Instead I came to understand that victimization and the mobilization of the criminal law in response presented a unique opportunity to cultivate 'the capacity of citizens to rise to the demands of justice in their own political lives'.[2] An opportunity that not only considered what had happened and what should happen next, but also to debate and deliberate the issues that confronted both victim and offender, and the social, political, economic and cultural aspirations they held for themselves and for others. The usual approach is the allocation of justice in a particular distributive pattern with parties as passive recipients of decisions made by legal professionals in a context where state institutions maintain an ideology of hegemony. Another is to see the opportunity provided in a sequence of procedural and institutional spaces for citizens to *produce justice*.

This book aims to describe and understand this capacity of citizens, and to consider the implications within this institutional 'culture of control'. It is not a book about retributive or restorative or any other particular way of doing justice. Neither is it a book that settles questions of what victims want or victims' needs after violence. Rather, it presents argument that the mobilization of the criminal law in response to victimization and subsequent engagement with criminal justice processes

---

Commissioner. The administration of justice involves diverse processes in police, prosecution, courts and tribunals, probation and corrections, and encompasses youth and adult jurisdictions as well as criminal and civil areas of law.

[2] Austin Sarat and Thomas R Kearns, *Justice and Injustice in Law and Legal Theory* (U Michigan P 1996) 17.

are practices arising from and an enactment of people's membership of a political community, a community of citizens; practices that contribute to governance. They are citizenship activities founded on peoples' justice *interests* rather than an articulation of their justice *needs*. As citizens, the justice they seek is that which is due to all.

DIFFERENT TALES, ONE STORY

Of course, as I heard in my working life and discovered anew during the research conducted for this book, there are many tales in the story of justice. In one such are the vast majority of victims of crime who vote with their feet and do not engage with authorities, particularly if the offence against them involves physical or sexual violence. Part of this version, extensively told, is about the structured alienation of people from access to justice. Another tale is about the astonishingly rare people who report the incident to police and who then see that case proceed through the criminal justice system. While an individual may be propelled by the circumstances of the victimization to report to authorities, there is no coercion to do so. This tale commonly tells of hurdles, barriers and casual discourtesies.

A different thread speaks of those who believe (albeit tentatively) that a wrong may – or perhaps should – be recognized; where they, with their torn human dignity, will be treated with respect and where fairness is paramount. At this point of the tale different interests and influences converge, conflate and conflict. Yet in this particular story ordinary people perhaps reasonably assume that the meaning both of *rights* and their status as *citizens* will be recognized. Indeed, that these two aspects of their social and political identity will be foundational to the way the system will operate, whether responding to them as victim or as offender. Embedded within the telling is a perspective that the system is designed to deliver justice, 'pure and simple', for all its citizens.[3] Indeed, that the system, as an embodiment of the state, is somehow a partner to them all – victim, offender and community – in that honourable purpose. This story is about how justice is valued in the wider social world.

Is this a fairy tale? Across the common law world in Australia, the United Kingdom (UK), the United States (US) and elsewhere so bruising are people's actual encounters, so taxing the process and so disappointing are its outcomes that a very real question hangs over what could be

---

3 Ibid., 2.

described as fanciful expectations. So the idea and ideal of justice leads the book's enquiry. It is examined mainly through the eyes of ordinary people but also through the narratives of legal officials. Rather than a philosophical ideal, it seeks an idea of justice in the real world. For the people in this study – ordinary and official – justice mattered very much.

The stories of these two groupings are often posed in counterpoint. Nils Christie famously charged the state and its agents as thieves of the private disputes of citizens.[4] This critique precipitated calls for complete or partial redesign of state-administered criminal justice. It also, in part, led to an explosion of interest in different approaches to and mechanisms for delivering justice. One activity that has come to dominate this area is restorative justice. While it is a diverse field, restorative justice commonly claims to return the dispute to private citizens. This book takes a different tack. Rather than see the 'dispute' as one thing *or* the other, I argue that it is defined and co-determined by private *and* public interests. As such it is brought by citizens into the public realm *because* it is a public space with particular and unique characteristics. In so doing, these citizens ask for deliberation on the nature of the conduct alleged and a determination on its wrongfulness to standards contained in the criminal law. They do so for a combination of personal and public policy reasons. By undertaking this engagement they make a contribution to public governance. This perspective views people as victims less as a law problem and more as social, political and legal actors.

THE CONTESTED PLACE OF VICTIMS IN JUSTICE

My arguments speak back to academic and policy debates where people as victims are presented either as 'a favoured constituency' driving redefinition of criminal justice[5] or as a 'pariah' to that same system[6] notwithstanding that they are also institutionally irrelevant.[7] Within these boundaries and in the domestic criminal justice environment of liberal

---

[4] Nils Christie, 'Conflicts as Property' (1977) 17 *The British Journal of Criminology* 1.

[5] David Garland, *The Culture of Control: Crime and Social Order in Contemporary Society* (OUP 2001) 121.

[6] Paul Rock, 'New Labour Policies for Victims' (2007) 67 *Criminal Justice Matters* 38, 39.

[7] Doreen McBarnet, 'Victim in the Witness Box – Confronting Victimology's Stereotype' (1983) 7 *Contemporary Crises* 293.

democracies, legal and conceptual recognition of victims is mired in endless controversy.

The irrelevance of victims to criminal justice in common law jurisdictions was not always the case. The centuries-old practice whereby victims had initiation and carriage of prosecution in England and Wales made the transport to the Australian colonies where much of the research that informs this book was undertaken. But in the modernist epic, bureaucratic centralization and professionalization was as rapid in Australia as it was episodic and inexorable at the centre of Empire. By the twentieth century, in both countries, people as victims had become instruments for institutional ends. Rationalizing this process involved weaving different historic threads into a blanket account of an abstract and universal 'public' owning the common good and the state's agents owning its definition. More recently, people victimized by crime have come to make a trenchant critique of their exclusion and thereby to question how that public is constituted and considered. They claim the system could not function without them. It is this person, group or entity who suffers the intrusion, articulates the violation, decides whether and how to inform and cooperate with formal or informal authorities, provides primary evidentiary and forensic information, is interrogated as a witness and is offered in validation (or not) of the outcome. They are also a part of the public.

This person, however, is subjected to innumerable indignities – as is the individual accused – in a system that espouses principles of respect, rights and equal treatment. These indignities do not appear by happenstance but are manifest as statements of institutional authority. Prior policy and academic debate has probed this disregard. In particular, critical scholars have found wanting the differential ways the law and its practice, as well as practitioners and institutions, dealt with particular offences and associated characteristics of victims such as their gender, age, sexuality, ethnicity or race. For many individuals and communities, the law is both over-applied and under-used. However, I argue that these characteristics are secondary to the primary structural and conceptual exclusion of persons as victims from criminal justice.

This exclusion is not globally uniform. Looking back in history as well as looking sideways to inquisitorial and other legal systems, more recent argument has emerged seeking recognition of victims with inherent civil and human rights, and – controversially – as parties.[8] At the level of

---

[8] Jonathan Doak, *Victims' Rights, Human Rights and Criminal Justice: Reconceiving the Role of Third Parties* (Hart 2008).

international criminal justice and in post-conflict justice, initiatives there have been rapid and radical adjustments made over the past 20 years to recognize, respect and represent victims.[9] In these domains it is possible to assert that 'victims are at the heart of human rights thinking'.[10] This more central role for victims internationally is not undisputed[11] but the changes have opened new and rich lines of scholarly reflection and advocacy about victims and justice.

The arguments for inclusion that I develop in this book, tap into the general tide of discontent with and alienation from institutions of democracy and governance. Here the agitation is for participatory practices and participatory institutions that are re-centred on the inherent power of citizens.[12] This agitation demands institutional humility and greater devolution of power. Participatory ideas that draw upon democratic theory have crept slowly towards criminal justice.[13] Positioning victims within this space conceives them as members of the social mass – the public. This public (or 'publics') is at once singularly sovereign and plural. It can be derided as populist or lauded as the source of 'strong democracy'.[14] In either guise these publics ask awkward questions about accountability of authorities, in particular about the normative roots of that authority. They turn a harsh light on the representational claims that justice entities make. My argument for inclusion and participation places people as victims in a political relation to state institutions; as rights bearers in a relation with duty holders.

---

[9] Rani Mani, *Beyond Retribution: Seeking Justice in the Shadows of War* (Polity Press 2004); Anne-Marie De Brouwer, 'What the International Criminal Court Has Achieved and Can Achieve for Victims/Survivors of Sexual Violence' (2009) 16 *International Review of Victimology* 183; Cheryl White, *Bridging Divides in Transitional Justice: The Extraordinary Chambers in the Courts of Cambodia* (Intersentia 2017).

[10] Francesca Klug, 'Human Rights and Victims' in Ed Cape (ed), *Reconcilable Rights? Analysing the Tension Between Victims and Defendants* (LAG 2004) 111.

[11] Brianne McGonigle Lehy, *Procedural Justice? Victim Participation in International Criminal Proceedings* (Intersentia 2011).

[12] Carole Pateman, *Participation and Democratic Theory* (CUP 1970); Iris Marion Young, *Inclusion and Democracy* (OUP 2000); Archon Fung, 'Continuous Institutional Innovation and the Pragmatic Conception of Democracy' (2012) 44 *Polity* 609.

[13] Albert Dzur, *Punishment, Participatory Democracy and the Jury* (OUP 2012); Marijke Malsch, *Democracy in the Courts: Lay Participation in European Criminal Justice Systems* (Routledge 2009).

[14] Benjamin Barber, *Strong Democracy: Participatory Politics for a New Age* (U Cal P 1984).

VICTIMS AND IDEAS OF JUSTICE

To date, however, many tales of victims and justice narrow their interests away from this broader public towards end points. In these confined spaces, assessments about justice or injustice are on the 'culmination outcome' and the influences upon it.[15] From this place justice is viewed as a singular standard. Moreover, as research subjects, people as victims are commonly asked just once about their justice views and retrospectively. Confining their viewpoints and assessments in this manner leads to an impoverishment of the idea and institutions of justice. The messages that are conveyed discourage citizens from their intrinsic and highly situated complex conceptualizations. They discourage thinking that justice matters, that they matter, or that the infraction matters. These messages are personal, social and political. They communicate information about values, about who and what is important, and about where power lies and how it operates.

In this book, I move away from single representations to explore complex realizations of justice. For the Justice Study upon which this book is based, I spoke on three occasions with women and men who were victims of violence and who engaged with the criminal justice system. These were conversations held 'beneath the constitutional surface' of the law.[16] Most people display a disengaged cynicism about the law and its institutions whether in Australia, Britain or elsewhere. But for those who become victims of violence this quickly becomes insupportable when they enter the portals of the criminal justice system. They have to think about what they think. They have to think about what to do, what to say, and why. Over time and in interactions with different entities, thinking about justice *unfolds*. Victims are informed both by the practical and the objective context in which they find themselves, as well as by their own moral and social intuitions. They become everyday philosophers of their situation.

Unsurprisingly this research approach opened space for articulating interpretations about justice that *layered* interpersonal, social and institutional influences. The reflections brought to light were partial, ambiguous and yet at times both firm as well as contradictory. There was nothing single or simple to victims' contemplation on the idea of justice. Their thinking was refracted through a spectrum of ideas, principles,

---

[15] Amartya Sen, *The Idea of Justice* (Harvard UP 2009) 215.

[16] John Dryzek, *Deliberative Democracy and Beyond: Liberals, Critics, Contestations* (OUP 2002) 2.

rules and criteria that act as heuristics. As victims of violence, people felt acutely the presence of power and the absence of justice. For them, the shift in the meaning of justice as a utopian ideal (Imogene's comment) to 'just a word' can be jolting.[17] In the rough and tumble of the real world, a malleable and more human construct appears, one that interacts with the idea of justice from a range of different positions.

THE IDEA OF JUSTICE IN THE REAL WORLD

Even as we are stimulated to look for justice, however, it emerges with an 'immense variety and complexity of meanings, applications and ideological associations'.[18] Vast libraries speak to earnest and erudite depictions of justice. Much of this is abstracted and removed from the actual injustice. Injustice can be messy, bloody and painful and, as Judith Shklar has argued, justice theory tends to avoid it.[19] So when I found Amartya Sen's book, *The Idea of Justice*, it came like the discovery of a cool pond in heated and treacherous terrain. His attention to how justice lives and moves in the real lives of ordinary people proved a refreshing draught. Sen engages with justice in its social and political dimensions. In doing so, he explicitly incorporates 'the presence of remediable injustice' as 'connected with behavioural transgressions' as well as with 'institutional shortcomings' (p. x). He suggests that justice need not be about prioritizing one good over another, nor about 'getting the basic institutions and general rules right'. He asks, 'Should we not also have to examine what emerges in the society, including the kind of lives that people can actually lead, given the institutions and rules, but also other influences, including actual behaviour, that would inescapably affect human lives?'[20]

What is inescapable in human lives, Sen argues, is a complex account of beliefs, motivations and interactions. His theorizing is imbued with respect for these diverse lives in many settings – in any of which people may apply different criteria when claiming what is just or unjust. There is no point, he says, in attempting to find a transcendent principle and calling that 'justice' as it will always leave something behind. Justice in the real world finds a plurality of grounds (or injustices) from which diverse reasoning flows (about justice criteria, what is right, and what

[17] Eric Stover, *The Witnesses: War Crimes and the Promise of Justice in The Hague* (U Penn P 2011) 139.

[18] Tom Campbell, *Justice* (2nd ed., Palgrave Macmillan 2001) 9.

[19] Judith Shklar, *The Faces of Injustice* (Yale UP 1990).

[20] Sen (n 15) 10.

emerges). Different contexts to and components of injustice and the resultant thinking about justice, will elicit attention to different objects of value, says Sen. In the new empirical research discussed in this book, those objects emerged as victim, offender and the wider publics in which the former two are embedded.

Sen further argues that the judgments about justice that revolve around these different objects of value 'take on board the task of accommodating different kinds of reasons and evaluative concerns' for the range of interests that flow from them. How this is done – the process of realization – embraces emotion, reasoning, scrutiny and dialogue. Justice is not an allocation to a single reason. Rather, in the real world, justice inevitably sees 'incomplete resolution'. Plausible outcomes, as 'rankings of alternatives that can be realised', are distinguished from those which might be clearly rejected. Sen proposes that realizable justice makes room for non-congruence and partial resolutions. That is, going 'as far as we reasonably can' is justice in the real world. It can never be absolute.[21]

As a theoretical framework and an analytic argument, Sen creates bridges between accounts that confine justice in the law to its rectificatory purpose, those who present justice as a supreme obligation, those who propose that justice is about maximizing particular goods for the maximum number, and those who see justice as a rights-based conception. He does this principally by presenting justice coming through dialogue. It is decision-making and not solely about decision. Thus, the departure Sen makes from predominant ways of presenting justice is away from transcendence and towards particularity. He proposes an approach to justice that enriches 'reasoned engagement through enhancing informational availability and the feasibility of interactive discussions'. By this I take Sen to mean drawing information from different relevant sources and into deliberation on justice. Perfect justice is not what transpires from such an approach. Rather, we advance towards it.[22]

In the arcane and rather closed world of contemporary criminal justice this type of approach may be tolerated on the fringes in diversionary practices, restorative conferences and therapeutic courts, for example. Dominant legal and scholarly opinion concede that common law criminal justice may benefit from some tinkering but deems the system to be essentially sound. Even though criminal justice systems in liberal democracies lay claim to long histories of organic evolution, there is little acknowledgment that change is a continual process. Tomorrow is viewed

---

21 Ibid., 395, 17, 401.

22 Ibid., xiii.

as more of the same. However, the principles of inclusion and participation that underpin Sen's approach are ribs to an umbrella of justice whether delivered through innovative *or* conventional mechanisms.[23] By drawing on the democratic underpinning to Sen's idea of justice as a discursive exercise,[24] I aim to contribute a different and perhaps radical re-positioning of ordinary people in relation to state-centric and law-centric versions of justice.

JUSTICE INTERESTS AS POLITICAL INTERESTS

The approach I develop asks for re-examination of the relationship(s) between the state's agents in criminal justice and the publics it encounters and dominates. Institutional interests in justice argue that they represent a higher embodiment of the public in the form of the state. The various publics, it is said, are free to self-regulate with minimum interference. Limits are set in standards and rules for which there exists a normative social consensus. As Antony Duff says, criminal law thus forms a kind of law of the public.[25] The state then represents that consensus through the criminal law. Should these norms and that law be transgressed, then the state will take what the victimized person proffers and says 'we will take action not for you but for all of you'. Furthermore, the state then says, 'we take the right and responsibility for punishment of those transgressions in order for you not to punish'. Doing these things becomes 'achieving justice' or 'delivering justice' for the public's common good. A universal conception of the common good, in turn, permits sacrifice of individuals or of smaller interests. Ironically, this depiction of a paternalistic and monolithic state lends itself to 'capacious interest' in its controlling and punitive nature.[26] This vision sutures the idea of

---

[23] Kathleen Daly and Brigitte Bouhours, *Conventional and Innovative Justice Responses to Sexual Violence* (Australian Institute of Family Studies 2011). These authors use the term 'innovative justice' to describe 'non-traditional' practices and procedures such as circle sentencing, restorative justice and special courts.

[24] Dryzek (n 16). An emphasis on discursivity seeks to detach deliberation from institutional structures. It does not, however, pose these democratic dynamics as in conflict.

[25] Anthony Duff, 'Towards a Theory of Criminal Law?' (2010) 84(1) *Aristotelian Society Supplementary Volume* 1.

[26] Adam Crawford (ed), *International and Comparative Criminal Justice and Urban Governance: Convergence and Divergence in Global, National and Local Settings* (CUP 2011) 17.

justice to both the state and its institutions, as well as to the centrality of punishment. The characterization fuels different narratives. One says that the state and its institutions of justice reflect, adhere to and uphold the values and norms of the public, while at the same time are neutral to and removed from the disputing publics; and the other narrative says that the state sustains social order and control through the harsh instrument of criminal law.

Into the gaps created by this state-centric and schismatic portrayal, the victimized person falls. Indeed, both victim and offender are extracted from the public, de-contextualized and used in performance roles to an institutional script. The narratives characterize victims as moralizing and interested in private goals and therefore not legitimate in a public interest system. So what are they to do? In the main they keep private pain private. They deal with it themselves. They do not approach the state. Only a small proportion turn to criminal justice institutions that claim to represent the public they came from and ask that the injustice they have experienced be acknowledged and addressed.

The larger frame to this story asks what is that relationship between citizens and the state at this site of criminal justice? In answering this question, the presence of the state in the lives of offenders is well recognized, but there is blindness to 'seeing the state' in the lives of victims.[27] But, if the state is present with both accused and victim and when they are in dispute or conflict with each other, the questions are shared: what does the state owe to each of them at the site of criminal justice? What constraints are placed on citizens and on the state that we can approve of, take to ourselves and impose on others? What is the convergence and divergence between ideas of justice envisaged by state entities and those of its citizens – those directly affected and those more indirectly concerned? These questions go to the *interests* of persons who are citizens, whether victim or offender. As questions, they are political in that they 'raise and address issues of the moral value or human desirability of an institution or practice whose decisions affect a large number of people'.[28] They maintain an open question over the extent to which citizen interests, specifically for those citizens who are victims, coincide with the interests of the state through its justice entities. They

---

[27] Robyn Holder, 'Seeing the State: Human Rights Violations of Victims of Crime and Abuse of Power' in Leanne Weber, Elaine Fishwick and Marinella Marmo (eds) *The Routledge International Handbook of Criminology and Human Rights* (Routledge 2017) Ch 39.

[28] Iris Marion Young, 'Impartiality and the Civic Public' in Seyla Benhabib and Drucilla Cornell (eds), *Feminism as Critique* (U Minn Press 1987) 73.

ask for re-examination of the portrayal of public and private interests as rigidly and necessarily distinct. They take seriously the offer of law to citizens. This is a different kind of civic politics to the idea of justice.

CITIZENS, JUSTICE AND DEMOCRACY

Within my characterization of the debate, claiming the status of 'citizen' for victims may seem obvious to some and deeply troubling to others. As a former practitioner within the criminal justice system, I found the 'victim' label to be sticky as well as unsteady. Its stickiness accreted where, for example, a person had particular characteristics such as being a child or was assessed as traumatized. In which case, special allowances such as witness facilities might be extended to them. The victim label was unsteady in that similar institutional kindnesses were also likely to be extended if the grateful individual performed as a 'deserving' victim. But in the everyday of criminal justice, people as victims were way more complicated and diverse than these representations and woe betides an individual who was angry or not fully literate or demanding in some other way. So I wanted a way of situating *any* person in relation to state institutions that was more stable, more robust and more comprehensive. Thus, at one level, using citizen-status recognizes that people are more than what happened to them at a moment in time. At another, it arises from noticing how simple and singular representations of victims act for the convenience of authority; how it blurs what is at stake. Citizens have *interests* in the way public systems work and how they work for all; whereas ideas of victim 'needs' shift people into the personal.

It is important to recognize that, if the demand for inclusion and participation in the justice space challenges narrow representations, it also requires a more rounded portrayal of all involved – without assumptions or absolutes. The citizen term may provide a kind of constitutional stability, but inclusion and participation also argue for recognition of diversity alongside what is shared, and hence recognize context and contingency. The term sees people not solely or only as a victim, or indeed as offender. Neither can be said to be fully represented by the concept of 'community' any more than either 'represent the community'. The citizen term further acknowledges that victims do not speak with one voice, and that the individual and the many victims have different ways of seeing justice. From this perspective, the idea of 'public interest' requires more open acknowledgement of many publics and a range of interests. Including this diversity and difference in participatory practices is core to citizenship in a mature liberal democracy. Inclusion and participation both reflect and generate a thick belonging. More than an afterthought to institutional legitimacy, they are foundational.

This call for inclusion and participation in justice is not uncontested. In highly charged debate it is claimed that the crime victim has become the 'idealised political subject ... whose circumstances and experiences have come to stand for the general good'.[29] The critical attention paid to the role of crime and victimization in the politics of law and order has ensured that the victim identity and experience remains subject to divisive and heated controversy. Justice, it is said, is not only about the victim. Jonathon Simon's work, *Governing Through Crime* (2007), deals with penal politics in the US but has been influential in Australia as in the UK. He expands arguments against victim inclusion by claiming that new forms of knowledge to bring victim 'truths' into the criminal justice process 'undermine the forms of solidarity and responsibility necessary for democratic institutions'. He infers that citizens who become victims of crime and engage with authorities constitute dangerous anti-democratic actors.

This claim seems to attack the legitimacy of *any* role in criminal justice for persons as victims, but leaves open the question: what then are citizens expected to be and do when victimized by violence and crime? Leave it to the professionals seemed to be Simon's answer. While unpacking the meaning of justice to ordinary people is the book's focus, questions about what justice was in a democracy and what democracy had to say to justice emerge strongly, some may say rashly.

To help orient readers, I place these questions firmly to the front in this book. Some will find this a challenge, although readers interested in victims and criminal justice will find much that is familiar in these pages. More unfamiliar ideas of normative justice, of the democratic citizen, and of participation and deliberation are subject to early critical attention in the chapters that follow. For now, it is important to know that, following Iris Marion Young, I hold that democratic practice, here through an inclusive norm, is not confined to representational events. Further, and unconfined only to administrative decision-making, I build on the principle of affected interests which says that 'individuals should be able to influence decisions that affect them'.[30] I argue that deepening democratic practices within criminal justice deepens justice itself. I also signal an

---

[29] Jonathan Simon, *Governing Through Crime: How the War on Crime Transformed American Democracy and Created a Culture of Fear* (OUP 2007) 77.

[30] Archon Fung, 'The Principle of Affected Interests and Inclusion in Democratic Governance' in Jack Nagel and Rogers Smith (eds) *Representation: Elections and Beyond* (U Penn P 2013) 237.

interest in the justice system(s) as institutional arenas 'in which competing demands can be listened to, argued about, and negotiated'.[31] These are civic spaces as well as places of and for law. The possibility of (re)connecting criminal justice to its essentially democratic footings considers the courtroom (and other justice sites) as a place for the validation of belonging, a subjective experience of it, and a site of challenge in which social relations are made and re-made.

Ultimately the book leads readers down two main pathways which I suggest are converging. One contemplates the meaning of justice (mainly) through the eyes of men and women victimized by violence who engage with the criminal justice process. The second considers how the idea of justice may be arrived at. This is about the participatory ideal, its origins in democratic theory and what it says to justice as an institution.

LOCATING THE JUSTICE STUDY

As a research study, the book is more grounded than these introductory remarks may suggest. It focuses on criminal justice in a common law setting. The institutional setting is evoked through the narratives of Australian and British prosecutors. Victim perspectives are based on exploratory research conducted in the Australian Capital Territory (ACT), a city-state located more-or-less the same distance from Sydney as Manchester is to London, or Washington is to New York. For this component women and men victimized by violence were interviewed on three occasions as their case progressed through the ACT criminal justice process.

In this locality, when a member of the public calls for police assistance following an incident of violence, what follows would look similar to that in most other common law jurisdictions. There may be the taking of statements, gathering of evidence, locating a suspect(s), and consequent decision-making about whether all the information police have gathered amounts to an alleged criminal offence. If a charge results then a prosecution may proceed. All criminal offences in the ACT are prosecuted by the statutory office of the DPP, unlike most other Australian states and territories where police prosecutors deal with summary offences. The function is similar to that of the Crown Prosecution Service (CPS) in England and Wales. In Australia as in Britain, the separation of

[31] Ian Loader, 'Policing, Recognition, and Belonging' (2006) 605 *The Annals of the American Academy of Political and Social Science* 201, 214.

prosecution from politicians and the political process is jealously guarded, unlike in the US where boundaries are porous. Once a charge is laid, the prosecutor will review the criminal charges, and will (usually) liaise with both the investigating officers and with defence counsel on the nature of the charges and the evidence. The prosecutor will come to her own decision about whether to prosecute and on what charges. If a charge is preferred then it will most likely be heard and finalized in the lower court before a magistrate. Discretion is a huge part of the common law criminal justice process and there are a lot of mays, maybes and likelys.

In many common law jurisdictions including the ACT, victim of crime legislation places some requirements on authorities to give certain information, to provide case status updates, and to provide information on aspects of the process as they affect witnesses.[32] Authorities may also let a victim know of the availability of opportunities for further input such as a concerns made to bail hearings about individual safety, the making of a Victim Impact Statement (VIS) if an offender is convicted, or submissions made for parole hearings. In the ACT, in matters of domestic assault or sexual assault then – as a result of extensive and sustained local reform efforts – the process of keeping individuals informed is almost uniform.[33] If it is a different type of assault then it is much more hit-and-miss.[34] In other common law countries similar scenarios are likely.

While victim legislation often invokes the language of rights, in reality, these are anything but.[35] At the time of the research, nothing in the ACT victims' legislation constituted a legal duty on any institution or an actionable right for the victim. Having been responsible for this particular statute for 15 years I probably know too much about the compromises justice agencies make in juggling all their functions with the volume of

---

[32] Tyrone Kirchengast, *Victims and the Criminal Trial* (Palgrave Macmillan 2016).

[33] Tracy Cussen and Matthew Lyneham, *ACT Family Violence Intervention Program Review* Technical and Background Paper No.52 (AIC 2012); Jessica Anderson and others, *Evaluation of the ACT Sexual Assault Reform Program (SARP): Final Report* Technical and Background Paper No.51 (AIC 2013).

[34] For a critical overview of the experiences of crime victims in general conducted when I was the statutory advocate, see Robyn Holder, *The Quality of Justice: Operation of the* Victims of Crime Act 1994 *in the ACT 1996–2007* (VoCC 2008).

[35] Rights litigation for victims of crime in the US has evolved considerably in the past decade. See Douglas Beloof and others, *Victims in Criminal Procedure* (Carolina Academic Press 2017).

cases. For sure I know that the rights-promoting and rights-protecting role of the statutory advocate for victims of crime has limited authority and few powers.[36] The inadequacy of rights protection is similar to that for victims in the UK, the US, Canada, and countries in Europe.[37] Although the ACT has a Human Rights Act, since its commencement in 2004 and at the time of writing, the legislation has not been invoked in relation to victims of crime in any court proceedings. Where law reform submissions from the Human Rights Commission (HRC) have touched on the interests of crime victims, comment has tended to be extremely cautious.[38] In the UK, human rights have been invoked, for example, in reviewing the investigation of deaths and reviewing the disclosure of complainants' medical records in sexual offence cases.[39] Overall, however, real rights for people as victims are distant.

STUDYING JUSTICE IN THE REAL WORLD

In such a complex environment, arguments about what is just/unjust, objective/subjective, and public/private are more than an academic binary. Therefore any examination of justice needs to allow people to voice contradiction and inconsistency even as it attempts to illuminate what is similar and different about the influences on individual thinking

---

[36] Holder (n 34).

[37] For the UK see Marie Manikis, 'Navigating Through an Obstacle Course: the Complaints Mechanism for Victims of Crime in England and Wales' (2012) 12 *Criminology and Criminal Justice* 149; for the US see Douglas Beloof, 'The Third Wave of Crime Victims' Rights: Standing, Remedy, and Review' (2005) 2 *BYU Law Rev* 255; for Canada see Marie Manikis, 'Imagining the Future of Victims' Rights in Canada: a Comparative Perspective' (2015) 13 *Ohio State J Crim Law* 163; and countries in Europe see Helga Ezendam, and Frida Wheldon, 'Recognition of Victims' Rights Through EU Action' in Felix Mukwiza and others (eds) *Justice for Victims: Perspectives on Rights, Transition and Reconciliation* (Routledge 2014) 51.

[38] For example, a 2008 submission from the Human Rights Commission in relation to proposed legislative changes aimed at improved protections for victim witnesses in violent and sexual offence proceedings expressed concern about the proposal to restrict direct cross-examination of the complainant witness by the accused in violent matters, and to require an accused to be legally represented. More recently, the HRC and the Victims of Crime Commissioner have produced a practical guide, *Victim and Witness Rights under the ACT* Human Rights Act 2004 (nd).

[39] Equality and Human Rights Commission, *Human Rights in Action: Case Studies from Regulators, Inspectorates and Ombudsmen (RIOs)* (EHR, 2014).

and action. Equally, it must notice what is dominating or what is marginal in portrayals of justice, and how realities are structured. Several small workplace studies I had conducted during my time working within criminal justice showed how these 'tensions and conflicts'[40] might be addressed in research design. These studies had exposed the importance of context and timing in survey responses, as well as nuance and perspective. They revealed that victims of all types experienced similar as well as different issues.[41]

One of the workplace studies derived from a group of 39 victims of domestic violence interviewed at the finalization of their matter at court. About a quarter of those first interviewed displayed considerable ambivalence if not hostility to the justice process and its outcome. Twelve months later, 15 of the earlier group were re-interviewed. At this second interview most women reported feeling very or fairly safe, expressed satisfaction and agreed that 'justice was done'.[42] These results showed that to sample at one occasion locked individuals into a single and simple statement. A static reflection of opinion at a particular point in time becomes the research outcome. However, surveying a person twice showed attitude formation to be a dynamic process and one that was influenced by the context and timing of the questioning.

A second study involved women and men answering a client evaluation survey from a community-based advocacy service – the Domestic Violence Crisis Service (DVCS). In one particular year, 41 per cent of clients indicated that the prosecution of the violent incident was 'not beneficial' to them. Nine of those who expressed this view participated in a follow-up telephone interview exploring further their preferences for decision-control,[43] their justice objectives and indications about future engagement. The sample said that they wanted to be listened to but declined decision-making control and, if faced with similar circumstances in the future, would re-engage with the system even when they had

[40] Jan Nespor, 'Morphologies of Inquiry: The Uses and Spaces of Paradigm Proliferation' (2006) 19 *International Journal of Qualitative Studies in Education* 115, 123.

[41] The workplace studies were conducted on (separately) victims of residential burglary, domestic violence, sexual assault and victims of crime as a general category.

[42] Robyn Holder and Nicole Mayo, 'What do Women Want? Prosecuting Family Violence in the ACT' (2003) 15 *Current Issues in Criminal Justice* 525. Only one woman indicated that there had been a new incident of assault.

[43] Discussed as victim 'choice' in the literature – see Linda G Mills, 'Killing her Softly: Intimate Abuse and the Violence of State Intervention' (1999) 113 *Harvard Law Review* 550.

expressed dissatisfaction.[44] The study showed the language of personal objectives overlapped with that of official public objectives of justice. These follow-up interviews showed that it was not only important to ask people what they think but why they think it. The perspective that time and distance provided suggested that individuals could and did talk in layered ways and from different positions about the one issue.

Workplace studies such as these have their own unique objectives and characteristics but much of the academic literature examining victims of violence and their experience of criminal justice is also constrained.[45] The victim of crime constituency is an extremely diverse population. Researchers and activists tend to respond to this diversity by focusing on offence-specific characteristics. The relevance of findings to victims of other types of offences is then open to contention. Commonly, research subjects self-select into studies and are usually sampled at one time and in retrospect. Finally, what is not measured in justice studies is as important as what is and in what context. Measures of emotional resolution, cooperation, safety, fairness and advocacy have been examined. In the main, however, the research on victims and justice has tended to focus on satisfaction.[46] There is very little knowledge of peoples' journey and still less of the beliefs and expectations they held at the outset. The resulting representation of peoples' perspectives is at once static, flat and passive.

Studying Victims' Ideas of Justice

The Justice Study sought to do something different. First, it sought to ground people's lived experiences in the broader context of their beliefs,

---

[44] Holder (n 34).

[45] See, e.g., discussion from a US perspective in Laura Moriarty and Robert A Jerin (eds), *Current Issues in Victimology Research* (Carolina Academic Press 2007); from a UK perspective in Jo Goodey, *Victims and Victimology: Research, Policy and Practice* (Pearson Education 2005). In Australia, while there are a number of small-scale and scattered studies derived from non-academic research, there are no comparable volumes or compilations. The report *Victims' Needs, Victims' Rights: Policies and Programs for Victims of Crime in Australia* prepared by Bree Cook and others in 1999 comprised a desk-based review of practice.

[46] Robyn Holder, 'Satisfied? Exploring Victims' Justice Judgements' in Dean Wilson and Stuart Ross (eds) *Crime, Victims and Policy: International Contexts, Local Experiences* (Palgrave Macmillan 2015) 184; Malini Laxminarayan and others, 'Victim Satisfaction with Criminal Justice: A Systematic Review' (2013) 8 *Victims and Offenders* 119.

expectations and motivations. Second, the nuance with which people struggled to bring to their understanding of what was happening to them and around them, was to be teased out in real time. Thus a longitudinal design was chosen to account for peoples' engagements with different criminal justice agencies.[47] Semi-structured interviews were conducted with a panel of victims on three occasions: at Time 1 after police had charged an alleged assailant and before the matter went to court; at Time 2 after the matter had finalized in the criminal court; and at Time 3 some six to eight months after court finalization (see the Appendix for more detail). However, keeping track of participants in longitudinal research is challenging. Having commenced at Time 1 with 33 adults (27 women and six men), numbers dwindled. At Time 2 there were 26 (21 women and five men), and by Time 3 the sample ended at 19 (14 women and five men). Overall, 58 per cent of the original sample stayed the full course of the research.

Prospective longitudinal research on victims and justice is infrequent. Some studies, focused on women as victims of domestic violence, have conducted two or three interviews.[48] One English and one Dutch longitudinal studies interviewed women and men victimized by different offences. The first interviewed a panel of victims of violence on different occasions from initial reporting to police to its outcome. At Time 1, 276 people were interviewed and 215 (78 per cent of the original sample) were interviewed at Time 3. Of 54 victims who had applied for compensation, 40 were additionally interviewed on a fourth occasion.[49] The Netherlands' study is more properly a pre- and post-test. This research was designed to evaluate the effects of new guidelines and legislation. Victims of property crimes and minor assault (13 per cent of

---

[47] Robyn L Holder, 'Untangling the Meanings of Justice: A Longitudinal Mixed Methods Study' (2016) *Journal of Mixed Methods Research*, online DOI: 10.1177/1558689816653308.

[48] Those interviewed twice are in Margaret Bell and others, 'Battered Women's Perceptions of Civil and Criminal Court Helpfulness: The Role of Court Outcome and Process' (2011) 17 *Violence Against Women* 71–88 and Ruth Lewis and others, 'Protection, Prevention, Rehabilitation or Justice? Women's Use of the Law to Challenge Domestic Violence' (2000) 7 *International Review of Victimology* 179–205; and on three occasions are in Ruth Fleury-Steiner and others, 'Contextual Factors Impacting Battered Women's Intentions to Reuse the Criminal Legal System' (2006) 34 *Journal of Community Psychology* 327–42, and Judith McFarlane and others, 'Women Filing Assault Charges on an Intimate Partner' (2000) 6 *Violence Against Women* 396–408.

[49] Joanna Shapland, Jon Willmore and Peter Duff, *Victims in the Criminal Justice System* (Gower 1985) 7–9.

the sample) were surveyed after their contact with police but prior to contact with the prosecutor and again, some five months later, after the prosecution had 'taken their case into consideration'. A total of 315 people were interviewed before the legislative change and, of these, 193 (61 per cent) completed a second interview. After the changes were put in place, another group of 325 people were interviewed and, of these, 242 (74 per cent) completed a second interview.[50] Findings from the English and Dutch studies are threaded through discussion of results from the Justice Study in this book.

For this new research, only victims of violence were recruited so as to constrain differences in victimization experience but also in recognition that the experience of violence carries a unique assault on human dignity. This characteristic transcended the gendered nature of individual experiences. None of the people who ultimately participated in the research are intended to stand for all victims. Those recruited were adult women who had been victims of a domestic assault from a male partner or ex-partner, and adult men who had experienced a non-domestic assault from another man. Domestic assault victims were 82 per cent of the study sample at the first interview, 81 per cent of the sample at the second interview, and 74 per cent at the third interview. Individuals were recruited via local victim advocacy and police liaison services in one region. The localized recruitment constrained irrelevant sources of variation in institutional responses. It was also a practical decision about access to and the conduct of face-to-face interviews with individuals over a long period of time. Data collection occurred over four years, from 2009 to 2013.

The Justice Study was initially conceived with a deductive focus on victims' experiences of procedural justice. The Time 1 interview comprised a mix of open and closed questions, some of which were answered directly on a survey form by the interviewee. This instrument contained a number of pre-coded questions that focused on the experience of respect, fairness, and being informed. Questions also asked about the decisions made, whether people felt their views had been considered, and that they had been given an honest explanation for the decisions. They were asked questions that revolved around the legitimacy of the decision-makers and the procedures: were they right, fair and effective. Some questions, asked

---

50 Combining the two datasets produced N=640 interviews at Time 1 and N=435 at Time 2 (68 per cent). The Netherlands sample comprised victims of theft (73 per cent), assault (13 per cent), vandalism (11 per cent), and crimes against public order (3 per cent) (Jo-Anne Wemmers, *Victims in the Criminal Justice System* (Kugler Publications 1996) 106, 115, 117).

on all three occasions, were repeat measures. Other questions were open-ended.

However, as the study progressed to the second and third interviews, the procedural justice focus shifted and became subsumed in a broader conceptualization of justice. The opportunity to be interviewed on three occasions gave people space and time to speak more expansively about the justice they sought. They spoke about what motivated them to mobilize the law, what they sought, and what their feelings were about the person who had been violent towards them. I asked about their perceptions, expectations and experiences of the institutions of police, prosecution and court. Perhaps above all I asked for their reasoning. From these open-ended questions, more thematic and critical perspectives emerged. In discussing these perspectives in the chapters that follow, I describe respondents in different ways as lay participants, lay people, victims and as citizen-victims. When quoted, each person is given a pseudonym.

At the first interview people were also asked closed questions derived from other Australian surveys so as to locate them within a national sample. One survey examined the micro foundations of Australian democracy and asked about trust, beliefs and values.[51] Another looked at citizen attitudes towards crime and policing,[52] and a third examined attitudes to sentencing and confidence in courts.[53] A number of scales were created from which to compare the study group with these larger samples. Because of the large N differences between the national samples and that in the Justice Study, only broad comparisons are made.

Studying Prosecutors and Their Ideas of Justice

This focus on individual victims, however rich and thick, would only enable a partial telling of the everyday justice story. The institutional landscape also needed to be brought into view. For this purpose, the book

---

[51] Valerie Braithwaite, *The Community Hopes, Fears and Actions Survey: Goals and Measures* Working Paper No.2 Centre for Tax System Integrity, The Australian National University 2001. The sample was N=3,558.

[52] Kristina Murphy and others, 'The 2009 Public Safety and Security in Australia Survey: Survey Methodology and Preliminary Findings' (2010b) Working Paper No.17 Alfred Deakin Research Institute, Deakin University, Geelong. The sample was N=1,204.

[53] Geraldine Mackenzie and others, 'Sentencing and Public Confidence: Results from a National Australian Survey on Public Opinions towards Sentencing' (2012) 45 *ANZJC* 45. The sample was N=6,005.

focuses on the public prosecutor. I first conducted semi-structured interviews with a small number of ex-Directors of Public Prosecution in Australia. Their justice story was dominated by a picture of criminal justice as a civilizing force and of their role as protectors of that tradition. A second phase of interviews conducted in 2016 with serving and ex-senior prosecutors in the UK demonstrated that the storybook was similar but with some intriguing differences. All prosecution interviewees were assured that no personal or professional characteristics would be used to identify them. Their comments are not individuated for this reason, a decision which highlights an institutionalized narrative.

In combination, the 12 prosecutors were invited to reflect on the underlying features to the concept of 'public interest' and where, if at all, private citizens stood within the criminal justice system. I also asked what conception of justice they carried with them in their working lives, and how they understood the different demands that victims put on prosecuting authorities.

Analysis Overview

Although there are obvious differences between the lay and legal interviewees in the Justice Study, several common conceptions of justice guided analysis of their narratives. The conceptions, drawn from political philosophy and social psychology, emphasized the normative and duty-oriented features of justice, ideas of fairness and accountability, moral and practical reasoning, relational and contextual aspects, process as well as outcome, and the public and private reach of justice. In addition, for the lay group, a number of repeat scale measures anchored the narrative analysis. These included 'overall satisfaction' and 'justice being done'. Although I am critical of victim research that splinters people's stories, my analysis did not fully overcome the problem.

The analysis of the lay sample primarily treats them as a single population rather than disaggregating by gender or nature of the offence. However, at Time 1 the difference between the sub-samples of domestic assault victims (N=27) and non-domestic assault victims (N=6) allowed some limited disaggregation. A separate analysis of the views of the women as victims of domestic violence is published elsewhere.[54]

In the end, the meanings given to the idea of justice by both victims and legal officials were far richer than the original procedural focus.

---

[54] Robyn Holder and Kathleen Daly, 'Sequencing Justice: A Longitudinal Study of Justice Goals of Domestic Violence Victims' (2017) *British Journal of Criminology* online doi:10.1093/bjc/azx046.

Ironically, the courtroom created a space where the two groupings shared (if different) interests in justice – though this is unacknowledged and unrecognized. Neither of the lay or legal narratives is claimed as truth or as representative, but their ideas of justice appeared as a dynamic construct. The analysis of these constructs attempts to make visible that which power renders invisible, and to scope multi-dimensional meaning where one (or even two) predominates. Feminist and other critical theorists encourage not only different ways of seeing, but also demand interrogation of dominant world-views. In the institutional setting, my analysis followed Pierre Bourdieu in order to examine ways in which the 'force of law' reveals and deconstructs power relations.[55] Developing upon Bourdieu's approach, I mine historical legacies and justifications that the interviews with public prosecutors revealed. This critical approach enables us to see 'what the law does' as well as to understand 'what the law is'.[56]

One final 'real world' comment needs to be made. I began and remain deeply cognisant of critical scholarly opinion that the law routinely and persistently fails to live up to its promise. But I do not subscribe to positions that would see it diminished or abolished. Undoubtedly the 'myth of rights' described by Stuart Scheingold seduces attention from the more 'ambivalent relationships to law and legal institutions' that research reveals.[57] But I have seen what violence does and the power it wields in the lives of women and men. I know there is a place for guardians of individuals and of the public interest. The problem is how comprehensively and exclusive that place is conceived.

PLAN OF THE BOOK

The book is structured in a slightly unorthodox manner with a preponderance of conceptual discussion in Chapters 1 to 3. These explore the literature; first, on justice and second, on legal mobilization. Usually this type of conceptual and theoretical discussion is restricted to an introductory chapter or inflects the final. However, I place it early to help the reader orient to how later analysis of the three waves of victim interview

---

[55] Pierre Bourdieu, 'The Force of Law: Towards a Sociology of the Juridicial Field' (1987) 38 *Hastings L J* 814.

[56] Susan Silbey, 'After Legal Consciousness' (2005) 1 *Annual Rev Law and Society* 323, 324.

[57] Ibid., 340. Stuart Scheingold, *The Politics of Rights* (2nd ed., U Mich Press 2004).

is developed. Chapter 2 opens with a brief critical examination of contemporary representations of victim interests in justice. I interrogate the nature of the 'public' in the civic realm, in the criminal law, and as an embodiment of difference. I particularly draw on Iris Young's critique of the private/public divide and the manner in which this serves a picture of justice as universal, rational and objective. I then explore the idea of justice through selected literature from political philosophy and the social sciences. Given the enormous breadth of this work, a number of dimensions to the idea of justice are developed that, in later chapters, then serve to frame both victims' and professionals' narratives as well as act as analytic codes. Specifically, these dimensions pose justice as normative guide, as duty, as accountability, as fairness, as relational, and as contextual. In order to accentuate the critical turn of the analysis, I expand on justice as an interpretive conception and as a heuristic in social and political consciousness.

In Chapter 3 I sketch ways in which law is both 'strange and familiar', accessible and remote to people who have experienced injustice.[58] I emphasise the influences at work that open or shut down awareness of law whether as a boundary or an available resource. From an analysis of theories of legal mobilization, I identify and highlight key concepts as either 'top down' or 'bottom up'. The distinction allows us to see that the movement people make from their everyday world to connect with legal authority is not a simple and direct instrumental choice, but is beset by complex decision-making. I outline the research that shows recourse to law to be a minority exercise and disentangle the evidence on victim motivations. The pathways (interpersonal, social and institutional) that are available (and not available) to people following a disruptive event are presented as both real and imagined; and as created by them as well as for them. There is nothing automatic or certain about turning to the law following violence.

Stepping from these theoretical and review chapters, Chapters 4–8 comprise findings from the Justice Study that are new to the field. In Chapter 4 I introduce perspectives on justice from serving and ex-public prosecutors. These perspectives are situated in the present day and as products of certain historic transitions that are selectively told. I unpick core prosecution concepts of independence and public interest. The construct of public interest is presented as both boundary setting and as a gap in the rules in which discretion flourishes.

---

[58] Patricia Ewick and Susan Silbey, *The Common Place of Law* (U Chicago P 1998) 16.

Chapter 5 focuses in to explore the grounded perspective of the 33 individual men and women I interviewed who turned to the law following violence. They are re-framed as voices from below; less as 'victim' and more as 'ordinary people', an alternative rendering that is drawn from cultural theory. From here I then link people to their citizen-status situated in a political arrangement to authorities. The lay participants are introduced and located within data drawn from larger Australian samples. People's comments about law and justice are sharpened by reflection on their objectives and reasoning in reporting the violent incident to police.

Looking through a substantive justice lens, Chapter 6 explores what matters in the idea of justice. Using Gromet and Darley's concept of *justice goals*,[59] I show these are multiple and face in different directions. I develop the notion of a justice trilogy to encompass the concerns the participants show for themselves as victim, for the offender and their community of others. The analysis of victims' multiple goals presents an understanding of fairness that is both contextual (individual, social and institutional) and consequential (constructed over time and experience). In Chapter 7, I shift to examine how people's ideas about justice hold up against their lived experience within the criminal justice system. Here, both procedural and an outcome justice lens illuminate what lies behind assessments of satisfaction. To this analysis are added people's reflections about their treatment. In the different contexts of the justice process the idea of justice becomes slippery and unstable.

Chapter 8 narrows discussion to those lay participants who contributed in all three interviews comprising the longitudinal study. I do this in order to explore how participation works and the extent to which individuals might want to influence decision-making. The discussion is placed within a broader literature about citizen and user participation in public and service spaces, and describes participation in the justice sphere as a unique citizenship practice. I demonstrate that some participatory roles in criminal justice derive from state-centric priorities around the 'decision' and fail to delineate the nature of the interests that the state and victims may (or may not) share. Rather than insisting upon a rigid distinction between public and private, I show that these interests are co-determining. The architecture of the criminal justice system enables

---

59 Dena Gromet and John Darley, 'Punishment and Beyond: Achieving Justice through the Satisfaction of Multiple Justice Goals' (2009) 43 *Law and Soc Rev* 1.

the sequencing of justice objectives and a series of spaces in which mutually constitutive public and private interests can be articulated.

In the final chapter I develop, from the key findings of the research, an argument for participatory justice that draws upon deliberative democracy literature. I argue that not only is justice foundational to the concept of citizenship, but that people's interaction with justice institutions, as a deliberative system, is constitutive of democratic governance. I contend that the exclusion of constituencies of directly affected interests represents a democracy deficit and one that trends against contemporary demands for involved publics and the integration of pluralism within justice.

2. Approaching justice

> To me justice ... you say the word and you know almost what it means. (Edward, 2011)

> When we come to say 'we just don't speak the same language' we mean something more general [than obvious variation]: that we have different immediate values or different kinds of valuation, or that we are aware, often intangibly, of different formations and distributions of energy and interest. (Williams, 1976, 9)

> The pursuit of a theory of justice has something to do with the kind of creatures we human beings are. (Sen, 2009, 414)

JUSTICE MATTERS

In a familiar media spectacle, an individual, often surrounded by family and friends, is standing in front of a court building. To the assembled media, they say, 'this is not justice'. Everyone, from viewers to journalists and to passing lawyers, assume we know what the person means. Despite the ubiquity of justice as a word, a referent and a claim in occasions such as these, it has been under-examined in literature on victims of violence. Like Edward (interviewed for this book), it is as if 'you know almost what it means'.

Justice clearly matters, but why and in what ways? Justice encompasses both actual realizations in people's lives, and acts as an imaginary against which we might evaluate and compare what has happened and what we might aspire to. It is a social and legal value that is not bound to law but may be found there. It can be invoked as a claim and as a weapon, and can also act to settle disputes and to distribute from them. It is the stuff of moral and political philosophy. So diverse and vast is justice theory that it is tempting to skip over it. However, so frequently is justice invoked by victims and the legal fraternity and so loosely is it used in the academic literature on victims, that it demands a more extensive discussion. The chapter makes a path through the diversity of justice literature to identify meanings relevant to victims of violence. This exercise is selective of a panorama of thinking. Reflections on justice, especially those articulated in the everyday, have an unfortunate habit of slipping from one association to another. Justice is a norm, a philosophical ideal, a standard, an outcome and also an institution. Rather than fight this slipperiness, I come to emphasize the manner in which the *idea* of justice *works*; that is, as an interpretive tool,[1] a trope in discourse, and as an analytic and critical code. In this manner justice is conceived as a commonplace and *public* idea that is also vernacularized in interpersonal worlds. In these more intimate spaces, the terms what is *fair* and what is *right* are more commonly used by ordinary people. Justice is a word more generally reserved for public discourse. Therefore it works as a *connecting* idea; something that links private to public, and offers opacity to language that, paradoxically, communicates what is important.

Our guides in this endeavour are critical political philosophers Iris Marion Young and Amartya Sen. They question dominant theorizing which divides private from public, and which separates emotion and moral discourse from the notion of reason. They maintain that critical analysis is historically, socially and politically situated. Furthermore, while arguing from a normative or ideal basis, they are cautious of claims for the transcendent and universal. Critical theory, says Iris Young:

> does not derive such principles and ideals from philosophical premises about morality, human nature, or the good life. Instead the method of critical theory … reflects on existing social relations and processes to identify what we experience as valuable in them, but as present only intermittently, partially, or potentially.[2]

The chapter works with the analytic and interpretive characteristics that the idea of justice offers to victims of violence, located in existing social relations and processes. I find these provide a unique capacity for the idea to work at particular and general levels, and with social and political implications. The features of the word, I will show in later chapters, enable ordinary people to raise possibilities, to ask questions, to communicate, and to think broadly within the context of criminal justice. Finally, in highlighting dimensions to the idea of justice that facilitate critical analysis, I consider the distinction between justice *interests* and *needs*.

---

1 Nathan Gibbs, 'The Nature of Law as an Interpretive Practice and its Associated Modes of Inquiry' (2009) *Legal Studies* 29. Gibbs discusses the law as 'an interpretive social practice'. He grounds this idea in the 'practical understanding of legal agents'. Both of us are interested in the way agents act to bring meaning.

2 Iris Marion Young, *Inclusion and Democracy* (OUP 2000) 10.

The difference applies a more political hue to the relationship between people as victims and criminal justice entities.

The classical concept of justice entails 'giving people what is due to them, and not giving them what is not due to them'. This concept, dominant in moral and political philosophy, gives rise to a duty on us and on our institutions. However, it is useful to distinguish, as political philosopher Adam Swift suggests, between a 'concept', and 'conceptions' of justice. The former, he says, is the broadly agreed 'general structure' of the term and the latter is a 'particular specification of that "concept", obtained by filling out some of the detail'.[3] Whereas Swift confines his discussion to the notion of social justice, I use the concept of justice as that which is due as undergirding the idea (or ideas) of criminal justice. The interpretive rendering of the idea of justice – explored in this book through the reflections of people who are victims of violence – are conceptions. It is in their real-world settings that a more intangible, fluid and ambivalent conception of justice comes alive.

VICTIMS AND JUSTICE CLAIMS

I cannot explore these different ways of seeing the idea of justice without first taking note of some contemporary claims that are made about victims and justice. The debate is riven by a number of schismatic separations – between private and public interests in justice, between victim and offender, between outcomes that are retributive or restorative, between legal and communal justice, and between elite technocratic visions of justice and those that are more ambiguous and contingent.

The discussion can only touch on deeper debate about the nature of human behaviour, especially in communal settings, and whether justice can be pinned to a universal and single standard. The pursuit of justice has been conceived as a product of social learning, of moral development, of cognition, and as a personal contract within the wider social contract.[4] Early debate pitched the duty ethic of justice against relational

---

[3] Adam Swift, *Political Philosophy: A Beginner's Guide for Students and Politicians* (3rd ed, Polity Press, 2014) 13.

[4] For social learning see Albert Bandura, *Social Learning Theory* (Prentice-Hall 1977); of moral development see Jean Piaget, *The Child's Conception of the World* (Rowman & Littlefield 1929); of cognition see John Levine and others, 'Social Foundations of Cognition' (1993) 44 *Annual Review of Psychology* 585–612; as a personal contract within the wider social contract see Melvin

conceptions.[5] These, in turn, connected to philosophical argument about justice being what was *right* and that which was *good* in consequence.[6]

What is said to be important to victims draws in a rather confused manner from these (and other) very wide fields of enquiry. Two assertions in particular are frequently used against them. In the first instance, people who are victims are said to be focused on winning their own ends – the substantive outcome. A related contention is that people who are victims are unwilling or unable to see beyond their own position. Through these arguments it is suggested that victim interests are inimical to justice.

Victims and Outcome Justice

On the first claim it is said that, for victims, getting justice is getting what they want.[7] The idea – discussed later in Chapter 3 – suggests that it is a rational calculation to maximize the utilities law brings. Moreover, the maximization sought is characterized as vengeance or, at least, retributive punishment.[8] The privileging of substantive justice rests, to some extent, on studies that connect victim satisfaction with criminal justice with outcomes such as arrest, prosecution and conviction.[9]

Lerner, 'The Justice Motive: Some Hypotheses as to its Origins and Forms' (1977) 45 *Journal of Personality* 1.

[5] The duty ethic of justice is Lawrence Kohlberg, 'Moral Stages and Moralization: The Cognitive-Development Approach' (1976) *Moral Development and Behavior: Theory Research and Social Issues* and relational conceptions are from Carole Gilligan, *In a Different Voice: Psychological Theory and Women's Development* (Harvard UP, 1982).

[6] There are many writers on these aspects but see Amartya Sen, *The Idea of Justice* (Harvard UP 2009), and John Rawls, *A Theory of Justice* (Harvard UP 1971).

[7] Matt Matravers, 'The Victim, the State and Civil Society' in Anthony Bottoms and Julian Roberts (eds), *Hearing the Victim: Adversarial Justice, Crime Victims and the State* (Willan 2010) 1.

[8] Dale Miller and Neil Vidmar, 'The Social Psychology of Punishment Reactions' in Melvin Lerner and Sally Lerner (eds) *The Justice Motive in Social Behaviour* (Academic Press 1981); Austin Sarat, 'Vengeance, Victims and the Identities of Law' (1997) 6 *Soc and Legal Studies* 163; David Garland, *The Culture of Control: Crime and Social Order in Contemporary Society* (OUP 2001).

[9] Edna Erez, 'Integrating Restorative Justice Principles in Adversarial Proceedings' in E Cape (ed), *Reconcilable Rights? Analysing the Tension between Victims and Defendants* (Legal Action Group 2004); Emmy Whitehead, *Witness Satisfaction: Findings from the Witness Satisfaction Survey 2000* (2001) Home Office Research Study 230.

What people 'get' from their encounters with others and with authorities is said to deeply influence their assessments of fairness. This suggests that justice is a matter of exchange in which cost-benefit assessments of fairness are embedded. Yet, there is no single standard upon which assessments of fair exchange rest. Distributive justice studies argue equity, equality, merit, need and desert as criteria to assess fairness in distributions of a 'good'.[10] Central to these lines of thinking are the *consequential* implications of the distribution.[11] Moreover, it is argued that people who pursue self-interested advantage will prefer an adversarial process that achieves it.[12]

However, other studies examining the relationship between assessments of justice and process and procedure, say that it is being treated well that is important to people.[13] Procedural justice argues that the perception of their in-group value generates compliance with authorities. It is argued that, if legitimacy is the goal, then institutions must make (and be seen to make) an effort to discharge respect and courtesy in fair decision-making procedures. In combination, the attention to fair process is said to address both the compliance of the governed and the legitimacy of the entity.[14] In other words, regardless of actual outcome, if the process is fair then institutions have done their job. Procedural justice is thereby ameliorative if people do not secure their ends.

---

10 Classic texts about these criteria are J Stacy Adams, 'Inequity in Social Exchange' (1965) 2 *Advances in Experimental Social Psychology* 267–99; Peter Blau, 'Justice in Social Exchange' (1964) 34 *Sociological Inquiry* 193–206; Morton Deutsch, *Distributive Justice: A Social-Psychological Perspective* (Yale UP 1985); and Elaine Walster, William Walster and Ellen Berscheid, *Equity Theory and Research* (Allyn and Bacon 1978).

11 'Just desert' is a common term that is linked to distributive and substantive justice. There are two key distinctions in the idea. One refers to 'legitimate entitlement' and the other refers to some type of 'compensation or equalization' (Swift (n 3) 45–8).

12 John Thibaut and Laurens Walker, *Procedural Justice: A Psychological Analysis* (LEA Pub 1975).

13 The group value theory has not been examined with regard to victims of crime. However, the theory is generally relevant to interactions between citizens and authority. See E Allan Lind and Tom Tyler, *The Social Psychology of Procedural Justice* (Plenum 1988).

14 Tom Tyler, *Why People Obey the Law* (PUP 1990); Tom Tyler, 'A Psychological Perspective on the Legitimacy of Institutions and Authorities' in John Jost and Brenda Major (eds), *The Psychology of Legitimacy: Emerging Perspectives on Ideology, Justice and Intergroup Relations* (CUP 2001) 416.

Victim Self-Interest and Justice

People who are victims are also said to be motivated by self-interest in engaging the law and consequently to perceive justice in terms of achieving their desired ends (discussed above). Not only does the observation frown on an apparent inability to see beyond their own position, it places self-interest outside the frame of justice itself. More specifically, if justice is what we owe others or what is owed others, then it is not that connected to a self-regarding imperative; that is, to preferences that are personally beneficial. Therefore, when acting from self-interest, human beings are motivated by advantage and any social or collective benefits are incidental.[15]

However, individualized accounts simplify, narrow, flatten, and de-contextualize human motivation and behaviour, while holding it static. They also tend to extract individuals from their interpersonal and social connections and to abstract them from their class, cultural, gendered and racial identities. In effect, the accusation of self-interest undermines the social legitimacy of persons as victims seeking a role within the public sphere of justice. This representation of the unencumbered individual has been criticized by communitarian and feminist philosophers, as well as social psychologists.[16] Their more multi-dimensional conceptions of humanity conceive of individuals as reflective and adaptive rather than calculative and passive.

Victim self-interest is further categorized as 'private', a notion that is historically and politically situated.[17] As an example, violations of women and children that took place in the domestic sphere were for centuries excluded from public justice. More generally the rejection of the 'private' denies affective and relational concerns in aspirations for

---

[15] What we owe to others is conceived as a duty and, therefore, cannot be incidental (Swift (n 3) 13). The position then argues that we must necessarily share willingness 'to modify our private demands in order to find a basis of justification that others also have reason to accept' (Thomas Scanlon, *What We Owe to Each Other* (Harvard UP 1998) 5).

[16] Michael Sandel, 'The Procedural Republic and the Unencumbered Self' (1984) 2 *Political Theory* 81; Iris Marion Young, *Justice and the Politics of Difference* (Princeton UP 1990); Melvin Lerner, 'The Justice Motive: Where Social Psychologists Found It, How They Lost It, and Why They May Not Find It Again' (2003) 7 *Pers & Soc Psy* 388; Leo Montada and Melvin Lerner (eds), *Responses to Victimization and Belief in a Just World* (Plenum 1998).

[17] Tony Kearon and Barry Godfrey, 'Setting the Scene: A Question of History' in Sandra Walklate (ed), *Handbook of Victims and Victimology* (Willan 2007).

justice. Iris Young further critiques positioning the private realm in opposition to an 'ideal of the civic public'. The ideal, she says, rests on an 'assumption of normative reason as impartial and universal' that 'exhibits a will to unity' which is, ultimately, exclusive of difference.[18] This abstract image of a universalist public is discussed, in Chapter 4, as a critical component of the rationale public prosecutors use to deflect justice claims by victims.

VICTIMS AND PUBLIC JUSTICE

Core to criticism of the assumed outcome focus and self-interest of victims is that justice is a public ideal. Thus it does not belong to any single constituency and is composed of the interests of many. A number of key dimensions to the public character of justice are useful to explore this perspective: the nature and scope of the public realm, what is 'public' about the criminal law, and the nature of people's relationship to criminal law and justice.

Conceptions of the Nature and Scope of the Public Realm

One conception of the civic rests in 'the public realm of sovereignty and the state'. This comprises a representation of a universal and homogenous public in and through which 'citizens express their rationality and universality, abstracted from their particular situations and needs and opposed to feeling'.[19] What remains untouched is the primacy of institutional dominance and institutional arrangements. It is the citizen who is problematized against a state that is purportedly neutral.[20] The state itself is conceived in two principal ways: first, it is minimally facilitative of citizens pursuing their own ends, with no obvious other normative obligation; or second, it is deeply implicated in structures and

---

[18] Iris Marion Young, 'Impartiality and the Civic Public' in Seyla Benhabib and Drucilla Cornell (eds), *Feminism as Critique* (U Minn Press 1987) 59.

[19] Ibid., 63, 73.

[20] This has also been discussed as the triumph of a 'managerialist' approach to criminal law as opposed to one that centres a 'moralistic' conception (Nicola Lacey and Celia Wells, *Reconstructing Criminal Law: Text and Materials* (Buttterworths 1998) 6).

relations of power in which 'the common good' acts to blanket difference, contestation and privilege.[21]

Another conception of the civic emphasizes openness and accessibility. This sense of the public incorporates variability arising from a 'particularist and affective experience of moral life'. This is not just an idea of the public as multiple and messy. It is one where public is constitutive of private and vice versa. The representation is of embodied persons with history, and with diverse identities and community memberships who comprise the public. People's occupation of the individual and group identity of 'victim', therefore, is at best temporary and transitional. They still carry with them prior identifications and statuses. In this civic realm, 'no persons, actions or attributes of persons should be excluded from public discussion and decision-making'.[22]

This latter conception of a deep civic public incorporates a discursive dimension.[23] It envisages dialogue and scrutiny of matters of shared and particular importance. It incorporates scope for 'witness', and opportunities to respond and discuss.[24] While in discursive engagements 'reason and emotion play complementary roles in human reflection', Sen suggests there is good reason to be wary of 'reason' itself. He argues the notion of *reasoning* is more useful in allowing space for the expression of reasons, motivations, preferences and connections that may derive from the private but are given voice in public.[25] Discussion on the nature and causes of injustice draws upon different experiences, observations and ideologies. Therefore the subjective is necessarily present. These then constitute the 'plural groundings' and 'plural reasons' in discussion on justice.[26] A consensus is not required.

---

21 The subject of 'the state' is itself much debated. See e.g., Stephen Mulhall and Adam Swift who provide an overview of debates about the state in *Liberals and Communitarians* (Wiley 1996). Iris Young addresses the different conceptions through an extended discussion on the politics of inclusion in *Inclusion and Democracy* (OUP 2000).

22 Young (n 18) 58, 59.

23 John Dryzek, *Discursive Democracy: Politics, Policy, and Political Science* (CUP 1990); Young (n 21).

24 Young (n 18) 73.

25 Sen (n 6) Part II. However, Sen's depiction of 'public reasoning' has been criticized for its potential to 'disadvantage those for whom this is an unfamiliar or uncomfortable form of communication' (John Dryzek, 'The Deliberative Democrat's Idea of Justice' (2013) 12 *European Journal of Political Theory* 329, 333).

26 Sen (n 6) 2–3.

As theorists with their feet firmly in real worlds, neither Iris Young nor Amartya Sen presumes that the spaces that are public are singular (an open-air domain for example) or are confined to certain moments (such as an election). Their publics are many, as are the spaces they inhabit and visit. Because of this, they recognize that ideas about 'universal' standards and the 'unity' of the public can act to smother heterogeneity, dissonance and the incomplete resolutions that mark contemporary societies. The abstracted 'public' to which criminal justice institutions frequently refer similarly ignores this diversity.

The Public Justice of Criminal Law

It is one of the ironies of criminal justice that it claims to 'own' harms and wrongs on behalf of the public while – at least in dominant discourse – setting aside particular features of individuals, diverse communities and, in part, diverse offences. It does so in the interests of consistency and treating like with like. Part of the reasoning for the state's ownership of the wrongs of crime is that there are 'public dimensions' to the harm that arises, and because of its role as a guarantor of overall security.[27] Thus criminal law is a distinctive kind of public law that is intimately tied to the sovereignty, core functions and legitimacy of the state. Exercising sovereign discretion, the state not only decides who or what is a suitable subject for the protection of the law, but also to whom it owes any rights at all. Thus, within criminal justice, it may owe human rights to some but not to persons as victims.[28] In this domain, individual persons may be used for some version of the common good that the state decides upon. When used as an instrument for other ends, the individual is not owed a duty of respect or accorded a human right of dignity or accorded the human right of *rights*.

---

[27] Matravers (n 7) 7.

[28] Ed Cape (ed), *Reconcilable Rights? Analysing the Tension between Victims and Defendants* (LAG 2004) 14. See Robyn Holder, 'Seeing the State: Human Rights Violations of Victims of Crime and Abuse of Power' in Leanne Weber and others (eds), *The Routledge International Handbook of Criminology and Human Rights* (Routledge 2017) Ch 39 for a contrary discussion of the human rights that are owed victims. Doak also offers extensive discussion of the application of human rights to persons as victims with a focus on the UK and the European Union, see Jonathan Doak, *Victims' Rights, Human Rights and Criminal Justice: Reconceiving the Role of Third Parties* (Hart 2008).

Alternative abolitionist arguments that claim conflict as the private property of citizens do not allow any room for the state.[29] These assume certain homogeneity of persons and that cohesion and commonality are the desired goal. They further lament segmentation and differentiation of social groups and neighbourhoods. However the abolitionist approach does not envisage the multiple publics having a vested interest in the state's protection; such as sexual minorities seeking protection from homophobic attack, for example. This interest is not evenly distributed because, individually and collectively, people are situated differently in spaces laced with oppressive and discriminatory features. Different types of offending, in these contexts, are not neutral engagements around property.

Thus a different case for recognizing a role for the state in criminal justice is that civil society is not uniform and does not have unified goods. As Iris Young says, 'those who wish to undermine injustice cannot turn their backs on state institutions as tools for that end'.[30] There remains a regulatory role for the state in responding to the disadvantage that victimization (of various types) brings. This role encompasses decision-making and enforcement.

Beyond focus on the state, another account of the public nature of criminal law and justice sees it as grounded in and intelligible within human practices and the social world. The 'normative moral language on which the law draws' follows 'thick ethical concepts' that are shared – even when the specifics are vehemently contested.[31] The wrong of crime as a public one is twofold: first that it goes against a law that we accept, and can impose on ourselves and others by 'virtue of [our] shared membership of the political community'; and second that these 'are wrongs in which the community shares'.[32] This theoretical basis for criminal law is wider than the older proposition of justice as rectificatory; that it is only concerned with the justification of punishment. It is instead a far broader exposition of a normative[33] system that seeks to take

---

[29] Nils Christie, 'Conflicts as Property' (1977) 17 *The British Journal of Criminology* 1.

[30] Young (n 21) 8.

[31] R Anthony Duff, *Punishment, Communication, and Community* (OUP 2001) 191.

[32] Ibid., 63; R Anthony Duff, 'Philosophy and "The Life of the Law"' (2009) 26 *Journal of Applied Philosophy* 245, 254.

[33] By normative in this context I mean relating to standards or rules or norms of what 'ought to be'. A norm has a moral basis. A normative institution derives its authority and rationale from those norms.

account of the basis of laws, the different spaces in which they are applied, and their relationship to the polity. These points, Antony Duff suggests, create different meaning to the notion of criminal law as a 'common law'.

The bringing in of the political community to the realm of justice is of course not new.[34] For my purpose, however, there are two key things to notice. The first is that Duff directs attention to the moral authority of criminal law as vesting in its constitutive relationship with the values of the collective. The second is to highlight the status of people's pre-existing relationship as citizens to the state and hence to state authorities. Neither of these claims obviates contestation around those values, nor presumes a stable and solitary relationship between citizen and state.

VICTIM AS CITIZEN AND MEMBER OF THE CIVIC PUBLIC

It is this 'citizen first' perspective that directs attention from the exercise of human practices to their meaning in a social and political context.[35] Ascribing citizen status to the victim gives pause on the significance of the term because the 'citizen' is the ultimate source of authority and accountability. It then asks what being a citizen *does*. First, it invites consideration of claim-making as a citizenship activity. Citizens – responsible, irresponsible or more commonly both – are said to make claims upon authority, indeed, do so on the basis of their status, while at

[34] The term *communitarian justice* has been given to the ideas of a number of different theorists who (in part) want to refocus on 'our moral and social attitudes and commitments' (Alasdair MacIntyre, *After Virtue* (Duckworth 1984) 259). See also, Iris Marion Young, *Justice and the Politics of Difference* (Princeton UP 1990); Michael Sandel, *Liberalism and the Limits of Justice* (CUP 1982); Michael Walzer, *Spheres of Justice* (Basic 1983). Antony Duff puts a different argument for an interlinked liberal-communitarian account of the relationship between the state and persons (n 31 Ch. 2).

[35] Daniel Gilling, 'Crime Control and Due Process in Confidence-Building Strategies: A Governmentality Perspective' (2010) 50 *The British Journal of Criminology* 1136–54. In crime-control literature the 'citizen' is usually problematized as an instrument of government policy. However, this is a top-down perspective that does not consider citizens as plural or as agents in situated localities, or as having relationships of cooperation as well as challenge with the state.

the same time having a collective responsibility to the ways in which that authority works and works for all members.[36]

Secondly, it creates a means of unifying people in their various relationships to a state which has different faces. From this vantage the criminal law is opened out as a site of challenge where, as a member of a political community, the citizen-victim acts to bring the criminal law to life. Similarly the person alleged to have committed a wrongdoing, as another citizen member of the political community, also acts to bring the law to life. Their shared political interest is in specification.[37]

Thirdly, it is in this manner that citizens are '*connected through* the practices and values of that community to their fellow citizens … in a distinctive enterprise of *living together* [emphasis added]'.[38] For my purpose this interpretation by Duff helpfully merges two contesting notions of the citizen – that it is bounded (in some manner) and rights possessing, and that it rests in the 'extent and quality … of one's participation' in a community.[39] Citizens are said to enact their status at micro and macro levels – formal and informal, social and political – in equal and mutually respectful ways in the civic enterprise.[40] Their *citizenship* (as activity and practice) connects explicitly with those schools of democratic theory that emphasize the involvement and participation of citizens.[41] These points leave open (and are explored in later chapters) the nature and specifics of the unique citizenship activity that the citizen-victim enacts.

---

36 Citizenship texts upon which I rely are Engin Isin, 'Citizenship in Flux: The Figure of the Activist Citizen' (2009) 29 *Subjectivity* 367; Egin Isin and Bryan Turner (eds), *Handbook of Citizenship Studies* (Sage 2002). Jane Mansbridge adds the proviso 'provided these fall within the range permitted by the broad constraints of human rights and morality and the deliberative constraints that run from mutual respect to mutual justification' (Mansbridge and others, 'The Place of Self-Interest and the Role of Power in Deliberative Democracy' (2010) 18 *The Journal of Political Philosophy* 64, 77).

37 Antony Duff speaks of the shared interest in persons being brought to account before their fellow citizens for their law (2009 (n 32); Duff, 'Towards a Theory of Criminal Law' (2010) 84(1) *Proceedings of the Aristotelian Society Supplementary Volume* 1–28).

38 Duff 2010 Ibid., 5.

39 Will Kymlicka and Wayne Norman, 'Return of the Citizen: A Survey of Recent Work on Citizenship Theory' (1994) 104 *Ethics* 352, 353.

40 Duff 2010 (n 37) 5.

41 Classic texts are Benjamin Barber, *Strong Democracy: Participatory Politics for a New Age* (U Cal P 1984); Carole Pateman, *Participation and Democratic Theory* (CUP 1970); Young 2000 (n 21).

MAPPING ANOTHER PATH TO JUSTICE

Thus far I have formulated an inclusive public where affected persons with a direct interest in a matter ought to be involved. In the next sections I consider this involvement by examining various ways of placing justice within human practices. To do so requires mapping another path through justice theory. Debates on justice as outcome or process connect only lightly to ancient dialogue about justice as a stern and virtuous end (what's *right*), and justice being that which comes in consequence (what's *good*). There is another story of justice as constitutive of human engagements with one another in contexts where fairness matters.

The dichotomy that is often posed between right and good has deep epistemological roots. The dialogue has, through the ages, been imbued with the colours of the world around it.[42] Since the ancient Greeks, scholars have discussed whether justice is *the* virtue or *one of* the virtues, and have presented nuanced conceptions of the nature of the outcome justice serves. Justice has been posed as universal or particular; and presented as either humane and benevolent, or chilly and remote. Still others have focused on justice as an evaluative framework for the arrangement of institutions and about procedures for the allocation of resources or decisions. There is extensive argument that justice is grounded in moral value; or that it is bound by pure reason excluding all other considerations. Some claim that justice is about the rules or, if not that, then it is about the rights. Philosophical approaches to justice *also* reveal divergence and contestation.

The different approaches in part reflect the different domains in which the idea of justice is important. Context and standpoint clearly matter. The *language* of justice is very different if one is reading philosophy or economics or psychology or law. Nonetheless, it also reverberates through everyday life.[43] Here the expression of justice is about what is *fair* or what is *right* or what is for the *good*. Since it is towards these everyday and ordinary interpretations that I look in this book, I map a path through this literature in three steps. First, I lay out some conceptions of justice and draw out core components or dimensions to the idea of justice that resonates in the everyday world. Secondly, I discuss justice as interpretation. I suggest that, when linked to injustice, the idea of

---

[42] Isiah Berlin, *The Crooked Timber of Humanity* (Princeton UP 1990).

[43] Michael Ross and Dale Miller (eds), *The Justice Motive in Everyday Life* (CUP 2002).

justice works as a heuristic in rights and legal consciousness. I then summarize where this different map of justice takes us.

CONCEPTIONS OF JUSTICE

This mapping of some (and by no means all) conceptions of justice draws upon the social sciences, as well as from moral and political philosophy. In doing so, I do not mean to elevate these conceptions to empirical truths. Rather, these are a *fleshing out* of the concept of justice *for* people who are victims. I could also ascribe these conceptions to particular domains. It may seem logical, for example, to locate 'justice as duty' to institutional settings; or 'relational justice' purely to civil society. However, I resist the temptation. That type of schematic is unhelpful to the task of mapping complexity. The key conceptions I highlight are:

- justice as normative guide
- justice as duty
- justice as accountability
- justice as fairness
- justice as relational
- justice as contextual.

Justice as Normative Guide

A normative conception of justice says what *ought to be*. Setting out what ought to be or ought to be done can also be understood as a norm, some of which have a moral basis while others do not. A normative conception is also a way of describing the rules, standards or norms that comprise a particular specification.

However, this leaves open how justice norms operate and are constituted. The normative question, according to moral philosopher Christine Korsgaard, is the way in which certain standards 'make claims on us. [Claims that can] command, oblige, recommend or guide'.[44] Whether claimed in desires, beliefs or judgments, normativity can be posed as ethics that operate to prioritize and organize our commitments and actions in personal, social and political realms. The idea of justice as a normative guide is that it makes a claim on how and why we might act (or not). Indirectly, guiding norms can act as a kind of algorithm for framing if not determining action.

[44] Christine Korsgaard, *The Sources of Normativity* (CUP 1996) 8.

For people victimized by violence, a normative conception of justice provides a way of thinking through 'what's the right thing to do'. While this has a simple surface, the conception does hide 'a more complicated picture'.[45] It does not, for instance, say what justice itself *ought* to be comprised of.

Justice as Duty

This is left to the conception of justice as duty. This is perhaps the most ancient of conceptions and is closely connected to justice as a normative guide or system.[46] Justice in this realm is imperative and demanding. It is about constraint. Justice as duty aims to be rational, objective, impartial and neutral as to consequence. It prioritizes what is *right* over what might be *good* and is even said to be a 'natural duty'.[47] Justice is giving people what is their due, and not giving what is not their due.

Justice as duty and right speaks strongly to legal systems. It offers some explanation for why legal systems assert an obligation to obey. Institutional arrangements and rules emphasize this obligation by maintaining transparency, consistency, predictability and the absence of bias. Justice here prides itself on its rigour in the face of scrutiny. An institution will claim it is just through the existence of such rules. It will draw much of its legitimacy as well as its authority from them.

This stern justice can reflect 'unattractive or even incoherent assumptions about human interests and human community'.[48] It requires thin information for what is rich decision-making.[49] Obviously the conception of justice as duty has implications for how people act towards each other. It also has implications for the ways in which institutions act towards persons.

---

45 Michael Sandel, *Justice: What's the Right Thing to Do?* (Farrar, Straus and Giroux 2009) 9.

46 Raymond Wacks, *Philosophy of Law: A Very Short Introduction* (OUP 2009).

47 Rawls (n 6) 115.

48 Will Kymlicka, 'Rawls on Teleology and Deontology' (1988) 17 *Philosophy and Public Affairs* 173.

49 John Braithwaite and Philip Pettit, *Not Just Deserts: A Republican Theory of Criminal Justice* (Clarendon Press 1990) 28.

Justice as Accountability

Justice as duty is closely related to justice as accountability. The Aristotelian idea of 'rectificatory' justice addresses harms or wrong. Many streams then flow from action that brings a wrongdoer to account. Justice may generate effects that are retributive, punishing, restorative, rehabilitative, and that denounce and deter. These can be described as some of the aims of justice. Bringing wrongdoers to account (or ending impunity) is a common call to justice in many settings.

Deeply embedded within the idea of justice rectifying harm or wrong lies consideration of the responsibility of people for their conduct, and hence their deservingness. It has an enduring, even common-sense, place within conceptions of justice.[50] Desert further connects to principles of merit, equity, equality, need or entitlement. Assuming the conduct does involve choice or intent, then responsibility and accountability informs the nature and content of what follows and could be just.

The idea of responsibility and accountability is foundational to belief in a just world.[51] Melvin Lerner's influential hypothesis says that an individual's expectation of justice constitutes an internalized personal contract derivative of its environment and of the wider social contract. It is said that we believe just outcomes will eventually follow from our psychological, material and physical investments, and therefore we are able to accommodate short-term injustices.[52] The proposition suggests that self-constraint is a component in a just world.

Justice as Fairness

John Rawls' corpus re-introduced *fairness* as a (if not *the*) central component to justice.[53] Fairness emerges as a key determinant to the justice of allocations, of procedures, and of decisions. It works to calibrate the distribution of benefits and burdens.

Furthermore, fairness as a rubric performs routine even mundane assessment across a wide variety of human activity. Thinking about and

---

[50] Wojciech Sadurski, *Giving Desert it's Due: Social Justice and Legal Theory* (Reidel 1985).

[51] Lerner (n 4) 1–52.

[52] Melvin Lerner, *The Belief in a Just World* (Springer US 1980). Lerner says that our belief in a just world is a delusion.

[53] The avowal of the centrality of fairness is made in relation to liberal democracies. It is open as to whether or not, and the extent to which, fairness is a key determinant in other societies.

asking what is fair in a given situation is a common human guide. In the discourse about justice, fairness operates as a vernacular grounded in the moral powers people have. Fairness brings to justice the consideration of others and moderates rational self-interest. Thus fairness is a 'cognitive shortcut' that steers decisions about investments with others and in situations; and also guides assessments about these various involvements.[54] It is responsive to information-rich environments. Fairness as a guide is influential on the ways in which persons assess their relationship to others and in groups. It is particularly evident in situations of flux and change in relationships – features relevant for victims of violence.

Justice as Relational

In a relational universe, people's lives are deeply connected rather than individuated and separated.[55] People's justice judgments in this world emerge not just from their own needs or the particular needs of others, but as evolving from particular relationships *with* others. This 'ethic of care' is cast as animated and multi-dimensional. It does not draw boundaries, nor pin down and suppress subjectivity. Relational justice challenges the ideal of impartiality.

A relational conception of justice is often posed as gendered in noticing that a disconnected and detached masculine justice represents itself as a full account of civilization and humanity. Rather than strive for universalism, justice that is relative performs as 'a marker of the human condition'.[56] From this perspective, the answer to the question 'what is justice?' becomes, *it depends*.

Relational concerns in justice are not confined to the familial or to in-groups. Justice is claimed as 'fundamentally an interpersonal construct' because we do not live in isolation from others and regardless of the distance between persons.[57] This particular reflection says that to think in terms of justice *necessarily* asks us to think of others. To do so

---

[54] E Allan Lind, 'Fairness Heuristic Theory: Justice Judgments as Pivotal Cognitions in Organizational Relations' in Jerald Greenberg and Russell Cropanzano (eds), *Advances in Organizational Justice* (Stanford UP 2001) 56, 190. See also Lind and Tyler (n 13).

[55] This depiction does not assume connection that is cooperative or conflicting. Rather it simply says there is inter-dependence.

[56] Carol Gilligan, *In a Different Voice: Psychological Theory and Women's Development* (Harvard UP 1982) xviii.

[57] Linda Skitka, 'Of Different Minds: An Accessible Identity Model of Justice Reasoning' (2003) 7 *Personality and Social Psychology Review*, 286, 293.

then argues room is made for the views and suggestions of others. From this point, conceptions of justice appear as provisional, multiple and even contradictory.

Justice as Contextual

Relational justice recognizes people as situated in a variety of ways in their social and political space. Identities are multiple and shift, merge and form. People are not singular. The spaces they inhabit are generally not settled or discrete. Highlighting different contexts in which the need for justice might arise thus questions any universalized standard. In making assessments and thinking what is just, people will draw on moral reasoning, a sense of fairness in distribution, and judgment about their treatment. That is, justice is context-sensitive, and emerges as contingent.

In different contexts there is 'complexity and flexibility of people's justice reasoning', and justice judgments are seen to 'vary both between and within persons over time'.[58] This point is particularly important for victims who not only engage with a number of different institutions, but maintain varying levels of connection and distance with others (including the offender). The wider frame around the social and institutional spaces that victims traverse allows consideration of multiple assessments of justice using different criteria. This gives rise to the possibility of partial ordering of priorities for justice, as well as incompleteness.[59] Imperfect, though comprehensive, outcomes may result. Incompleteness, however, does not mean dropping particular concerns.

With a wider frame, different dimensions to people's individual and social lives come more clearly into view. For example, personal identity characteristics such as age or gender may become more salient. Similarly, emergent features consequent upon the victimization, such as mental health or financial harm or family breakdown, will also become more apparent. People inhabit spaces and lives where concrete social and political practices precede their engagement with and search for justice. Casting and recasting ideas of justice in these fluid environments suggest it is a never-quite-filled vision.

---

[58] Linda Skitka and others, 'Knitting Together an Elephant: An Integrative Approach to Understanding the Psychology of Justice Reasoning' in Ramona Bobocel and others (eds), *The Psychology of Justice and Legitimacy: The Ontario Symposium* 11th Vol. (Taylor and Francis 2010) 1–26.

[59] Sen (n 6) 102–5.

MAKING MEANING ABOUT JUSTICE

The different conceptions that I have highlighted do not indicate a fixed perspective of justice. They demonstrate a conception that is enlivened in human hands. To understand justice as a malleable idea requires understanding more of the human context. That is, how people find and make meaning, how reason and reasoning relate and are different, how important injustice is to the search for justice, and the various ways in which interaction facilitate meaning-making.

Finding Meaning in the World

It is apparent that the idea of justice is open to different interpretations in different contexts. Herbert Blumer has shown that three key premises underpin interpretation. First, 'human beings act toward things on the basis of the meanings that the things have for them'. Secondly, the meanings attributed to things 'is derived from, or arises out of, the social interaction that one has with one's fellows'; and finally, 'meanings are handled in, and modified through, an interpretive process used by the person in dealing with the things he encounters'. Interpretation is a process 'through which the individual handles his world and constructs his action', and from which he might 'map and construct lines of conduct'.[60] Human beings are profoundly social in this process.

Contributing to meaning-making are 'stocks of knowledge' that presume a degree of shared understanding.[61] The ideal of justice, therefore, is a 'sensitising concept' that is facilitative of action. Justice becomes an *imaginary* that serves as 'a word of magic evocations'.[62] The idea acts as a pull to those who have experienced injustice. Furthermore, institutionalized manifestations of justice can act as a symbol of 'outer power' through which indeterminate experience may be mediated and managed.[63] As a theory, Blumer's symbolic interactionism accommodates the constraints that context and situation impose on people by recognizing

---

[60] Herbert Blumer, *Symbolic Interactionism: Perspective and Method* (U Cal P 1969) 2, 14; Jonathan Turner, *A Theory of Social Interaction* (Stanford UP 1988) 18.

[61] The term is from Alfred Schutz (1932), *Phenomenology of the Social World*, Trans. George Walsh and Frederick Lehnert (Northwestern UP 1967) 80 and is discussed in Turner Ibid., 79–83.

[62] Edmund Cahn quoted in Eric Stover, *The Witnesses: War Crimes and the Promise of Justice in The Hague* (U Penn P 2011) 1.

[63] Franco Crespi, *Social Action and Power* (Blackwell 1992) 99.

adaption, adjustment, re-definition and re-presentation. Many interactions and influences – interpersonal, cultural, and institutional for example – contribute to appraisal and reappraisal.

Reasoning and Agency

The different conceptions of justice form a prism through which to see, understand and engage with the world. Exploring this idea further requires identifying core features of the human condition. The first is our capacity to think and to reason.[64] This capacity interacts with other features of our makeup: values, emotions, beliefs and attitudes. Secondly, human reasoning also interacts with our moral and relational sensibilities. Finally, I assume that human beings have agency; not of the individualist and atomized kind, but that which is encumbered with our social and political relations as well as burdened by responsibilities, and by experiences of injustice and disadvantage.

Presenting people in this manner does not require that persons are all rational or reason rationally; one simply has to acknowledge that especially (but not only) we think about what to do. While there are different understandings of practical reasoning, I take a simple definition that it is 'the sorts of reasoning that we attempt in contexts of action'.[65] Reasoning will not take place on a blank canvas either. Values, norms, and beliefs form an existing infrastructure. However, these can be 'too abstract, general and incomplete to guide specific concrete action in specific concrete situations'.[66] Thinking and reasoning about what to do and how to interpret justice will be an information-rich exercise. Appraisal and assessment will weigh many aspects including features of the situation, prevailing norms, contextual power relations, and relevant criteria such as desert. Reasoning these combinations shows the idea of justice as a method of evaluation.

Of course, static portrayals of persons do not emerge from these assumptions. Neither is their agency unconstrained. The 'space for action' is not the same between persons.[67] Yet they emerge with moral status and ethical standing. They are conceived as whole persons who act in relation to prevailing norms in a relationship with a 'range of bodies

---

[64] Here the capacity to reason is posed as the activity of *reasoning*. This does not presume or prioritize reason as rational and objective.

[65] Onora O'Neill, *Bounds of Justice* (CUP 2000) 11.

[66] Morris Zelditch, 'Theories of Legitimacy' in Jost and Major (n 14) 33, 51.

[67] The 'space for action' is a concept developed by Maddie Coy and Liz Kelly in *Islands in the Stream* (Trust for London 2011).

and people who are continuously mediating their daily lives'.[68] To conceive of persons as rights-bearing citizens makes their sacrifice for some larger social good more troubling.

Finding Justice from Injustice

But something must make it occur to us to think about justice. It is people experiencing, claiming, perceiving and acknowledging victimization, oppression, disadvantage, domination or discrimination that brings to life the idea of justice. Injustice animates thinking and signals certain human values at risk. Only looking at justice misses these deep roots. In recognition of this, Sen opens *The Idea of Justice* with a story about the indignity and affront of violence victimization. An excerpt from Dickens' *Great Expectations* describes Pip's reflection on the violence in his childhood. Sen uses the story to pose 'the identification of redressable injustice' in the 'lives and freedoms of the people involved' as central to his theory of justice. The experience or perception of injustice with its 'inequities or subjugations' moves us, he says. It is the emotional (indeed, moral) power of injustice that stimulates scrutiny.[69]

Violence – as an experience of injustice – acts as an instrument to undermine, if not destroy, human flourishing. Philosopher Christine Korsgaard claims that '[i]f justice is what makes it possible for a person to function as a single unified agent, then injustice makes it impossible'.[70] If there is an immorality in violence such that it stirs a moral response, it is that it targets human dignity and autonomy and makes self-respect, 'worthiness', equality and freedom contingent.[71]

However, not all injustice is perceived as such. Human beings in a range of situations have been shown to believe powerfully that their world is just when it is, on objective fact, patently not.[72] Therefore the interpretation of injustice is one often done with third parties. This 'ideal

68 Charles Pattie, Patrick Seyd and Paul Whiteley, *Citizenship in Britain: Values, Participation and Democracy* (Cambridge UP 2004) 110.

69 Sen (n 6) vi, xii, 40.

70 Christine Korsgaard, *The Constitution of Agency: Essays on Practical Reason and Moral Philosophy* (OUP 2008) 108.

71 Drucilla Cornell, *The Imaginary Domain: Abortion, Pornography, and Sexual Harassment* (Routledge 1995) 11–12.

72 Lerner 1977 (n 4); 2003 (n 16).

observer'[73] is said to be 'in the realm of justice' rather than in 'the realm of fortune' where ill luck, disadvantage and misfortune (the natural and social contingencies) are determinative.[74] From this distanced standpoint, we are invited to consider difficult dilemmas or decisions as they affect others.

Empirical work unsettles suggestions that injustice acts as an imperative for action. Studies reveal a complex picture. For example, it is possible for victims of injustice to live with or neutralize an awareness of the injustice or to not perceive a situation as unjust against objective criteria that reveals it as such.[75] Victims may minimize harm and deflect fault. They may assess the cost of doing something in relation to victimization as too high. The experience of injustice does not necessarily prompt a feeling of discomfort or disadvantage, nor necessarily prompt action. Key to these scenarios may be *judgments* about something as just or unjust. That is, a perceived violation of rights or entitlements involves 'attributions of causality, controllability and intent to an agent who is not the victim, as well as perceived lack of justification'.[76] Furthermore, the responsibility attributed to the harm-doer and the degree of intention in particular 'affect the evaluative, emotional and behavioural reactions of victims and third parties'.[77] Taken together these findings suggest that the emotional weight of injustice may assume and carry more consequence than the perceived violation of entitlement or right.

Justice in Interaction

As Anthony Giddens has argued, this rich reflexive capacity to interpret and draw meaning is foundational to contemporary understandings of social action.[78] Central therefore to specification about injustice and justice is dialogue. Dialogue is information gathering and information

---

[73] The concept originates with Adam Smith and is discussed in BC Postow, 'Ethical Relativism and the Ideal Observer' (1978) 39(1) *Phil and Phen Research* 120.

[74] Francis Snare, 'Misfortune and Injustice: On Being Disadvantaged' (1986) 16 *Canadian Jrn of Phil* 39, 41.

[75] Gerold Mikula and Klaus Schlamberger, 'What People Think About an Unjust Event: Toward a Better Understanding of the Phenomenology of Experiences of Injustice' (1985) 15 *Euro Jrn of Soc Psych* 37; see also Sen (n 6).

[76] Gerold Mikula, 'On the Experience of Injustice' (1993) 4 *Euro Rv of Soc Psych* 223, 229.

[77] Gerold Mikula, 'Testing an Attribution-of-Blame Model of Judgments of Injustice' (2003) 33 *Euro Jrn of Soc Psych* 793, 805.

[78] Anthony Giddens, *The Constitution of Society* (Polity Press 1984).

assessing. It brings forth different interests and different criteria in an evaluative exercise that takes account of different points of view. Justice on this account is dialogically constructed and constituted, and comes 'within the human horizon'.[79] Furthermore, the dialogic nature of interpretation, communication and action potentially repositions individuals in a fundamentally powerful role in the polity. Dialogue and dissention inform a stronger civil society in relation to the state.

Although justice's call on the individual may be to ask questions, seek clarification and articulate principles, it is through a dialogic process that the self is understood *in* the world. In Sen's terms, 'the evaluation needed for the assessment of justice is not just a solitary exercise but one that is inescapably discursive'.[80] This invitation to reciprocate and collaborate on an understanding of the meaning of justice involves not simply a confirmation but is also a creation – that is, an invitation to re-pattern common interests and shared values. The call to justice 'involves the transformation of existing interests and the creation of new, shared interests'.[81] These shared interests may involve alterations to the enterprise of living together, or the articulation of emergent norms. These too are not necessarily fixed.

Reflecting on Conceptions of Justice

In this section I have drawn together strands of intellectual thought about justice that are current and which circulate in society; and traces of which are found in debate about victims. Knitted together into conceptions, these thought-strands can be used uncritically and unreflectively by ordinary people, and thus can appear conflicting and contradictory. Equally, the thinking resonates strongly precisely because it comes from and is used by people in the everyday.

These conceptions do not find fixed meaning – perhaps because the classic concept of justice being what is due to persons remains open to context: how then is this figured and decided? What will it mean between this person and the next, or between persons in conflict situations? These questions come when real lives, diverse social groupings, and actual institutions interact.

None of these conceptions of justice is argued as a human *need* (although arguably fairness is a human need). Rather, the emphasis is that

---

79 Berlin (n 42) 11.

80 Sen (n 6) 337.

81 Susan Mendus, 'The Importance of Love in Rawls' Theory of Justice' (1999) 29 *Brit Jrn of Pol Sci* 57, 68.

people have *interests* in justice that derive from their status as citizens in the first instance, and as persons who have become victims in the second. Iris Young restricts 'interests' to those which are 'self-referring' and 'whatever is necessary or desirable in order to realise the ends the agent has set'.[82] Her definition focuses on means to ends, and thus 'instrumentalises' the notion of interests. I prefer Jane Mansbridge's definition of interest as an 'enlightened preference. That is, what hypothetically one would conclude after ideal deliberation was one's own good or one's policy preference, including other-regarding and ideal-regarding commitments'.[83] My argument, consistent with the conceptions I have outlined, is that interests expand beyond but do not dismiss the self and incorporate individuals in their diverse social worlds.[84] Citizens have interests in how others are treated, as well as themselves, and interests in the manner in which civic and state institutions work. Citizen's interests comprise an instrumental and ethical meld.

I do not argue against the notion that persons who are victims have justice *needs*,[85] although a needs focus has diverted attention to various therapeutic arguments about what justice could be.[86] What I do suggest is that resolution of the justice *interests* of citizen-victims is their priority when engaged with criminal justice. The resolution of their *needs* may be consequential upon the satisfaction of their interests. To have interests in justice speaks to a form of civic membership, engagement and participation that has its roots in democratic ideals.

SEEKING JUSTICE IN THE REAL WORLD

This chapter has analysed the fluidity of and contextualization to ideas about justice. I have departed from a search for 'transcendent' justice

---

[82] Young (n 2) 134.

[83] Mansbridge and others (n 36) 68.

[84] I note others' difficulty with the question of victim interests. For example, the Victims' Rights Working Group, established to promote the rights and interests of victims before the International Criminal Court, can agree no shared theoretical or practical view on 'interests' except that it 'requires special attention' and that 'voices' should be heard.

[85] Judith Herman, 'Justice from the Victim's Perspective' (2005) 11 *Violence Against Women* 571; Leslie Sebba, *Third Parties: Victims and the Criminal Justice System* (Ohio SUP 1996).

[86] Edna Erez, Michael Kilchling and Jo-Anne Wemmers (eds), *Therapeutic Jurisprudence and Victim Participation: International Perspectives* (Carolina AP 2011).

while acknowledging the ways in which this ideal *works*. Ideas about justice help to connect people's experience of violation, victimization and injustice to wider public concerns. In this manner conceptualizations of justice animate consciousness of rights, and open possible lines of action.

One of these lines of action ponders the offer of law. There are practical and actual concerns that violence gives rise to, involving self and others. It creates a focal point from which we might begin to talk about *approaching law*. But if the idea of justice feels malleable, then *law* feels solid, 'thing-like', and something like a device.[87] It feels instrumental. It stands in contrast to the ductile nature of justice. The next chapter explores the way law is considered within social settings and ways in which it may interact with ideas of justice. It charts how the phenomenon of law also shifts in people's hands. Here too we encounter a similarly wide range of ideas about what law is, what law does and how law can be acted upon; all of which mean that questions why and how citizen-victims might mobilize the law in response to violence have few simple answers.

---

87 Naomi Mezey, 'Out of the Ordinary: Law, Power, Culture, and the Commonplace' (2001) 26 *Law and Social Inquiry* 145, 158.

3. Approaching law*

I would have said [the law is] there for our benefit. (Roslyn, 2010)

We tell ourselves stories in order to live … We look for the sermon in the suicide, for the social or moral lesson in the murder of five. We interpret what we see, select the most workable of the multiple choices. We live entirely, especially if we are writers, by the imposition of a narrative line upon disparate images, by the 'ideas' with which we have learned to freeze the shifting phantasmagoria which is our actual experience. (Didion, 1979, 11)

THINKING ABOUT LAW

If justice is a dynamic concept responsive to human practices then what about law? Law leans towards certainty rather than to indeterminacy. So is it for certainty that a citizen-victim may turn to it? How might they view the relationship between justice and law, if any? A separation of these is neither a new nor an uncontroversial proposition. Upholding law, applying law, and maintaining the rule of law is a *raison d'être* of criminal justice, so where does justice stand? At a more grounded level, where does the citizen-victim stand, and what is the law to them? This person is generally viewed as having private interests whereas the institutions of criminal justice represent themselves as embodiments of the state. This stance presents neutrality as set in opposition to the private realm but as responsive to a disembodied public. So why, when and how do members of that public turn to law in search of justice? It is not an obvious choice.

This chapter maps the landscape around these questions in a number of steps. First is a sketch of the dominant ways in which law presents itself. Then everyday consciousness of the law and its constitutive relationship

* Portions of Chapter 3 first appeared in Robyn Holder, 'Victims, legal consciousness, and legal mobilisation' (2017) in the edited collection from Antje Deckert and Rick Sarre, *The Palgrave Handbook of Australian and New Zealand Criminology, Crime, and Justice*. Reproduced with permission by Palgrave Macmillan.

to social life are foregrounded as counterweight to law-centric and state-centric visions. The schema embedded within legal consciousness illuminates connections and disconnections between the meaning people make of events and the action they may take. This focus on law and consciousness provides a different way to understand citizen-victims' engagements with criminal justice. When and how they report crime following victimization has been extensively described, but less so how they interpret what has happened to them as a precursor. The interaction between meaning-making about the event and the availability of law is explored through different theories of legal mobilization. Some theorists emphasize the attracting power of law while others suggest citizens understand its limited and uncertain role.

One obvious aim in the chapter is to decentre formal legal institutions and procedures to take 'seriously the idea that ordinary people can be legal actors'.[1] The proposition views the mobilization of criminal law as much a social and civil practice as it is a means to some self-interested end. As a practice, it is influenced by cultural as well as legal schemas and emerges from people's membership of a bounded polity of citizens. The perspective highlights the interconnected and derivative nature between behavioural standards embodied in criminal law and wider social norms. Through legal mobilization people re-inscribe these norms and seek to re-establish their collective context. Yet law's offer and how people understand its relationship to their situated selves varies. The collective public is heterogeneous. A community of citizens experience law in ways that are different and similar. It is through this orientation that I re-focus attention on the broader political character of ordinary people's engagement of the criminal law as victims. It is *political* in that the interaction signifies and activates a relationship with state authority that has wider public implications.

LAW'S IMAGE

Law projects different images. In ordinary and everyday worlds law is close and distant, peculiar and familiar. In their ground-breaking ethnographic study of legality in everyday American life, *The Common Place of Law*, Patricia Ewick and Susan Silbey identify a range of commonplace ideas or schema about the law. They argue against ascription of any particular schema to one or other demographic or to one or other event.

---

[1] Anna-Maria Marshall and Scott Barclay, 'In Their Own Words: How Ordinary People Construct the Legal World' (2003) 28 *Law and Soc Inq* 617.

Rather, the ideas act to illuminate how law works in the everyday. Usually law's 'own story' emphasizes its centrality to liberal democracy through the rule of law and its separateness to that which is common and unremarkable.[2] It is a formal presence and formal entity comprising lofty adherence to rule and principle, and to immanent rationality. Legal text, legal doctrine and legal actors such as judges, lawyers and legal academics are posed as a reality of authority, continuity, form, truth and internal cohesion where law is its own master. Within this view, law is foundational to the consensus basis of the sovereign order. Here law is command and its subjects are organized, ruled, and sanctioned.

From this perspective, the impact of law and legal practices is unidirectional but works in different ways. Ordinary people – as citizens, complainants, defendants and litigants – are acted upon. If they approach law they do so cautiously. They are submissive 'before the law'. Law is taken to transcend individuals and moments, and justness is presumed. If law, legal procedure and law's institutions are experienced in some frustration, this does not weaken their authority. If approached by law, ordinary people are most often portrayed as resisting, evading and re-casting law and legality.[3] They are said to be 'against the law' and may be mulish, resentful or defiant.[4] However, this perspective minimizes the 'institutional autonomy and operational elasticity' of the law.[5] In consequence law is lifeless.

A view of law as self-governing also detaches it from its social context. This is particularly so for criminal law. A law-centric and state-centric position accentuates the threat and control of criminal sanction. However, de-centring law asks a different question: it asks, 'what kind of criminal law, serving what ends and expressing what values, is appropriate for … citizens of a particular kind of polity'. Here there is a very direct connection: 'the law should see and address those whom it claims to bind as citizens'.[6] This proposition from Antony Duff joins other critics of legal centralism. A law-centric stance renders ordinary people as external and passive, and invests law and legal

---

[2] Patricia Ewick and Susan Silbey, *The Common Place of Law* (U Chicago P 1998) 83.

[3] Sally Merry, *Getting Justice and Getting Even: Legal Consciousness Among Working-Class Americans* (U Chicago P 1990).

[4] Ewick and Silbey (n 2) 47–8.

[5] Kam Wong, 'Black's Theory On The Behaviour Of Law Revisited' (1995) 23(3) *Int'al Jrn of the Soc of Law* 189, 221.

[6] Antony Duff, 'Towards a Theory of Criminal Law' (2010) 84(1) *Proceedings of the Aristotelian Society Supplementary Volume* 1, 3, 5.

institutions with the power to attract and repel. Although the law is 'all over' in ways that people – indeed whole constituencies – experience differently,[7] Duff's account says that it is also true that people 'understand and use law'.[8] How they do this, however, is highly responsive.

LEGAL CONSCIOUSNESS, LAW AND SOCIAL CONTEXT

The Everyday

We see this responsivity by looking at law and justice from below, from the everyday. This everyday is lived and common. It is a place of shared meanings and understandings where the ordinary is dignified as well as a place where marginality is encountered. At the same time, it is a product of decisions, activities and histories in which ordinary people do not participate and about which they may not even be aware. French sociologist, Michel de Certeau, however invests weight, authority and challenge in the 'tactics' people employ in the everyday.[9] He stresses that, in the everyday, people are active. They act, react, interact and connect; they ignore, interpret and re-construct; and they negotiate, manipulate, manage, mobilize and plan in a complex reality that is material and imagined. The everyday comprises spaces where power is exercised, understood and resisted in lived experience. Multiple, often overlapping, realities jostle; where the 'intimate intrusions' of sexual and physical abuse are found,[10] and racial discrimination is 'everywhere'.[11] The everyday is riven with stereotype and competing narratives. It is not necessarily a beatific place.

---

[7] Austin Sarat, 'Law is all Over: Power, Resistance, and the Legal Consciousness of the Welfare Poor' (1990) 2 *Yale Jrn of Law and the Humanities* 343.

[8] Merry (n 3) 5.

[9] Michel de Certeau, *The Practice of Everyday Life*, Trans. Steven Rendall (U Cal P 1984).

[10] Elizabeth Stanko, *Intimate Intrusions: Women's Experiences of Male Violence* (RKP 1985).

[11] Coles as cited in Kristin Bumiller, *The Civil Rights Society: The Social Construction of Victims* (Johns Hopkins UP 1988) 70.

The activities of the everyday take place beneath the radar and the notice of the world of formal rules and formal institutions.[12] In contrast to law-centric perspective, the everyday is as much places, spaces and occasions where rules and laws are evaded, reinvented and discounted as it is where they are made, re-made and respected. The deep patterning of rules comprises habits of legality. Consciousness of the boundaries, standards, possibilities and mitigations of the social world do not require the formal institutions of the state. They are submerged frames and guides to social practices and interactions. The 'discourse of law' is one such frame. It provides language for meaning-making and 'shaping our taken-for-granted understandings of the social world'.[13] This legal consciousness works hand-in-hand with rights consciousness. Consciousness of rules and rights influences a look away from law or a turn towards it.

Looking Away From Law

Legal consciousness considers the 'ways in which people make sense' of law. Ewick and Silbey's ethnography suggests three dominant approaches. One way takes together the beliefs, attitudes and actions of individuals and social groups to 'determine the form and texture of social life'. Liberal political and legal theory stresses the consensus forged around ideals of fairness and equal treatment. A second way conceptualizes law and legal consciousness as 'epiphenomena because a particular social and economic structure is understood to produce a corresponding or appropriate legal order, including legal subjects'. An aspect of this perspective concentrates on the legitimating functions of law within the social order. Finally, legal consciousness can be identified as cultural practice. It is conceived as 'part of a reciprocal process in which the meanings given by individuals to their world, and law and legal institutions as part of that world, become repeated, patterned and stabilised, and those institutionalised structures become part of the meaning systems employed by individuals'.[14] Here human action and structural constraint are integrated and law is *produced.*

---

[12] However, see Walklate's discussion on the use and misuse of victims of crime in policy and political debate in Britain. Sandra Walklate, *Imagining the Crime Victim* (Open UP 2007).

[13] Catherine Albiston, 'Legal Consciousness and Workplace Rights' in Benjamin Fleury-Steiner and Laura Neilson (eds), *The New Civil Rights Research: A Constitutive Approach* (Ashgate 2006) 55, 56.

[14] Ewick and Silbey (n 2) 35–9.

Looking away from law itself sees legality as constructed and mediated through signs, signals and storytelling in a socialized discourse. These narratives encode and position people, places and events. However, they tell many complex and contradictory stories; stories which interact with other schemas such as those of political consciousness, the 'injustice frames' of feminism, workplace ideology, legal imaginations, legal norms, and local cultures.[15] Legal consciousness is soaked in context and contingency.

Law in Social Context

The law-centric and state-centric view tends to accentuate the instrumental functions of law; that it is 'used by the state to achieve the community's chosen collective goals'. In doing so law is 'authoritative rules backed by coercive force, exercised by a legitimately constituted (democratic) nation-state'. It is both threat and umpire.[16] Law both shapes behaviour and gives expression to community standards.

Yet this version of law in social context is insufficient. Constitutive theorists argue that 'legal life and everyday social life are mutually conditioning and constraining'.[17] Law and legality are something created and acted upon. They are manifestations of social bonds and of the collective. They signal boundaries and ways to do things that are devised by people in their diverse social contexts. Thus, a bottom-up engagement with law and legal institutions is as influential on law's meaning as

---

[15] The texts I am referencing here are: Michael McCann, *Rights at Work: Pay Equity Reform and the Politics of Legal Mobilization* (U Chicago P 1994) on political consciousness; Anna-Maria Marshall, 'Injustice Frames, Legality, and the Everyday Construction of Sexual Harassment' (2003) 28 *Law and Soc Inq* 659 on the 'injustice frames' of feminism; Elizabeth Hoffman, 'Legal Consciousness and Dispute Resolution: Different Disputing Behaviour at Two Similar Taxicab Companies' (2003) 28 *Law and Soc Inq* 691 on workplace ideology; Kathleen Daly, 'Mind the Gap: Restorative Justice in Theory and Practice' in Andreas von Hirsch and others, *Restorative Justice and Criminal Justice: Competing or Reconcilable Paradigms?* (Hart 2003) on legal imaginations; Frances Zemans, 'Framework for Analysis of Legal Mobilization: A Decision-Making Model' (1982) 7 *Law and Soc Inq* 989 on legal norms; Carol Greenhouse and others, *Law and Community in Three American Towns* (Cornell UP 1994) on local cultures.

[16] Bronwen Morgan and Karen Yeung, *An Introduction to Law and Regulation: Text and Materials* (CUP 2007) 4–6.

[17] Alan Hunt, 'Law, Community, and Everyday Life: Yngvesson's Virtuous Citizens and Disruptive Subjects' (1996) 21 *Law and Soc Inq* 173, 179.

top-down imposition. In this guise, there can be more of the servant in law's image. Law in social context incorporates ideas about legal consciousness, mediated practices, law's imaginative capacity, and its discursive and definitional capability.[18] The 'stylized concepts' of law as threat, umpire and servant are useful 'to summarise patterns of empirical variation'.[19] What then do these empirical patterns of victimization, legal consciousness and legal mobilization tell us?

LEGAL CONSCIOUSNESS AND VICTIMIZATION

Thinking about Victimization

The perception and experience of victimization, unfairness, disadvantage and discrimination enliven the conceptual frameworks to law in its social context. These injustices lie deep within legal consciousness literature. As everyday experiences, they invite questioning and act to sharpen definition to legality and rights. However, neighbour problems, abusive partners, employment issues and stranger transgressions are everyday experiences that are not automatically scripted as law problems or even as problematic.

Consciousness of wrong or harm ranges from experience, to perception and recognition. Indeed, actual victimization is not determinative of an assessment of disadvantage, harm or injury.[20] The formation of a consciousness of victimization is itself rooted in internal psychological and cognitive processes that constantly interpret, re-interpret, construct and re-construct the bounds of normal and understandable or even permissible and expected. What is culturally acceptable and unacceptable and therefore subject to considerations of what is wrongful or unjust are historically and socially situated. There are different perceptions of what

---

18 The texts referenced here are Ewick and Silbey (n 2); Franco Crespi, *Social Action and Power* (Blackwell 1992) on mediated practices; Clifford Geertz, *Local Knowledge* (Basic Books 1983) on law's imaginative capacity; Austin Sarat and others (eds), *Crossing Boundaries: Traditions and Transformations in Law and Society Research* (NW UP 1998) on law's discursive and definitional capability.

19 Morgan and Yeung (n 16) 339.

20 William Felstiner, Richard Abel and Austin Sarat, 'Emergence and Transformation of Disputes: Naming, Blaming, Claiming' (1981) 15 *Law and Soc Rev* 631; Joe Clare and Frank Morgan, 'Factors Affecting Perceived Criminality: Evidence from Victims of Assault' (2009) *Trends and Issues in Crime and Justice* (AIC).

actually happened, different situational and social contexts, differences of 'self-definition as a victim', differential impacts of race, gender and relationship, and the disorienting effects of victimization itself.[21] Diverse cultural and structural conditions reveal enormous variety in the manner and style of handling interpersonal, group or social problems, disputes and victimizations.[22] Victimization then is only part of a puzzle.

To Act or Not to Act

The complex interaction between victimization and consciousness of it as problematic becomes clearer in studies of victim decision-making. These show that the decision by a citizen to mobilize law is not a simple or singular reaction to a problem or event. Some emphasize the 'subjective rationality' of the individual decision-maker[23] and others emphasize what are 'culturally available motives for action'.[24] While problem perception

---

[21] The texts referenced here are Roy Baumeister and others, 'Victim and Perpetrator Accounts of Interpersonal Conflict: Autobiographical Narratives About Anger' (1990) 59 *Jrn of Pers and Soc Psych* 994 on 'what happened'; on different situational and social contexts see Martin Greenberg and others, 'Decision Making by Crime Victims: A Multi-Method Approach' (1982) 17 *Law and Soc Rev* 47; Eva Jonzon and Frank Lindblad, 'Disclosure, Reactions, and Social Support: Findings From a Sample of Adult Victims of Child Sexual Abuse' (2004) 9 *Child Maltreatment* 190; Neil Vidmar and Regina Schuller, 'Individual Differences And The Pursuit Of Legal Rights' (1987) 11 *Law and Human Behaviour* 299; on differences of 'self-definition as a victim' see J Shapland, J Willmore and P Duff, *Victims in the Criminal Justice System* (Gower Publishing 1985) 16; Catherine Kaukinen, 'The Help-Seeking Decisions of Violent-Crime Victims: An Examination of the Direct And Conditional Effects of Gender and the Victim-Offender Relationship' (2004) 17 *Journal of Interpersonal Violence* 432 on differential impacts of race, gender and relationship; and Judith Herman, *Trauma and Recovery: the Aftermath of Violence – From Domestic Abuse to Political Terror* (Basic Books 1992) on the disorienting effects of victimization.

[22] Laura Nader (ed), *Law in Culture and Society* (U California P 1969); Donald Black, *Towards a General Theory of Social Control* (Academic Press 1984); Richard Miller and Austin Sarat, 'Grievances, Claims, And Disputes: Assessing The Adversary Culture' (1981) 14 *Law and Soc Rev* 525; Carrie Menkel-Meadow, 'From Legal Disputes to Conflict Resolution and Human Problem-Solving: Legal Dispute Resolution in a Multidisciplinary Context' (2004) 54 *Journal of Legal Education* 7.

[23] Zemans (n 15) 1069.

[24] Barbara Yngvesson, *Virtuous Citizens, Disruptive Subjects: Order and Complaint in a New England Court* (Routledge 1993) 9.

and labelling are generally a requirement for action,[25] a solid body of research shows a strong tendency for people *not* to formalize an event or problem (of a wide variety) through recourse to law.[26]

Those who have experienced a 'justiciable event'[27] but who nonetheless do not turn to the law are variously described as 'lumpers', 'self-helpers' and 'the advised'. Those who might 'lump it' when confronted by a problem or event are cast as tolerant or accepting however grudging that may be. Self-helpers use available resources and opportunities relevant to the issue at hand. Some will access advice and proceed no further. People move in and out of these categories and may occupy all of them in relation to a problem.[28] Going deeper into these categories reveals more porous boundaries. Lumping a problem or event, for example, ignores coping strategies that can involve self-medication and self-harm.[29] Similarly, self-help may involve the deployment of multiple and multi-layered methods of resistance, accommodation, avoidance and negotiation. While the types of response to a justiciable event derive from studies of access to civil justice, they are relevant also to criminal justice. So widespread is non-reporting crime across countries with similar and dissimilar legal systems that 'legal inaction [is] the dominant pattern in empirical legal life'.[30] Perceived victimization and the availability of law are therefore only further parts of the puzzle.

Reasons for not turning to law enforcement authorities refer to prevailing social and legal norms, situational assessments, perceptions of authorities, and perceived efficacy. On contextual norms, people say the incident was 'not serious' or 'too trivial' or 'unimportant'. This was the most common reason given for non-reporting across 20 countries in the International Crime Victim Survey (ICVS), and also in national

---

[25] R Barry Ruback and others, 'Social Influence and Crime-Victim Decision Making' (1984) 40 *Journal of Social Issues* 51; Zemans (n 15).

[26] Marc Galanter, 'Justice in Many Rooms: Courts, Private Ordering, and Indigenous Law' (1981) 13 *Journal of Legal Pluralism* 1; Bumiller (n 11); Carlos Carcach, 'Reporting Crime to the Police' (1997) 68 *Trends & Issues in Crime and Criminal Justice*; Heather Genn, *Paths to Justice: What People Do And Think About Going To Law* (Hart 1999); Denise Lievore, *No Longer Silent: A Study of Women's Help-Seeking Decisions and Service Responses to Sexual Assault* (AIC 2005); Clare and Morgan (n 20).

[27] Genn defines a justiciable event as one for which a legal remedy exists, whether or not the subject recognizes the matter as being 'legal' (Ibid., 5, 21).

[28] Ibid., 19–21.

[29] Liz Kelly, *Surviving Sexual Violence* (Polity Press 1988).

[30] Donald Black, 'The Mobilization of Law' (1973) 2 *The Jrn of Legal Studies* 133.

surveys.[31] Holly Johnson's examination of the Australian component of the ICVS revealed similar reasons given for not reporting with 43 per cent of assault victims and 33 per cent of burglary victims indicating that the incident was not serious enough to warrant police intervention.[32] Similarly, in the UK, the most frequently cited reason for not reporting to police was that victims perceived the incident as too trivial, there was no loss or they believed that the police could not or would not do much about it. For violent crime, the most common reason for not reporting was that victims considered the incident to be a private matter and dealt with it themselves.[33] Gender and offence differences also influence reporting: respondents cite concerns, fear of reprisal and a desire to protect offenders.[34] The variations indicate a socially constructed deference to private worlds.

Also a strong feature in legal consciousness studies as well as access to justice literature is perceived efficacy of the law and legal institutions. Crime surveys expose assessment of the receptivity, efficacy and sensitivity of justice agencies, and of police in particular as influential on non-reporting. About a quarter of assault victims say that they did not tell police because they took care of it themselves, it would be inappropriate

---

[31] Jan van Dijk and others, 'Criminal Victimisation in International Perspective: Key Findings from the 2004–2005 ICVS and EU ICS' (WODC 2007) 112. Over one-third (34 per cent) of respondents surveyed for the ICVS thought the incident was not serious enough to report. Nearly half (48 per cent) of New Zealanders gave similar reasons for not reporting (Pat Mayhew and James Reilly, 'Victims' Experiences and Needs: Findings from the New Zealand Crime and Safety Survey 2006' (NZ MoJ 2008) 63). A third of Australian respondents felt that the assault against them was too trivial or unimportant to report (ABS, *Crime and Safety 2005*).

[32] Holly Johnson, *Crime Victimisation in Australia: Results of the 2004 International Crime Victimisation Survey* (AIC 2005) 43–44.

[33] Chris Kershaw, Sian Nicholas and Alison Walker, 'Crime in England and Wales 2007/08: Findings from the British Crime Survey and Police Recorded Crime' (Home Office 2008) 39.

[34] In Australia 42 per cent said that they dealt with the incident themselves, and 27 per cent said they did not regard it as serious (ABS, *Women's Safety Survey* 1996, 29–31). In the UK, 41 per cent of women and 68 per cent of men who had experienced domestic violence in the previous year did not report to police because they thought the matter too trivial, or that it was a private family matter (Sylvia Walby and Jonathan Allen, 'Domestic Violence, Sexual Assault and Stalking: Findings from the British Crime Survey' (Home Office 2004)). In NZ, 56 per cent of victims of 'partner offence' dealt with the matter themselves, 45 per cent felt the incident was too trivial to report and 20 per cent felt that police would not have bothered (Mayhew and Reilly (n 31) 64).

to do so, or because the 'family solved it'.[35] In New Zealand, a third of respondents felt that police could not have done anything, would not have been bothered, or were too busy to attend.[36] The ICVS found that a significant and substantial proportion of respondents felt that police could not or would not do anything, a factor that was higher in main cities.

The theoretical and empirical research outlined thus far points to ordinary people as actors in their world; not free and unburdened, but also not inert. Their assessments of victimization – of different kinds – are socially constructed as much as legally defined. While legal concepts do 'influence the goals, options, choices, and problems of ordinary individuals',[37] in the main, people tend not to involve formal law and instead 'deal with it themselves'. They may be burdened and bounded but encumbered agency is theirs.

LEGAL MOBILIZATION

Yet something must happen to bring forward law as a possibility following violence victimization. Naomi Mezey has commented that the law in legal consciousness could be lost except for legal mobilization.[38] What then are the explanations for people's recourse to law? This section considers a range of ideas about legal mobilization: that it facilitates governmental social control, invokes legal norms and involves the identification of redressable injustice. Others say that legal mobilization is about dispute transformation, citizen participation, rational choice and a part of strategic action. Each of these theories is intimately connected to ideas about the law in social context.

Legal Mobilization as Social Control

In one of the earliest studies of legal mobilization, Donald Black posed an 'entrepreneurial model of law' whereby citizens rationally pursue their own interests in a kind of 'self-help' system but without a role in the law's development. In so mobilizing the law, he said, 'the greatest legal good of the greatest number presumptively [arises] from the selfish

---

[35] ABS 2005 (n 31); van Dijk and others (n 31) 113; Mayhew and Reilly (n 31) 63.

[36] Mayhew and Reilley, Ibid.

[37] Marshall and Barclay (n 1) 617.

[38] Naomi Mezey, 'Out of the Ordinary: Law, Power, Culture, and the Commonplace' (2001) 26 *Law and Social Inquiry* 145, 153.

enterprise of the atomized mass'. Black suggested that a reactive legal system – such as a criminal legal system – 'acts to reinforce the tendency of citizens to use law only as a last resort, since it allows citizens to establish their own priorities'.[39]

Black situated his discussion within a larger enquiry in which law itself was quintessential 'governmental social control'.[40] From this perspective 'the common man' is posed either as a mere instrument of 'highly aggressive' government entities intent on 'ferreting out illegality' or as naive, ignorant and often mistaken in their 'legal intelligence'. Key determinants to legal mobilization Black suggested were the greater the 'relational distance between the parties in dispute the more likely is law to be used to settle the dispute' in addition to the event seriousness, the community and institutional context, and features of the parties. Furthermore, he suggested, the social conditions of event distribution, the availability of legal opportunities, the organization of mobilization and the 'countervailing normative system' all influence legal mobilization.[41]

Black's thesis of legal mobilization proposed that the mobilization of the law by private citizens is based on 'a margin of freedom or discretion'. Informing this discretion, he claimed, are 'the moral standards of the citizenry' and 'particularistic law enforcement'. For Black, these features rest upon moral diversity and prejudice and exemplify reactive legal systems as 'the more democratic form of legal process'.[42] The idea of the victim as a moral entrepreneur continues to resonate with scholars examining the social construction of deviance.

Legal Mobilization Invoking Norms

Richard Lempert critiqued Black's theorizing as narrow, unidirectional and formalistic. Instead he depicted legal mobilization as 'a process by which legal norms are invoked to regulate behaviour'. Legal norms, he suggested, are derivative of social norms and may influence actions taken even when law is not expressly engaged.[43] Lempert posed two key features to legal mobilization. In the first instance, it is a mechanism for transferring disputes from one arena to another, from the private sphere to the legal system. In this transition, third parties such as lawyers act as

[39] Black (n 22) 138, 134.
[40] Black (n 30).
[41] Black (n 22) 129–40.
[42] Ibid., 141–4.
[43] Richard Lempert, 'Mobilizing Private Law: An Introductory Essay' (1976) 11 *Law and Soc Rev* 173, 174.

gatekeepers to interpret, divert, forestall and facilitate access. Second, he said that the goal of legal mobilization is avoidance of future disputes or problems. Citizen perception of the cost, efficiency, efficacy, and relevance of legal avenues as well as of the uncertainty and contingency of outcomes, all contribute to understanding that 'it is not irrational to fail to invoke available ... law' and neither is it 'a simple reaction to problems'.[44]

Legal Mobilization as Transformative

Felstiner, Abel and Sarat developed upon Lempert's ideas in analyzing how the problem or event shifts from the immediate environment of the parties to something involving external authority. Their influential model of dispute transformation posits a three-step process. The first step involves acknowledging something is injurious ('naming'); secondly there is a perceptual shift to seeing the injurious experience as a grievance ('blaming'); and finally, a step to consciousness of the availability of some remedy ('claiming'). Felstiner and his colleagues acknowledge that this transformational process is influenced by social structural features as well as personal ones. They explain, therefore, that the characteristics of transformation are its subjectivity, instability, reactivity, and its complexity and incompleteness. Their answer to the question 'why so few people turn to law?' is to conclude that 'relief from trouble' is uncertain, contingent and costly.[45]

Legal Mobilization as Political Participation

Frances Zemans marked out the participatory essence of legal mobilization. She suggested it is a form of citizen 'demand' designed to influence or implement government policy and to receive entitlements.[46] Zemans claims that the legal system 'relies upon the individual actor to personally evaluate the burdens and benefits of invoking the law on his or her own behalf'. She sees 'legal mobilization as analogous though not identical to other forms of help-seeking and resource use behaviour'. 'The law', Zemans suggests, 'informs the citizenry of the circumstances

---

[44] Ibid 178–9. Zemans reinforces this point by expressly stating that 'it is rather perfectly rational not to expend scarce resources to pursue complaints if no positive results are reasonably expected' (n 15 999).

[45] Felstiner, Abel and Sarat (n 20) 637, 653.

[46] Frances Zemans, 'Legal Mobilization: The Neglected Role of the Law in the Political System' (1983) 77 *The Amer Pol Sci Rev* 690, 694.

under which the power of the state can be employed'. It provides 'an endorsement to action per se'.[47]

With its focus on the transformational, Zemans' decision-making model is similar to that of Felstiner and colleagues. However, she drew out the influences on and information required in this process. First, there is the perception of an event or situation that is 'potentially in need of a response'. The decision to act is described as a dynamic that is 'continuous and not perfectly sequential' where legal and social norms act alongside situational factors to stimulate or inhibit. The model further ponders attributes of the decision-maker and, in particular, the presence of 'rights consciousness'. She notes that it is not knowledge of the law that is determinative of a decision to act but rather 'the salience of rights on the one hand and the sense of justification in asserting them'. Rights consciousness is influenced by socialization as well as socio-economic and other demographic aspects. Perceptual variables such as expectations of success, cost, time and space, as well as calculations of the 'social costs'[48] further influence the decision to act. The uneven distribution of these resources and of the social costs results in 'an individualized system'.[49]

Taking action is posed not as a discrete and separate option, but more of a dynamic of conversation with others (formal or informal), acting for oneself, and engaging the intervention of others. The 'subjective rationality' embedded within the process acknowledges that, in practice, an individual's decision 'is bound by limited knowledge of alternatives and their consequences'. Zemans asserts that 'the citizen's assertion of perceived rights is central' to the operation of the legal system and that 'the public good' emerges from this fundamental point as an aggregation of demand.[50] As a political scientist, Zemans claims this type of citizen initiative defines the citizen regulator as a critical actor not only in the enforcement of the law but particularly in the implementation of public policy from which law derives political authority.[51] Her definition casts

---

[47] Zemans (n 15) 989, 1002, 1006.

[48] Social costs being the impact on interpersonal and social relations including on family and friendship networks, and reputation (Zemans Ibid., 1003, 1004, 1009, 1024).

[49] Zemans (n 46) 695.

[50] Zemans references the work of Edgar Cahn and Jean Cahn (1970) in her critique of the 'disenfranchisement' of non-lawyers in the process of legal mobilization and as a subject of scholarly enquiry (n 15, 995).

[51] Zemans (n 46) 1069, 995. Further, Zemans discusses the public policy outcomes from legal mobilization as the aggregation of individual demands

legal mobilization as 'a form of political activity by which the citizenry uses public authority on its own behalf'.[52]

Legal Mobilization as Strategic Resource

It is from this standpoint of legal mobilization as a mechanism for political participation that Michael McCann extended his examination of how law is used by social groups and social movements. His study of legal mobilization in pay equity campaigns in the US is interpretive and process oriented. Arguing against conventional understanding that legal mobilization is ineffective and that legal and other rights are myths, McCann posed law as a strategic resource. He conceptualizes rights as 'cultural conventions in social practice'. People's legal consciousness is joined to their interpretation of inherited and learned legal symbols and discourses through which social relationships may be negotiated and action strategies considered. However, as an inherited set of conventions, practices and structures, law is posed as contributing 'only limited, partial, and contingent constitutive influences in most domains of citizen activity'.[53]

In social and political contexts, the use of law is strategic. The diversity of settings in which legal ideas are deployed and the pluralism of the legal order suggest that turning to law is neither 'insular or autonomous' in people's lives. Instead, legal mobilization is 'one among many constitutive and strategic dimensions' of social movements. Legal consciousness is formative in that it 'structures meaning' even though it 'dictates no particular course of action'. McCann concluded that an analysis of legal mobilization needs to accommodate the context of contingent factors and relational dynamics to capture the unstable, ambiguous and contradictory effects of consciousness.[54]

Legal Mobilization in Summary

Theories of legal mobilization are intimately connected to ideas about the law and perspectives on the social context. One set of approaches are

---

(n 15 996). Democratic theorists differentiate between this type of aggregation, and the public interest or common good (see Robert Dahl, *Democracy and its Critics* (Yale UP 1989) 71). I consider that there is rather less emphatic distinction between the two.

[52] Zemans (n 46) 690.

[53] McCann (n 15) 5–8.

[54] Ibid., 10–11, 283, 287.

law- and state-centric. These emphasize the law's role in shaping, directing, modifying and controlling behaviour. The interaction between law and society is generally unidirectional and presupposes remedy as the primary objective. Another approach attempts to unsettle law and to foreground the social context. In so doing, the heterogeneity of peoples situated in various ways to each other and to sources of power is necessarily acknowledged. In consequence, the salience and availability of law is contingent. Thus, reciprocal meaning-making between the self, 'individual action and larger social structures such as law' is emphasized.[55] Ultimately legal mobilization is an uncommon enterprise whether initiated by individuals or social movements. Law looks different depending on insider and outsider perspective.[56] Problems are framed with diverse schema and invested with multiple meaning. At the same time, law itself frames and structures permissible action.[57] It is, at best, a 'structural opportunity' albeit one that is impregnated with deep ambivalence.[58]

LEGAL MOBILIZATION AND VICTIMIZATION

Proportionately few instances of victimization and injustice are brought to that ambivalent space. But what of those who do? Deciding whether or whom to tell about an incident is perhaps one of the most elementary help-seeking decisions for victims of any type of crime to make. Certainly, reporting to law enforcement, as a step in mobilization of a criminal legal response, is selective. It is a largely voluntary and self-motivated endeavour that starts as help-seeking.

Help-seeking

As an active behaviour, help-seeking is a form of communication 'directed towards obtaining support, advice, or assistance in times of

---

[55] Ewick and Silbey (n 2) 151.

[56] Mari Matsuda, 'Looking to the Bottom: Critical Legal Studies and Reparations' (1987) 22 *Harv Civil Rights-Civil Liberties Law Rev* 323.

[57] Gillian Hadfield, 'Framing the Choice Between Cash and the Courthouse: Experiences with the 9/11 Victims Compensation Fund' (2008) 42 *Law and Soc Rev* 645.

[58] McCann (n 15) 239.

distress'.[59] It constitutes single and multiple sets of actions, and is generally divided between informal networks and formal helping agents.[60] Actions can proceed through discrete stages but may not be linear.[61] Help-seeking is highly related to the nature of the problem and event, the characteristics of the help-seeker, and the availability and perceived efficacy of resources. It is deeply influenced by the socio-economic context.[62] There is a clear pathway from help-seeking in family and friendship networks to formal helping agents such as legal institutions.[63] Population-based surveys of crime victims support these findings. These especially show that women victims of physical and sexual violence seek succour and support predominately from personal networks.[64] In turn, these networks are influential on decisions to turn to the law.

Legal Mobilization Through Police

While few report to them, police can nonetheless be viewed as a helping agent and gateway to legal and other resources. Yet reporting is discretionary. Most crime investigated by police results from notification by

---

59 Nancy Gourash, 'Help-seeking: A Review of the Literature' (1978) 6 *Amer Jrn of Comm Psych* 413, 414.

60 Bernice Pescosolido, 'Beyond Rational Choice: The Social Dynamics of How People Seek Help' (1992) 97 *Amer Jrn of Soc'y* 1096.

61 Thomas Willis and Frederick Gibbons, 'Commentary: Using Psychological Theory in Help-Seeking Research' (2009) 16 *Clinical Psych: Science and Practice* 440.

62 Catherine Kaukinen, 'The Help-seeking Decisions of Violent-Crime Victims: an Examination of the Direct and Conditional Effects of Gender and the Victim-Offender Relationship' (2002) 17 *Journal of Interpersonal Violence* 432; Kaukinen (n 21).

63 Amy Blackstone and others, 'Legal Consciousness and Responses to Sexual Harassment' (2009) 43 *Law and Soc Rev* 631; Kaukinen 2002, Ibid.

64 Mayhew and Reilly (n 31) for NZ; Walby and Allen (n 34) for the UK; Jenny Mouzos and Toni Makkai, 'Women's Experiences of Male Violence: Findings from the Australian Component of the International Violence Against Women Survey (IVAWS)' (AIC 2004) and ABS 1996. For Canada, Kaukinen found that male victims of violence tend not to disclose and when they do it is to police, Ibid. On help-seeking patterns and behaviour in domestic violence see Belle Liang and others, 'A Theoretical Framework for Understanding Help-Seeking Processes among Survivors of Intimate Partner Violence' (2005) 36 *Am Jrn of Comm Psych* 71–84.

citizens and the vast majority of these are victims.[65] This is also true in relation to specific offences such as domestic assault.[66] Across comparable countries, the decision to report an incident of crime to a formal authority such as police is made by about half or less than half of all crime victims.[67] There is, however, considerable difference in reporting depending upon the type of offence. Property crime is generally highly reported but interpersonal offences are not.[68] Reporting patterns have also been shown to differ over time. For example, reports to police of sexual

---

[65] Donald Black and Albert Reiss, 'Patterns of Behavior in Police and Citizen Transactions' (1967) 2 *Studies in Crime and Law Enforcement in Major Metropolitan Areas* 1; Michael J Hindelang and Michael Gottfredson, 'The Victim's Decision Not to Invoke the Criminal Justice Process' (1976) *Criminal Justice and the Victim* 57; Michelle Sced, 'Public Satisfaction with Police Contact – Part II: Self-Initiated Contacts' (ACPR 2004).

[66] Ruth Fleury-Steiner and others, 'Contextual Factors Impacting Battered Women's Intentions to Reuse the Criminal Legal System' (2006) 34 *Jrn of Comm Psych* 327; Robyn Holder, 'Police and Domestic Violence: An Analysis of Domestic Violence Incidents Attended by Police in the ACT and Subsequent Actions' (2007) *Research Paper No.4* Australian Domestic and Family Violence Clearinghouse; Walby and Allen (n 34).

[67] Wes Skogan, 'Reporting Crimes to the Police: The Status of World Research' (1984) 21 *Jrn of Research in Crime and Delinquency* 113. More recent analysis suggests the proportions are lower. In the UK about 42 per cent of all crime is reported (see Kershaw and others (n 33)). In the US, between 1973 and 2005 only 40 per cent of non-lethal violence and 32 per cent of property crimes were reported to police (Eric Baumer and Janet Lauritsen, 'Reporting Crime to the Police, 1973–2005: A Multivariate Analysis of Long-Term Trends in the National Crime Survey (NCS) and National Crime Victimization Survey (NCVS)' (2010) 48 *Criminology* 131, 153). In NZ, just 36 per cent of crimes are reported to police (Mayhew and Reilly (n 31) 62).

[68] In Australia, 74 per cent of victims of a break-in will report to police, while only 31 per cent of victims of assault will do so (ABS 2005 (n 31)). In the UK, 93 per cent of victims of thefts from vehicles and 76 per cent of burglaries report to police, while only 34 per cent of assault without injury report (Kershaw and others (n 33). In the USA, 47 per cent of all violent victimizations and 40 per cent of all property crimes are reported (Michael Rand, 'Criminal Victimization 2008' (2009) *Bureau of Justice Statistics Bulletin* (US DoJ). In Australia, the UK, Canada, NZ and the USA the reporting of domestic violence is less than for other crimes (Mouzos and Makkai (n 64); Walby and Allen (n 34); Kaukinen 2002 (n 62); Mayhew and Reilly (n 1); Karen Rodgers, 'Wife Assault: The Findings of a National Survey' (1994) *Juristat Service Bulletin*, Statistics Canada).

assault and other forms of assault have increased in the US since 1973.[69] In the UK, however, the proportion of people participating in the British Crime Survey who indicated that they had contact with police fell from 43 per cent in 1981 to 27 per cent in 2005–06. In 1981 the reason most commonly given for the contact was to ask directions. In 2005–06 it was to report a crime.[70]

Reasoning Legal Mobilization

If few report, then a remaining question asks what informs citizen-based assessments of priority for mobilizing public law through police. This question has only recently become the subject of enquiry.[71] Attention has previously focused on barriers and inhibitions rather than incentives and pathways. In examining both incentives and costs associated with victim reporting using data from the US National Crime Victimization Survey 1992–98, Richard Felson and his colleagues consider the behaviour to be 'rational in the sense that victims are attempting to achieve something they value, whether it be something practical or something they think they ought to do out of civic duty or a sense of justice'. The goal orientation of motivation as 'something of value' accommodates both instrumental and non-instrumental objectives.[72]

Earlier research tended to focus on the situational characteristics driving reporting especially incident seriousness and assessment of 'durable harms'.[73] However, this emphasis obscured contextual and

---

69 Baumer and Lauritsen (n 67) 165. These increases were observed for violence against women as well as men, and stranger and non-stranger violence, as well as for victims from all ethnic and racial categories.

70 Krista Jansson, 'British Crime Survey: Measuring Crime for 25 Years' (2008) 22.

71 Richard Felson and others, 'Reasons for Reporting and Not Reporting Domestic Violence to the Police' (2002) 40 *Criminology* 617; Amanda Robinson and Meghan Stroshine, 'The Importance of Expectation Fulfilment on Domestic Violence Victims' Satisfaction with the Police in the UK' (2005) 28 *Policing* 301.

72 Felson and others Ibid., 619.

73 Skogan (n 67); Heike Goudriaan and others, 'Reporting to the Police in Western Countries: A Theoretical Analysis of the Effects of Social Context' (2004) 21 *Justice Quarterly* 933. Johnson's study of the Australian component of the ICVS confirms incident seriousness as a predictor for reporting, along with factors including older aged persons and lower household incomes. Controlling for other factors, Indigenous victims of assaults were also more likely than non-Indigenous victims to report to police (Johnson (n 32) 41). Carcach (n 26) 4

normative factors.[74] For example, features of the social context that tend towards 'collective efficacy' of neighbourhoods are influential on engagement with authorities.[75] The normative influence of the social network is also clearly pronounced on female victims of violence reporting to police.[76] Moreover, crime and safety surveys in three countries reveal clusters of motives around normative reasoning, a sense of civic duty and desire for protection. In the US, the primary reason victims of violence give for reporting is a belief that the incident was a crime (30 per cent). The second most common reason was self-protection (19 per cent prevent future violence, 17 per cent stop offender). A further 15 per cent express a concern for others.[77] Of those who reported crime to police in the UK, 43 per cent did so because they felt that crime 'should be reported' and 37 per cent reported because they wanted to see the offender punished.[78]

For violence categories, the motivations are similar. The majority of violence victims in the longitudinal study conducted by Joanna Shapland and her colleagues in the UK felt they ought to report and to protect others.[79] Responses to the 2000 ICVS Survey across 17 countries showed that victims of sexual incidents and assaults were (predominately) more interested to stop the violence and (secondly) for retribution, than were victims of property offences. Between a quarter and a third of victims of violence reported to police because they felt they 'should' and that it was 'serious'. A further quarter reported 'to get help'. Across all crime types, most victims reported because they felt they 'should' and that it was

---

also confirms seriousness as affecting victim reporting in Australia; and Mayhew and Reilly (n 31) 66 for NZ.

74 Martin Greenberg and R Barry Ruback, *After the Crime: Victim Decision-Making* (Plenum Press 1992).

75 Heike Goudriaan and others, 'Neighbourhood Characteristics and Reporting Crime Effects of Social Cohesion, Confidence in Police Effectiveness and Socio-Economic Disadvantage' (2006) 46 *Brit Jrn of Crim* 719; Jeffrey Morenoff and others, 'Neighborhood Inequality, Collective Efficacy, and the Spatial Dynamics of Urban Violence' (2001) 39 *Criminology* 517.

76 Kaukinen 2002 (n 62); 2004 (n 21).

77 Victims of more serious offences such as rape and sexual assault, aggravated assault and serious violent crime express more concern to protect others than do victims of other violent offences such as robbery or 'simple assault' (Timothy Hart and Callie Rennison, 'Reporting Crime to the Police, 1992–2000' (2003) *Bureau of Justice Statistic Special Report NCJ195710*, US DoJ 7).

78 Jonathan Allen and others, 'Policing and the Criminal Justice System – Public Confidence and Perceptions: Findings from the 2004/2005 British Crime Survey' (Home Office 2006).

79 Shapland, Willmore and Duff (n 21) 15.

'serious'.[80] Victims of domestic assault also reveal this mix of protective and other-regarding motivations in reporting to police. In the US, for example, women are 'more likely to desire protection, they are less likely to think that their partner's violence is a private matter, and they are less likely to think the incident was trivial'. This study concludes that 'the factors encouraging women to report to police are much stronger than the single factor that discourages their calling'.[81]

Summary

Considering these data, the victim of crime is an informed citizen making contingent choices – expressed transparently or otherwise – about which of the resources available in the community will assist her with her purpose(s). They identify and ignore, use, develop, and create what Blumer called 'networks of action'. They seek guidance from a range of personal and social supports. They do so according to different circumstances and with different expectations. As citizens, victims of crime make judgments about whether and who to access, why and when. In Black's terms, they use their discretionary authority and become legal actors. There is nothing automatic or certain, however, to the mobilization of law.

LEGAL CONSCIOUSNESS, MOBILIZATION AND JUSTICE

The theoretical and empirical discussion in this chapter has presented people's interpretation of events and problems as socially embedded and situated. Their meaning-making is influenced by the discourse of law and the legal, as well as through a justice imaginary. These ideas shape and guide but do not direct action. Perceiving victimization and injustice, seeing the availability of law, making assessments about law's salience, efficacy and relevance, and moving into the possibilities created by law all comprise part of the puzzle of legal mobilization. The component parts reinforce an image of the citizen actor exercising discretion in ways that are socially and politically situated. At the same time schemas

---

80 John van Kesteren and others, 'Criminal Victimisation in Seventeen Industrialized Countries: Key Findings from the 2000 International Crime Victims Survey' (WODC 2000) 68–9.

81 Felson and others (n 71) 640.

of legality interact with other frames to permissible and available action. The option of legal mobilization is hedged by constraints and contradictions.

A conception of the victimized citizen as an agent in determining the frame and thereby – at least in part – the response to an incident, event or problem, centralizes their role in civil society. Acting to invoke law and become a legal actor is but one option open to them. In aggregate, these actions draw attention *through law* to the boundaries set by public policy. The citizen-victim enacts law and 'create[s] the possibility of change'.[82] They give flesh and meaning to the flat letter of law. The discursive movement between peoples, laws and law's institutions fashion and re-fashion the everyday.

Republican theorists envisage these as 'communitarian sources of order … empowered with opportunities and resources to participate directly in any local area of collective-decision-making that has an important effect on their lives'.[83] It is more than social order, however, that this chapter has highlighted. In particular, the role of ordinary people in forming, reinforcing, re-ordering and offering definition and specificity to communal norms in collective settings is revealed as social practice with civic implications. From this perspective, Roger Cotterrell goes so far as to pose the option of legal mobilization as part of an 'individual's obligation to maintain mutual interpersonal trust in the form necessary for the particular relationships of community' such that 'betrayal of this trust … can give rise to liability, to some kind of sanctioning of the individual within the community'.[84] The proposition fuses legal mobilization as part of an individualist rights narrative to that of a broader social and political one. This narrative is a complex one where cohesion and contestation are in dynamic tension.

---

[82] Marshall and Barclay (n 1) 618.

[83] Ian Ayres and John Braithwaite, *Responsive Regulation: Transcending the Deregulation Debate* (OUP 1992) 17.

[84] Roger Cotterrell, *Law, Culture and Society: Legal Ideas in the Mirror of Social Theory* (Ashgate Publishing 2006) 164. At this point I do not explore critiques of the governmental trend 'responsibilise' citizens to undertake crime prevention or to participate in law as an obligation of citizenship. See Jo Goodey, *Victims and Victimology: Research, Policy and Practice* (Pearson Education 2005); Jacki Tapley, 'From "Good Citizen" to "Deserving Client": The Relationship Between Victims of Violent Crime and the State Using Citizenship as The Conceptualising Tool' PhD thesis (University of Southampton 2003); Alison Young, *Imagining Crime: Textual Outlaws and Criminal Conversations* (Sage 1996).

In this space law is not the neutral umpire it purports to be. It is potentially oppressive as well as liberating. How ordinary people as victims of violence view law and come to experience it comprise part of the new research in Chapters 4–8 of this book. The extent to which the law and legal institutions affirm or disabuse them of their faith in its fairness, the extent that it respects the equality and dignity of citizens emerge from an intense, long-term engagement. It is through a detailed examination of interaction with authority and involvement in commonplace conversation that the Justice Study considers the potential for justice through the law. Such potential, however, needs first to sketch the institutional landscape to the law that citizens encounter.

4. Mapping institutional discourse about justice

> You are not running a service for the victims who want to feel better. (P1, 2011)

> Competition for control of access to the legal resources inherited from the past contributes to establishing a social division between lay people and professionals by fostering a continual process of rationalization. Such a process is ideal for constantly increasing the separation between judgments based upon the law and naive intuitions of fairness. (Bourdieu, 1987, 817)

> Institutional fundamentalism may not only ride roughshod over the complexity of societies, but quite often the self-satisfaction that goes with alleged institutional wisdom even prevents critical examination of the actual consequences of having the recommended institutions. Indeed, in the purely institutional view, there is, at least formally, no story of justice beyond establishing the 'just institutions'. Yet, whatever good institutions may be associated with, it is hard to think of them as being basically good in themselves, rather than possibly being effective ways of realising acceptable or excellent social achievements. (Sen, 2009, 83)

WHERE POWER RESIDES

Individual and communal appraisal of the law does not exist in a vacuum. This chapter explores institutional and legal orientations to the victim in criminal justice, and to the idea of justice itself. The discussion looks back to identify some key conceptual transitions in the evolution of criminal law and justice, pauses on present-day realities, and then looks forward to touch on future possibilities. Although a rather panoramic depiction, the intention is to situate lay people and professionals – as well as their narratives – in a specific socio-historical context.

The chapter starts with a brief description of the processes and entities that comprise institutional aspects of this environment. In particular, I explore the evolution of public prosecution and contrast some differences between Australian and English histories. Interviews with prosecutors from both these jurisdictions help identify and trace the contours of thinking about victims and the public interest. The analysis is done as critique but also in appreciation as the role of public prosecutor is an extraordinarily difficult one. My ultimate aim, however, is to situate prosecutors' views within a political frame.[1] The analysis works *through* the question 'where power resides' in criminal justice[2] to locate it, in part, within prosecutors' routine practices. The chapter's argument is that the prosecution discourse on these justice practices is a form of 'institutional fundamentalism' that acts as an ideology through which power becomes hegemonic.[3]

WHY FOCUS ON PUBLIC PROSECUTION?

In today's world the institutions of criminal justice are imbued with an astonishing degree of power and authority over ordinary citizens. Mostly this is indirect and criminal justice lies in the background of people's everyday lives. Whereas police and the courts are sharper in focus, prosecutors conduct their business largely hidden from the public eye. Public prosecution has been described in neutral terms as forming 'the crucial link between law enforcement and penal sanction',[4] and – more caustically – as 'the most secretive, least understood and most poorly documented aspect of the administration of justice'.[5] The degree of discretionary privilege and independence enjoyed by prosecuting authorities has been noted in England and Wales, the US, Japan, Canada, New

---

[1] I extend Iris Young's conception of the political in order to attend here to the relationship of ordinary people to the state (through its institutions) ('Impartiality and the Civic Public' in S Benhabib and D Cornell (eds), *Feminism as Critique* (U Minnesota P 1987)).

[2] Tony Kearon and Barry Godfrey, 'Setting the Scene: A Question of History', in S Walklate (ed), *Handbook of Victims and Victimology* (Willan Publishing 2007) 33.

[3] Here I rely on Raymond Williams' exposition of hegemony as a dynamic process as much as it is a system of dominance. Hegemony is adaptive and not necessarily total (Raymond Williams, *Marxism and Literature* (OUP 1977)). See also David Sklansky, 'The Problems with Prosecutors' (2017) 14 *Annual Review of Criminology* 2.1, 2.3.

[4] Andrew Sanders (ed), *Prosecution in Common Law Jurisdictions* (Dartmouth Publishing Group 1996) xi.

[5] Law Reform Commission of Australia, *Sentencing of Federal Offenders* Report No.15 (AGPS 1980) 61.

Zealand, and in comparative perspective.[6] Prosecution is an under-researched practice and an under-theorized role, yet its central organizing concepts are emblematic of criminal justice as a whole.

Relations between police and victims of diverse offences have been extensively explored, and were touched on in the previous chapter; but there has been rather less for prosecutors. In recent years, dramatic and high-profile cases in Australia and the UK as well as sustained pressure from victim groups have highlighted tensions and challenges within the role and conduct of prosecution. In Australia, controversies periodically flare on decisions not to prosecute and have encompassed allegations of sexual assault (the Volker case in Queensland) and of homicide (the death of Lynette Daley in NSW); and failure to appeal (the Nemer case in South Australia). In England and Wales, the Crown Prosecution Service (CPS) has come under trenchant criticism over failure or delay in respect of prosecution of allegations of sexual abuse such as those involving Jimmy Savile and Greville Janner, and homicide prosecutions such as those involving Robert Trigg. In both countries, rights campaigners for those with intellectual impairments, for elders as well as children, for those subject to exploitation and human trafficking, and for those subject to hate crimes among others have mounted sustained criticism of the public prosecutor. Major public enquiries such as that of Macpherson (1999) into responses to the killing of Stephen Lawrence in London and the Australian Royal Commission into Institutional Responses to Child Sexual Abuse (2013–17) have revealed whole constituencies of persons who allege discriminatory and inequitable protection from the law. As an institution within criminal justice, the pressures on public prosecutors are immense and the job Sisyphean. At the same time, these controversies and cases all point towards the urgency of understanding that the victim is not the property of the prosecution; an item which hitherto has been picked up or set down if not at will then seemingly so.

---

[6] The texts I reference here are: for England and Wales, Andrew Ashworth, 'Developments in the Public Prosecutor's Office in England and Wales' (2000) 8 *European Journal of Crime, Criminal Law and Criminal Justice* 257–82; for the US, Bruce Frederick and Don Stemen, *The Anatomy of Discretion: An Analysis of Prosecution Decision-Making* (Vera Institute of Justice 2012); for Japan, David Johnson, *The Japanese Way of Justice: Prosecuting Crime in Japan* (OUP 2002); for Canada, Philip Stenning, *Appearing for The Crown: A Legal and Historical Review of Criminal Prosecutorial Authority in Canada* (Brown Legal Publications 1986); for New Zealand, Philip Stenning, *The Modern Prosecution Process in New Zealand* (Victoria UP 2008); and for a comparative perspective, Julia Fionda, *Public Prosecutors and Discretion: A Comparative Study* (Clarendon Press 1995).

However, for the best part of the twentieth century the work of public prosecutors was barely questioned.[7] The conceptual frames placed around their role and conduct went unchallenged. In particular, prosecutors' claim to represent the public interest and to decision-making guided by the public interest have been and remain central. Yet the public interest claim can serve as a protective cloak. In this chapter I use reflections on the public interest from Australian and English prosecutors as a lens through which to consider their role and to explore their approach to justice. Individual views are not compared but are used in single narrative form[8] in order to articulate and map institutional orthodoxies, and sketch the production and reproduction of power. The six Australians were all ex-Directors of Public Prosecution (DPP) and performed their public role in six different jurisdictions. Between them they had over 51 years of prosecuting experience (average 8.5 years). The six English interviewees included ex-Directors, and serving and ex-senior prosecutors. These had approximately 76 years' combined prosecuting experience ranging from five to 24 years. All the interviews were conducted in a semi-structured manner either face-to-face or over the phone, and comprised over 18 hours' conversation in total (1.5 hours per person on average).

Prosecutors may not view themselves as an elite. Those who have '220 Crown cases allocated' and are 'flying through cases and not able to cope' (E6) certainly will not. However, as legal officials, prosecutors inhabit a space where their decision-making in the name of the state or Crown – discretionary and unseen – moves them 'from the language of administration to the language of power'. In making decisions to prosecute or not, they decide what is to come under the purview of law and what is not. In a modern democracy, the public prosecutor enacts, in an evocative phrase from Sarat and Clarke, 'the logic of sovereignty'.[9] Their specific power consists in 'revealing rights': to acknowledge and

---

[7] Major inquiries in the UK have included the Royal Commission on Criminal Procedure in 1981 and the Glidewell Review of the CPS in 1998. However, I make the 'unquestioned' claim primarily with regard to members of the public.

[8] Quotations from prosecution interviewees are de-identified but differentiated numerically from P1 to P6, and from E1 to E6.

[9] Austin Sarat and Conor Clarke, 'Beyond Discretion: Prosecution and the Logic of Sovereignty, and the Limits of Law' (2008) 33 *Law and Social Inquiry* 387.

amplify or to discourage and veto.[10] At the same time, their disciplinary and institutional setting imposes 'cognitive and social norms' that are habituated and routinized in their professional lives, and which, in repetition, confers them particular authority.[11] Prosecutors' power is conferred as well as enacted. They are routine and royal.

As legal professionals, prosecutors abjure any suggestion of such monopolistic command. They situate themselves as one in a chain of decision-making sites, as 'just one cog in the process' (P3). Moreover, the power they do have is cautiously applied; they make decisions only when 'properly and fully informed' (E2). This managerialist approach presents prosecutors as administrative practitioners and dissociates them from the power and authority criminal justice wields. At the same time, prosecutors formally present themselves as 'ministers of justice' (P4, P5, E1),[12] a depiction that has been described as a 'silver thread' in the criminal law[13] but also criticized as over-stated, 'flawed' and 'outdated'.[14] As minister of justice, prosecutors are independent and beholden to no one. As legal officials, they contribute to shaping a 'dominant vision' while, in the minister of justice guise, invoking higher principles in ill-defined language.[15]

It is important to take prosecutors' accounts seriously 'without losing sight of the particular settings and circumstances in which they were developed and articulated'.[16] In the particular setting of criminal justice it is important to appreciate, as Robert Gordon suggests, 'the stakes, intellectual and political, that the managers of the legal system [have] in

---

10 Pierre Bourdieu, 'The Force of Law: Towards a Sociology of the Juridicial Field' (1987) 38 *The Hastings Law Journal* 814, 833.

11 Michael Meuser and Ulrike Nagel, 'The Expert Interview and Changes in Knowledge Production' in Alexander Bogner and others (eds), *Interviewing Experts* (Palgrave Macmillan 2009) 20; Bourdieu, Ibid., 819.

12 A contemporary statement is located in NSW Director of Public Prosecutions (2007), *Prosecution Policy*, Office of the Director of Public Prosecutions, Sydney, 5.

13 *R v Pearson* (1957) 21 WWR (NS) 337, 348.

14 David Plater and Lucy Line, 'Has the "Silver Thread" of the Criminal Law Lost its Lustre? The Modern Prosecutor as a Minister of Justice' (2012) 31 *U Tas LR* 55, 56. See also Richard Young and Andrew Sanders, 'The Ethics of Prosecution Lawyers' (2004) 7 *Legal Ethics* 190–209.

15 Robert Gordon, 'Critical Legal Histories' (1984) 36 *Stanford Law Review* 57, 71.

16 Susanna Blumenthal, 'Of Mandarins, Legal Consciousness and the Cultural Turn in American Legal History' (2012) 37 *Law and Social Inquiry* 167, 174.

their own constructs'.[17] It is from this starting point that I begin to trace some areas of dissonance and congruity in perspective between lay and official ideas of justice.

CONTEMPORARY CRIMINAL JUSTICE

The discussion first requires grounding in the present day and locating prosecution alongside other key justice entities. The notion of criminal justice as 'a sequence of decision situations'[18] is useful for this purpose as it emphasizes the pragmatic and administrative interdependence of the various justice entities and their work as social practice. In later chapters, I touch on the responsibilities of the various authorities to crime victims but in this section I draw a simplified picture capable of representing criminal justice in both Australia and in England and Wales. In doing so there is a risk of over- or under-stating some procedural or functional aspect. Likewise there is a risk of presenting the various justice entities in either country as having common purpose, shared values, and both internal and external coherence. These are all contestable presumptions. In the interests of brevity I also do not engage with the various debates and controversies associated with the powers of the respective agencies and the extent to which they fulfil their mandate.[19] However, it is relevant to acknowledge the expansive use of discretion across all criminal justice agencies in both countries.

Police are the most visible and accessible to ordinary citizens of all criminal justice institutions. As such they are a likely first port of call for those acting in relation to an incident.[20] They are 'official gatekeepers of

---

[17] Robert Gordon, 'Critical Legal Histories Revisited: A Response' (2012) 37 *Law and Social Inquiry* 200, 208.

[18] Mark Findlay and others, *Australian Criminal Justice* (4th ed, OUP 2010) Preface, xx.

[19] This section provides only a truncated depiction of the criminal justice process in describing the adult jurisdiction and does not touch on the correctional system or the varieties of victim support and advocacy.

[20] There are, of course, different ways of counting non-reporting of incidents to police (see Chapter 3). The criminal process acts as a sieve for the resolution of cases. It has been estimated that for every 1,000 incidents reported to police, a suspect is detected in 64, and 43 result in convictions with one person jailed (Russell Hogg and David Brown, *Rethinking Law and Order* (Pluto Press 1998) 10). It is important to note that police are not the only portal to criminal justice. In the US, for example, a criminal complaint can be made directly with public prosecution (David Ford, 'Prosecution as a Victim Power Resource: A Note on

the criminal justice process'.[21] They receive and harvest a wide range of information. The police function is an interpretive, selective and filtering one. Thus they may record an incident as a crime or not, and may (or may not) mount an investigation and determine the level of investigative effort. In electing whether to divert, caution or charge it is police who decide the resolution pathway for an incident. They determine whether to summons or to arrest an alleged offender (with resultant decisions about bail), and they decide the nature and number of initial charges.[22] It is the police preparation of the brief of evidence that provides prosecution with its preliminary orientation. In doing so, the investigator assumes the role of informant.

Prosecutors[23] present this early brief at court and will have carriage of the finalization of the matter on behalf of the state or the Crown. Usually at the first appearance of the defendant in court, prosecution will make further representations about bail. The prosecutor has discretion in framing charges and may amend, add to or discontinue charges – an authority that paves the way for charge negotiation.[24] Prosecution guidelines commonly describe a two-step decision-making process on whether to proceed to prosecute. The first step considers whether the evidence is sufficient to suggest that there is a reasonable prospect of conviction. The second step is that, having regard to the provable facts and the whole of

---

Empowering Women in Violent Conjugal Relationships' (1991) 25 *Law and Society Review* 313–34) and the capacity for individuals, corporations and other organizations to bring a private prosecution remains in the UK and Australia (Ashworth (n 6); Chris Corns, 'Police Summary Prosecutions in Australia and New Zealand: Some Comparisons' (2000) 19 *University of Tasmania Law Review* 280–310).

21 Findlay and others (n 18) 115.

22 In deciding whether to charge and for which criminal offence(s), the police may liaise with the prosecutor. How this is done and in what circumstances does vary across the Australian jurisdictions, England and Wales, and other common law countries.

23 In most Australian jurisdictions police prosecutors perform this function in summary proceedings and an independent DPP conducts indictable prosecutions. In the ACT – within which the lay respondents in this study are situated – the DPP conducts all summary and indictable prosecutions. There are no police prosecutors as is also now the case in England and Wales.

24 The practice of charge negotiation (or bargaining) in the Australian context was outlined by Gordon Samuels (2002) in his 'Review of the New South Wales Director of Public Prosecutions' Policy and Guidelines for Charge Bargaining and Tendering of Agreed Facts' (Attorney General's Department, Sydney).

the circumstances, it is in the public interest to prosecute.[25] The basis of this discretion derives from the statutory independence of prosecution and is unbound by any enforceable standard.[26] While most criminal matters are resolved by way of a guilty plea,[27] prosecutors will be central to decisions about which proceed to trial (often by way of committal proceedings) and will also determine the exact nature of the indictment.

The majority of all crimes prosecuted in Australia and England are usually resolved in a lower court before a magistrate – the vast majority by way of a guilty plea from the defendant. It is in higher courts that a trial is conducted before a judge and may also involve a jury. The low proportion of criminal cases resolved at this level has led some to suggest higher courts are a showcase of ceremony and formality.[28] It is here also that the adversarial performance is at its most ritualistic. In all levels of court, the role of the judicial officer is 'to supervise proceedings, to act as umpire, to determine questions of law, and to direct the jury in their task of determining the factual issues'.[29] The judicial officer will, upon a verdict of guilty, determine the nature of a sentence (if any) for the

---

[25] In the UK, *The Code for Crown Prosecutors* (2013) provides guidance to prosecutors on the general principles to be applied when making decisions about prosecutions. In Australia, each prosecuting authority publishes its own guidelines. However, there is broad commonality between them. Commonwealth Director of Public Prosecutions (2008), *Prosecution Policy of the Commonwealth*; Director of Public Prosecutions (NSW) (2007), *Prosecution Guidelines of the Office of the Director of Public Prosecutions*; Director of Public Prosecutions (ACT) (1991), *Prosecution Policy and Guidelines of the Director of Public Prosecutions (ACT)*; Director of Public Prosecutions (NT) (2005), *Director of Public Prosecutions Guidelines*; Director of Public Prosecutions (Qld) (2003), *Directors Guidelines*; Director of Public Prosecutions (SA) (1992), *Prosecution Policy*; Director of Public Prosecutions (Tas) (1994), *Director Public Prosecutions Guidelines*; Office of the Director of Public Prosecutions (Vic) (2010), *Director of Public Prosecutions Policy*; Director of Public Prosecutions (WA) (2005), *Statement of Prosecution Policy and Guidelines*.

[26] Sarat and Clarke discuss the case law on this point with regard to the US Supreme Court ((n 9) 394–404).

[27] In 2011–12, approximately 91 per cent of criminal cases were finalized in lower courts across Australia. Of those finalized at this level, 89 per cent were adjudicated, and 86 per cent were proven guilty or plead guilty, and of these 91 per cent resulted in a non-custodial sentence (Australian Bureau of Statistics 2013).

[28] And as 'the arena where the ideology of justice is put on display' (Doreen McBarnet, 'Magistrates' Courts and the Ideology of Justice' (1981) 8 *British Journal of Law and Society* 181, 195).

[29] Findlay and others (n 18) 166.

accused. In Australia and in the UK, the aims of sentencing are commonly described as retribution, deterrence, rehabilitation, denunciation and incapacitation. A sentence may seek to address one or more of these aims with varying degrees of coherence.[30]

SIMILARITIES AND DIFFERENCES

Australian prosecution authorities claim the country 'inherited the English system lock, stock and barrel in the beginning' (P3). The association made with an organic and lay-based system that is bound by the common law is a powerful legitimating feature for the transplant. Nonetheless, along with similarities between the two countries, there are some important differences.

The English Context

As a question of political history rather than legal history, the forces behind the inexorable centralization of power are empirically contested in the English situation.[31] It is generally accepted, however, that industrialization and urbanization in England over the eighteenth and nineteenth centuries provided the foundations to later consolidation and professionalization of state justice bureaucracies.

The institution of public prosecution was nonetheless a 'historical latecomer' in England.[32] From 'square one' (E1), public prosecution was

---

[30] Andrew Ashworth, *Sentencing and Criminal Justice* (5th ed, CUP 2010); Mirko Bagaric, *Punishment and Sentencing: A Rational Approach* (Cavendish Publishing 2001).

[31] In this section I draw on a number of classic texts: JM Beattie, *Crime and The Courts in England 1660–1800* (Lightening Source 2008); David Cairns, *Advocacy and the Making of the Adversarial Criminal Trial, 1800–1865* (Clarendon Press 1998); Douglas Hay and Francis Snyder, *Policing and Prosecution in Britain 1750–1850* (OUP 1989); Peter King, *Crime, Justice, and Discretion in England 1740–1820* (OUP 2003); and John Langbein, *The Origins of the Adversary Criminal Trial* (OUP 2003). There is particular contestation in relation to gender and class. See, e.g., Shani D'Cruze, *Everyday Violence in Britain, 1850–1950: Gender and Class* (Longman 2000) and Edward P Thompson, *Whigs and Hunters: The Origin of the Black Act* (Pantheon Books 1975).

[32] John Langbein, 'The Origins of Public Prosecution at Common Law' (1973) 17 *American Journal of Legal History* 313–35.

tightly restricted to treason and related state trials. It was more extraordinary than ordinary. Indeed, features such as adversarial trial procedure and the involvement of legal counsel (prosecution as well as defence) developed slowly and patchily over the eighteenth and nineteenth centuries.[33] Even with the establishment of an organized urban police service in 1829 and the gradual evolution of a 'system of police-conducted prosecution', by the mid-nineteenth century in England, prosecution counsel was used only in one in 20 cases.[34] Criminal procedure and hence the criminal justice system as a whole relied upon private prosecution well into the nineteenth century.[35] It was, says historian Douglas Hay, 'the paradigm of prosecution'.[36] While the indictment might be brought in the name of the Crown, it was usually carried by a private individual or a private association of individuals.[37]

---

[33] Indeed, aspects of trial claimed as traditional rights such as the 'right to a fair trial' were only settled and extended in the twentieth century (Simon Bronitt and Bernadette McSherry, *Principles of Criminal Law* (2nd ed., Thomson Law Book Company 2005) 101–3). See also Ian Langford, 'Fair Trial: The History of an Idea' (2009) 8 *Journal of Human Rights* 37–52.

[34] Langbein (n 31) 256.

[35] Private prosecution refers to the initiation of criminal proceedings from an individual victim or person acting as an agent of the victim. Persons could be members of an association for the prosecution of felons (Kearon and Godfrey (n 2) 21; Douglas Hay, 'Controlling the English Prosecutor' (1983) 21 *Osgoode Hall Law Journal* 165, 171–2). Estimates of the volume of private prosecution in England in the nineteenth century vary. One detailed regional study estimates that, in 1880, eight out of ten prosecutions for violence were initiated and conducted by individuals (Langbein (n 32) 317). A database of cases from 1880–1940 showed over three-quarters of prosecutions for violence were prosecuted by individuals (Barry Godfrey, 'Changing Prosecution Practices and their Impact on Crime Figures, 1857–1940' (2008) 48 *British Journal of Criminology* 171–89).

[36] Hay, Ibid., 167. However, there are differences of view as to the import of private prosecution. On the one hand, is the idea that because substantial numbers of people from lower socio-economic groups initiated prosecutions, the law and legal institutions enjoyed legitimacy (Langbein (n 31)). On the other hand, is the argument that the poor 'exploited the powers of the state' for malicious ends (Douglas Hay, 'Prosecution and Power: Malicious Prosecution in the English Courts, 1750–1850', in Hay and Snyder (n 31) 343–95). Argument about the motivations of victimized citizens who turn to the law remains current.

[37] Even in 1960 a legal scholar could write that 'every police prosecution is in theory a private prosecution; the information is laid by the police officer in charge of the case, but in so doing he is acting not by virtue of his office but as a private citizen interested in the maintenance of law and order' (Patrick Devlin, *The Criminal Prosecution in England* (OUP 1960) 16–17).

Pressure for reform of English prosecution was an intermittent and long-drawn-out affair. Through the various reform attempts in the nineteenth century, arguments for greater involvement of a public official in criminal prosecutions railed against the inefficiencies and inconsistencies of the existing *laissez faire* system. The greater capacities of the state were invoked as well as the spectre of an urbanized, fractious and unruly populace. Private individuals were castigated variously as frivolous, vexatious, unreliable, ignorant, helpless and easily intimidated.[38] They were described as blocked by the expense and inconvenience of prosecution, or diverted with bribes from accused persons, or simply uninterested in the effort to support a common good. At the same time arguments against centralization and professionalization found fertile ground in references to allegedly oppressive state practices in continental France and Cromwellian England, as well as fear of state indolence or indifference.[39] The 'monopolistic control of prosecutorial power' was generally viewed with some alarm.[40]

This centuries-old right to a private prosecution was not viewed as resulting from administrative oversight. Rather it was 'of great constitutional significance' to people's hard-won freedoms against tyranny and their sovereign status as citizen-subjects.[41] On the occasions establishing the Director of Public Prosecutions (1879) and the Crown Prosecution Service (1985), the retention of the right to private prosecution was protected as 'a valuable constitutional safeguard'.[42] Indeed numerous and diverse submissions to the Royal Commission on Criminal Procedure in 1981 argued for retention of the right to private prosecution as the 'ultimate safeguard against official inaction, whether due to corruption, inefficiency, or other causes'.[43]

A 'very small' office of the Director of Public Prosecutions was finally established in England in 1879, operating under the Attorney-General and

---

38 See, e.g., the comments of Denman CJ quoted in David Plater, *The Changing Role of the Modern Prosecutor: Has the Notion of 'Minister of Justice' Outlived its Usefulness?* PhD Thesis (University of Tasmania 2011) 70.

39 Paul Rock, 'Victims, Prosecutors and the State in Nineteenth Century England and Wales' (2004) 4 *Criminal Justice* 331.

40 Juan Cardenas, 'The Crime Victim in the Prosecutorial Process' (1986) 9 *Harvard Journal of Law and Public Policy* 358, 361; Hay (n 35) 173.

41 Sir James Stephen (1883) quoted in Hay, Ibid., 167.

42 Interestingly, both the DPP at the time and the Criminal Bar Association submitted to the Royal Commission on Criminal Procedure that the right to private prosecution should be retained (Thomas Hetherington, *Prosecution and the Public Interest* (Pergamon Press 1989) 57, 64, 153).

43 Hay (n 35) 181.

with an emphasis that prosecuting would be an exception rather than the rule. Notwithstanding these reforms, the principle endured – prosecutions 'remained largely private in law and in practice'.[44] The governing statute establishing the Director of Public Prosecutions in England and Wales in 1879 was explicit that this right to private prosecution was not to be interfered with. It would not be until 1985 that the prosecution of offences would finally be taken out of police hands by a new Crown Prosecution Service[45] albeit with 'a very backroom low profile function' (E2).

Clearly the assertion that private individuals had and have no place in the criminal justice system is a tale of late-twentieth-century construction. In his study examining the importance and ultimate disappearance of the English private prosecutor, Douglas Hay comments that it 'marks how far memories of executive tyranny have receded, as well as how far the assumption that a universal franchise ensures benign government has proceeded'.[46]

The Australian Context

The English emphasis on the constitutional importance of private prosecution as a defence against 'executive tyranny' was absent in the Australian environment.[47] Similarly, any assertion of a grounded evolution made in relation to the English common law and its lay institutions must become something different given the dramatic rupture of a penal

---

44 Rock (n 39) 333, 342.

45 Ibid.

46 Hay (n 35) 181.

47 David Plater claims that private prosecution and grand juries were 'never as prominent in Australia as in England' (Plater (n 38) 128). The Australian ex-directors interviewed for this study who mentioned the availability of private prosecution were nonetheless assertive in saying they 'took over' and discontinued all of them. The concern about constitutional protections against sovereign will was also not present in Canada (Douglas Hay, 'The Criminal Prosecution in England and its Historians' (1984) 47 *The Modern Law Review* 1). However, constitutional protection was very present in the US (Paul Marcus and Vicki Waye, 'Australia and the United States: Two Common Criminal Justice Systems Uncommonly at Odds' (2004) 12 *Tul J Int'l and Comp Law* 27–116). These differences suggest potential for deeper comparative historical research.

and later settler colony.[48] The profound differences in social, economic and political beliefs and practices – and not least in the geography of the colonies, dispersed European populations, and wars with Aborigines – caution against too many assumptions of commonality with English developments. The struggle of far-flung Australian colonies to survive – literally and as emergent state identities – has been evocatively drawn by Robert Hughes in *The Fatal Shore*.[49] In this environment, people's relationships to the slowly establishing instruments of law were both intensely intimate, and distant and uncertain.

David Neal has argued, in *The Rule of Law in a Penal Colony*, that New South Wales was colonized on the cusp of old and new systems then in transition in England. Despite or really because of the penal origins of the colony, he stresses the importance of law – especially the idea and role of law. A rule of law ideology[50] declared '... the law is the birth right of every subject, so wherever they go they carry their laws with them'. The colonists – whether convict or free – Neal argues, drew on the power and tools of this ideology as 'the means of expressing and contesting the differing conceptions of social and economic relations in the colony'.[51] These were a set of distinctions that did not encompass Australia's Indigenous and sovereign peoples. Australia's convict heritage – referred to delicately by Dowling J in 1831 as 'local difficulties and peculiarities'[52] – required attention from a legal tradition that could be both inclusive and exclusive. Thus the rule of law as inheritance and as tradition was important to the construction of identity among all classes in colonial Australia.

With this background, contemporary Australian prosecutors assert that 'we came to this country with the Magna Carta in our back pockets' (P5). However, while much archival historical research into colonial prosecution practices remains to be conducted in Australia,[53] it is apparent that,

---

48 Barry Godfrey and Graeme Dunstall (eds), *Crime and Empire – 1840–1940: Criminal Justice in Local and Global Context* (Willan 2005); John Braithwaite, 'Crime in a Convict Republic' (2001) 64 *The Modern Law Review* 11–50.

49 Robert Hughes, *The Fatal Shore* (Vintage 1988).

50 Described by Neal as, 'a set of concepts encompassing legal rules, institutions, processes of reasoning and powerful symbols' (David Neal, *The Rule of Law in a Penal Colony: Law and Power in Early New South Wales* (CUP 1991) xii).

51 Ibid., xii, 24; Hughes (n 49) xii.

52 Quoted in Plater (n 38) 91.

53 Plater's doctoral research marks a notable departure although he relies on high-profile cases to depict colonial prosecution (Ibid.). More recently The

as in England, the criminal law was 'put into effect by victims'. Indeed, 'it was the responsibility and obligation of individuals' to do so.[54] The penal administration provided for the establishment of civil and criminal courts but, for the first thirty or so years, decision-making was exercised by an autocratic executive with a 'military element'.[55] Legislative reform in 1823 placed initiation of the criminal process in the hands of an Attorney-General. However, the responsibility of Attorneys-General to initiate and conduct prosecutions was, as in England, restricted to serious crimes. Regulation of police in the 1830s and 1860s reflected the spread and demands of growing settler and emancipist groups for security as much as for good government. By the 1890s the institutionalization and centralization of policing in the colonies enabled development of permanent and specialist police prosecutors.[56] In Australia, as in England and Wales, legislation establishing independent and comprehensive prosecution authorities occurred later and over a similar time frame in the 1980s.[57] Nonetheless, this construction of government rule, legal institutions and laws was, in effect, a construction of the Australian state.

CORE CONTEMPORARY PROSECUTION CONCEPTS

This sketch of the main themes and markers of history affirms the rationalizing and bureaucratizing underpinnings to the appearance of the public prosecutor in both Australia and England. One face shows a

---

Prosecution Project at Griffith University, Australia, has created a database of higher court decisions in Australia from the earliest days of the colonies. See <https://prosecutionproject.griffith.edu.au/> accessed 10 October 2017.

[54] GD Woods, *A History of Criminal Law in New South Wales: The Colonial Period 1788–1900* (The Federation Press 2002) 108 and 192.

[55] Ibid., 49.

[56] New Zealand Ministry of Justice, *Examining the Prosecution Systems of England and Wales, Canada, Australia and Scotland: a background document to the Review of Public Prosecution Services in New Zealand* (NZ Ministry of Justice 2011).

[57] In 1896 the first police prosecution department was established in Van Diemen's Land. Directors of Public Prosecution began in 1973 with Tasmania (established by statute later in 1986), Victoria (1982), Queensland and the Commonwealth (1984), NSW (1986), the ACT (1990), Western Australia and the Northern Territory (1991) and South Australia (1992). To date, only in the Commonwealth, Tasmania and the ACT is the DPP responsible for both summary and indictable matters.

modest and administrative processor of matters brought before it;[58] another is of an institution with 'a great deal of power' (P3). Yet the history and function of an institution are but one element of prosecution authority. Its core organizational concepts do not 'passively exist as a form of dominance', but are 'continually to be renewed, recreated, defended, and modified'.[59] Such core concepts revolve around the criminal law itself, and the notion of the public interest.

Sovereign, State, and Society

Central to understanding the public prosecutor's role and system of thought is the classic doctrinal text, *Blackstone's Commentaries*. Written in the mid-eighteenth century, the text restated and consolidated the assertion that crime was an offence against the Crown 'because the sovereign, in whom centres the majesty of the whole community, is supposed by law to be the person injured by every infraction of the public rights belonging to that community'. In practice 'indictments … are preferred … in the name of the King, but at the suit of any private prosecutor'.[60] Acting on behalf of this public is 'converted into accepted facts'[61] by contemporary public prosecution notwithstanding its historically intermittent actual appearance in the daily court calendar.

Despite differences, prosecutors in both countries share normative and instrumental viewpoints on the criminal law and criminal justice. It is a mechanism:

> for keeping order … for controlling the power of other public officials … for protecting the community … for publicly expressing the community view of what ought to or ought not to be permitted … And essentially in its day-to-day activities it is a mechanism by which persons accused of things are prosecuted and dealt with …' (P1).

State-based institutions served a twin purpose: they took 'the power away to administer justice away [sic] from local landlords [and] barons' and

---

[58] Valerie Braithwaite has said that 'invisibility becomes the ally of durability and tradition' for administrative state entities such as, in her study, the Australian Tax Office (*Defiance in Taxation and Governance: Resisting and Dismissing Authority in a Democracy* (Edward Elgar Publishing 2009)).

[59] Williams (n 3) Preface.

[60] William Blackstone, *Commentaries on the Laws of England* (Book 4 1769) 12 and 303 <https://ebooks.adelaide.edu.au/b/blackstone/william/comment/index.html> accessed 10 October 2017.

[61] Bourdieu (n 10) 817.

fulfilled 'a desire to prevent vendetta' (E1). These ideas sustain a self-referencing worldview. Prosecutors' perspectives on the law in social context utilize both the stern threat image and the benign umpire (see Chapter 3). The criminal law, the emergence of centralized institutions and their statutory authority draw on an account of social, legal and political historical change that steadily progresses towards liberal democratic capitalism and which systems of laws naturally and properly enable.[62] From the rather lofty standpoint of public prosecutors, their role and function is liberal, progressive, and humane. If they are masters of their universe, they are benign ones.

The Public Interest

The term 'public interest' is ubiquitous. In the realm of public policy, a definition of the public interest 'can't be found by way of mathematical or political calculation'. At its most benign, the concept is claimed as an:

> indispensable as benchmark and guide. It requires us to think about means as well as ends. It commits us to good process as well as good policy. It broadens our understanding of the interests that are relevant when considering policy and it compels us to think and act beyond the constraints imposed by self-interest.[63]

The public interest is infinitely malleable in different contexts and is 'a highly political concept'.[64] The phrase has a unique capacity to silence questioning. Elish Angiolini QC, then Solicitor-General in Scotland, commented that it can serve 'as a useful decoy to dazzle those who would otherwise probe decisions taken under that label'.[65] Yet, because it is so normatively resonant, it holds a central place in the ideology of public prosecution. Prosecuting in the public interest means 'we have a

---

62 Gordon (n 15).

63 Geoff Gallop, 'The Curious Mix Known as the Public Interest', *Sydney Morning Herald* <http://www.smh.com.au/opinion/politics/the-curious-mix-known-as-the-public-interest–20100712-106cj.html> accessed April 2013.

64 Bronitt and McSherry (n 33) 58.

65 Elish Angiolini, Lord Advocate of Scotland from 2006 to 2011 in a speech entitled, 'Public Prosecutor: Hero or Villain' (2005) delivered at The Edinburgh Lectures 25 January 2005 quoted in David Plater, 'The Development of the Prosecutor's Role in England and Australia with Respect to its Duty of Disclosure: Partisan Advocate or Minister of Justice?' (2006) 25 *Uni Tas LR* 111, 112.

duty to justice, we have a duty to you [as a complainant], we also have a duty to be fair to the accused, and to be honest with the court' (E1).

Decisions taken in the public interest are not made 'in a vacuum' (E2) but are embedded in 'the underlying philosophy' (P2) of prosecution guidelines. These then specify a long list of criteria ('a peg to hang your coat on', P3) that may be taken into account when deciding what is in the public interest. While the criteria are similar in Australian[66] and UK prosecution guidelines, they are 'somewhat vague because it has to apply to any number of situations'. There are 'factors for and against [prosecuting], so it [the guidelines] will give examples of factors that may push you into the realm of prosecuting, and factors that may push you away' (E3). Whether the overarching objective is 'the deterrent effect of an appropriate prosecution' (P6), or a reflection of society's concern for the seriousness of the alleged offending (E4), determining what is in the public interest is 'tricky' (E5). With the core two-part test through which the assessment is made, it will either be on the sufficiency of evidence or on the public interest to which that criticism, or 'clamour' (E3), is directed whether from victims, politicians or the media. And, 'if there is no evidence there is no case, there is no public interest in prosecuting someone when there is no evidence' (E5). Notwithstanding the elasticity of the public interest, it acts 'almost like a lifejacket in these choppy waters of criminal justice. We'd say "I'm clinging to this because actually that's where the truth lies, that's what's real"' (E6). Nonetheless, the absence of transparency of much prosecution decision-making ensures definitions of public interest are consistently controversial.[67]

Engaging with the Australian public on the nature and scope of their interests is largely formal – through speeches and presentations – and cautious (P2, P3, P4, P5, P6). Doing otherwise whether through the media or direct to individuals including complainants is to engage in

---

[66] The criteria across Australian prosecuting authorities are mostly the same. For the jurisdiction of the Justice Study, the public interest is at para 2.9 *The Prosecution Policy of the Australian Capital Territory 2015*) <https://www.dpp.act.gov.au/__data/assets/pdf_file/0006/715506/PROSECUTION-POLICY-OF-THE-AUSTRALIAN-CAPITAL-TERRITORY.pdf> accessed 10 October 2017.

[67] The issue is discussed by Asher Flynn, 'Bargaining with Justice: Victims, Plea Bargaining and the *Victims' Charter Act 2006 (VIC)*' (2011) 37 *Monash Law Review* 73–96. In Australia, a decision to prosecute is reviewable by courts but the decision not to is 'largely immune from public or even judicial scrutiny and review' (Law Reform Commission of Australia, *Sentencing of Federal Offenders* Report No.15 (AGPS 1980) 61). Judicial review of prosecution decisions is open to UK courts (Plater (n 38)).

'inflammatory' discussion (P2). Prosecutors in England, on the other hand, emphasize community engagement through a variety of mechanisms (E3, E4, E5, E6). These have translated into a wide range of public policy documents from prosecuting assisted suicide or rape or cybercrime that are additional to the Director's Guidelines.[68] These enable the English prosecutor to see responsiveness 'on the policy level' and 'not on the individual case' (E5). Thus, these focused policy documents constrain discretion by making 'the tests slightly higher' but decision-making 'on an individual case by case basis' remains (E3). At a vernacular level, arriving at a decision about the public interest in a particular circumstance is what is 'buyable by the community' (P4). Responsiveness to changing community norms, for example in prosecuting offences such as domestic violence and child abuse as serious public concerns,[69] or indeed responsiveness to regional and local circumstances,[70] is set in contrast to perceived obligations to resist a punitive public (E1, E2, P1, P3, P6) and to resist notions of direct answerability to the public or specific publics.

Who that community is, what is the nature of 'the public' and where the victim fits in these terms is both clear and opaque. For most of the prosecutors interviewed, the figure of the accused person was in plain sight. It was to this person – a '15-year-old shoplifter' (E5) or a 'mentally defective fellow' (P1) – that procedural safeguards and legal rights accrue. In a classic depiction, Sir Thomas Hetherington as first head of the Crown Prosecution Service, describes the 'paramount duty' of the Director is 'to the public' and 'and every action he takes, and every decision, must be in the interests of the public as a whole or in the interests of an individual member of the public'. He then goes on to say these 'two interests sometimes conflict as, for example, when the prosecutor has to balance the interest in protecting society by prosecuting someone who appears to have committed an offence against society, against the interest of the individual who will benefit by not being

---

68 These 'Other Key Documents' are publicly available at <http://www.cps.gov.uk/publications/prosecution/index.html>. As at 10 October 2017, under 'Policy and Guidance by Group', there were ten policy documents devoted to particular constituencies or particular categories of offence.

69 Interviewees commented on the way their guidelines 'move' (P1) in relation to social mores. For further discussion on this point, see Hetherington (n 42) 139 and more generally Young and Sanders (n 14).

70 Hetherington, Ibid., 79 and Council of Europe, 'The Role of the Public Prosecution in the Criminal Justice System' Recommendation Rec(2000)19, 4 <https://rm.coe.int/16804be55a> accessed 10 October 2017.

prosecuted'.[71] Said one Australian prosecutor, 'we do bend over backwards to be fair' (P6). However, the figure of victim/complainant is present as someone who is 'vulnerable' (P2) but also as someone who is 'hysterical, out of control' (P1). Even the suggestion that a victim be believed is 'deranged' (E2) in a system in which such representations are contestable. Therefore, as rights-bearing individuals in the community, victims 'don't have any rights. No, certainly not' (P6).[72] For the public prosecutor, there can be a conflation of populist rhetoric with that of victims as a whole constituency or with that of an individual victim who is also a witness. From this standpoint, it becomes an article of faith to the public prosecutor 'to protect the prosecution process from all external pressures, whether blatant or subtle, which can arise in a divided society'.[73]

VICTIMS THROUGH PROSECUTION EYES

The victimized citizen is said to have 'surrendered' their constitutional authority to prosecute.[74] In the end is a system in which there is no 'legal or conceptual role for the victim'.[75] As there is no structured space or resources[76] for victim representation or advocacy of their interests, they may be avoided as carrying 'a foul disease' (E1) or 'ignored as a class of people' (P6), 'nowhere to be seen' (P4) and thus allowed to become 'forgotten'.[77] If there is a competition for the control of access to legal

[71] Hetherington, Ibid., 137.

[72] Some argue that the idea of victims' rights should more properly 'be assessed on general principles' rather than as 'rights' (Andrew Ashworth and Mike Redmayne, *The Criminal Process* (4th ed, OUP 2010) 49). In contrast to the rights of the accused, victims' rights in international law are regarded as 'soft'. Sometimes described rhetorically as 'rights' by different jurisdictions, the principles for the treatment of victims derive from the 1985 UN Declaration of Basic Principles of Justice for Victims of Crime and Abuse of Power, located at <http://www.un.org/documents/ga/res/40/a40r034.htm> accessed 10 October 2017.

[73] Kevin McGinty, Her Majesty's Chief Inspector of the Crown Prosecution Service, quoted in Nicholas Cowdery, 'Challenges to Prosecutorial Discretion' (2013) 39 *Commonwealth Law Bulletin* 17, 18.

[74] Plater (n 38) 71–2.

[75] Leslie Sebba, *Third Parties: Victims and the Criminal Justice System* (Ohio State UP 1996) 40.

[76] Where 'resources' are taken to encompass political, intellectual, material, financial and institutional capital.

[77] Paul Rock, 'New Labour Policies for Victims' (2007) 67 *Criminal Justice Matters* 38, 38.

resources, it is won, in the late twentieth century, by the professional legal elite. As an institution the public prosecution may argue for 'more resources to deal with people' (P1) but this still leaves untouched the structural void in which the citizen-victim finds him or herself.

From prosecution perspective – 'in the old days' (P3) – 'victims were simply another witness on the list and came and went and were given … no special consideration at all and treated quite heartlessly really' (P2, E5). They had to be 'genuine' (E1) or 'whiter than white' (E4). The victim was 'expected to put up with whatever happened to them [in the witness box] and too bad' (P3). They were 'caught up in the criminal justice system' (P3) and 'irrelevant' (P4). They could be conceived, on the one hand, as 'merely the vehicle by which the [community] norm has been broken' (P4) or simply as 'cannon fodder' (P6) for the machinery of criminal justice.[78] While there may be 'a whole range of influences that cause someone to come forward and complain' (P5), in such a heartless environment (P2), public prosecutors could reasonably 'wonder why' (P1) members of the public might come forward to report and cooperate with authorities. Nonetheless, prosecutors assume that people cooperate 'because they have got to' (P1). It is taken 'for granted' (P3).

In the present day, there is some recognition in common law countries that this state of affairs is no longer acceptable.[79] The drivers of change range from the political and social 'rise of victims in recent times' (P1, E2), to humanitarian recognition that victims are 'people for crissake' (P6), and to broader political pressure that 'people don't these days put their trust in authority figures who are opaque and unaccountable or unquestioned' (P4). Consequently, a range of legislative and administrative measures has been put in place in attempts to address victim concerns.[80] Public prosecution has 'moved a long way' (E3), especially for the 'fully enfranchised member of society' (E5). Nonetheless there remains 'an uneasy tension between prosecution and victim' (P4). At the

---

[78] In the early twentieth century 'the role of the victim in criminal justice processes was re-imagined and reconfigured, with the socially located victim of crime as a real actor in the day-to-day practice of criminal justice becoming usurped by the "victim of crime" as a symbolic and generic construct' (Kearon and Godfrey (n 2) 24).

[79] Jonathan Doak, 'Victims' Rights in Criminal Trials: Prospects for Participation' (2005) 32 *Journal of Law and Society* 294–316; Douglas Beloof, 'The Third Wave of Crime Victims' Rights: Standing, Remedy, and Review (2005) 2 *Brigham Young University Law Review* 255–370.

[80] For Australia, see Tyrone Kirchengast, *Victims and the Criminal Trial* (Palgrave Macmillan 2016); and for the UK see Matthew Hall, *Victims of Crime: Policy and Practice in Criminal Justice* (Willan 2009).

least, the reforms send 'mixed messages' (E3) and, at worst, are viewed as a 'danger' and a 'throwback to medievalism' (P1, E1). Authorities are – to some extent – 'frightened of being seen to be pandering to victims' (P4). As a constituency, victims are contaminated with this danger – notwithstanding acknowledgment of the diversity of expectations and responses to the formal justice process and its outcomes (P2, P3, P4, P5, P6, E3, E5).

Of course a question remains whether the reforms create (or recreate) legal and conceptual roles for victims. In the main, public prosecutors view communication as 'part of the solution to the problem' (P3). That is, communication with both the broader public as well as with victims. While occasionally spoken of as 'dialogue' (P3), the discourse reveals a predominant top-down emphasis consistent with prosecution's discretionary authority. Communication is informing. In this vein, some 'can't contemplate prosecuting a matter without keeping the victim informed' (P2), and some will go so far as to say 'there is an entitlement for the victim to have an explanation' for a decision (P4). Here prosecution is 'discharging a duty … to explain and to inform and that's where it ends' (P4). Communication is, in part, taking 'into account the views of the victim [but] not to act on them as instructions' (P3). At the same time, the institutional culture of prosecution challenges the consultative effort – 'the buggers wouldn't do it and we had to work like hell to get them to do it' (P6) – thus giving rise to a plea to fellow prosecutors that 'listening to people and caring about them doesn't impede your effectiveness' (P2). Notwithstanding these sentiments, contemporary offices of public prosecution will maintain they are as resource poor as other government services in meeting public demands (P1, P4, P5, P6, E3, E6). Consequently consulting is a 'second order consideration' (P4) and it is an 'unfortunate truth' (P3) that the individual victim remains a tool in the process, with no unique human rights,[81] identity or agency. Justice then 'is for somebody else' (E5).

Even though there is acknowledgment that, when 'caught up in the criminal justice process, the victim wants to have a champion, wants to have a representative, wants to have somebody working for them' (P3), this does not extend to welcoming the possibility of victim legal representation. It would 'distort what the court is on about' (P1) and challenge the 'theoretical foundations' of the current system (P3). The

---

[81] Contrary to this claim, Jonathan Doak has closely examined the scope and constraint of the human rights framework in the UK for victims of crime, *Victims' Rights, Human Rights and Criminal Justice: Reconceiving the Role of Third Parties* (Hart Publishing 2008).

individual is 'still sitting here alone' (E5). Existing requirements to keep victims informed and consult them in some circumstances to some extent recognizes interests that are distinct from the overall public, but there is no structural recognition (P3), and a sense that one 'can't take an independent prosecution to a more closer relationship than that' (P2). To recognize the victim 'more and more and more and more' (E5) would require authorities and civil society to 'clearly define what the role and expectations are' for a victim representative, 'to work it through' (P4). For public prosecution 'the big change has happened' (P3) with legislative reform modelled on the 1985 United Nations instrument.[82] While some 'absolutely' understand (E6) victim interests in representation, there is no 'particular juggernaut' demanding structural change. The shift to victim inclusion and participation at the level of international courts and tribunals is 'only a result of very strong lobbying' (P3) that does not exist in domestic systems.

THE JUSTICE OF PROSECUTION

It is of course possible to conceive conceptual space for victim inclusion and participation within prosecution objectives. However these are contested. On one hand, prosecution is ambiguously depicted as 'fearlessly' protecting 'the greater good' (P2) in the public interest where a wrong is to be 'set right' (E6); and on another, the prosecutor should not 'set standards' but do 'his job and that's it' (P3). In between these depictions it is suggested prosecutors may 'value add, to bring something to it' (P4) and that the reason for prosecution 'is to enable the court to do these things [apply the sentencing principles] (P6). Arguably, however, 'empty formalism' is what emerges from ticking the boxes of public interest criteria.[83]

A coherent, normatively-based conception of what is the public interest or of justice itself is missing. Procedural formality becomes the fall-back (P5, E6). Ideas of doing justice or achieving justice or delivering justice in their daily practice are articulated as being 'professional' because 'on a day-to-day basis you run the case that you are doing … the process takes over and you hope in some sort of way ultimately that it gets to, in general terms, a just result' (P1). Professional public prosecutors do 'the best we can with the tools we have' (P2) to 'manage expectations of a realistic outcome' (E6), and to 'achieve a generally acceptable outcome'

82 See 1985 UN Declaration (n 72).

83 Young and Sanders (n 14) 207.

(P3) 'according to the law' (P1). Prosecutors model constraint (P4).[84] Doing the best one can is described as scrutinizing the case 'as closely as you can' because 'justice can't be perfect' (P2). Not doing this means not being 'properly prepared' and being unable or unwilling to make an 'effort at persuasion' (P2). The idea of justice is – in the parlance of a modern bureaucracy – the prosecution 'mission' (P6). That is, to be independent, professional, effective, to operate with integrity and to be fair and just. Being fair and just with the accused is 'broad overall consistency', 'equality of treatment' (P5), 'dealing with the individual fairly' (P6), and ensuring that 'the same test applies to you and to me but not one for the high profile cases and not for others' (P2). In this frame, prosecution argues that it does not deal with 'some abstract concept of justice' (P1).

In the discourse, public prosecutors shy away from expressing what might constitute justice as values or the type of outcome that is just (P2, P4). These are 'going to depend on judgments that are made by people' (P3): 'the requirements of justice point in different ways which makes it difficult to define it in any comprehensive way' (P3). Victims may want that 'their experience [...] be validated' (E4), but the prosecutor, if pressed, may 'suppose you come out with a few basic things like convict the guilty and acquit the innocent, fairness, fair trial, sentences that were proportionate' (P4).

CONCLUDING DISCUSSION

Bourdieu argues that the skill of the modern bureaucratic state is to portray moderation – to look competent, appear benign and to nestle in neutral phraseology that 'is capable of compelling universal acceptance'.[85] Pronouncements on the body of ideas, beliefs and claims that comprise liberal legal ideology consecrate particular legal norms. These depict a way of seeing and engaging with the world. Hegemony becomes the capacity to both fashion a field according to that world view and to require it. Public prosecutors not only define what is correct, but have the authority to compel conformity. That they represent the public is a claim

---

84 Constraint is discussed as one component to the Minister of Justice conception of prosecution (Plater (n 38) 162). In a policy context, there is an example of the reference in the NSW Director's Guidelines (2007, 5) <http://www.odpp.nsw.gov.au/docs/default-source/default-document-library/prosecution-guidelines.pdf?sfvrsn=2> accessed 10 October 2017.

85 Bourdieu (n 10) 818.

of self-definition but it is also one where they get to say who is and who is not subject to the protection of the law. On this definitional authority rests the ideological and real power of the prosecutor.

Acknowledging the state monopoly of criminal justice is of course not new. However consideration of the state's use of its monopoly power has, in the main, focused on the rule-breaker. The implications of the sacrifice of individual members of the public, as victims, in furtherance of the law's role in promoting 'the common good' have been rather less explored.[86] The individuation of procedural and substantive fairness extended to the accused has only recently been proffered to victims. However these are not rights upon which citizens can rely. While victims cannot be said to be an 'opponent' of the public prosecutor, neither can or should they be presumed an ally.[87] Yet the legal ideology upon which prosecution authority rests has, to date, successfully promulgated the view that the interests of the individual victim correspond to the interests of the prosecution and that rights are an unnecessary encumbrance. 'Trust me' (P6) says the prosecutor. This trust is assumed in the exercise of discretion as it takes the legal official 'beyond the bounds of formal legality'.[88] In this 'gap' the exercise of discretion creates 'exceptions and exclusions' that impact directly on individuals.[89] It is within this capacity and authority to act unbound that power resides.

Yet the discourse of the public prosecutor is as textured as it is deeply patterned. Their narration on their work is redolent with complexity and nuance. Their daily exposure to claim and counter-claim lays bare that 'human beings are messy' (P1). Their retreat into a sanitized procedural version of justice and reliance on abstraction perhaps tells of this. But there is honesty enough to acknowledge that victims' 'sense of justice is as diverse as is the sense of justice in the community' (P4). What the narration also reveals is that the exercise of discretion does not exist only as a gap in the rules. Rather, discretion is enacted in a space where public

---

[86] But see Antony Duff, *Punishment, Communication, and Community* (OUP 2001).

[87] The terms were used by the European Court of Human Rights in *Berger v France* (2002) ECHR 48221/99 in determining that a victim, here in a *partie civile* matter, had a right to express interests alongside those of the state and the defendant.

[88] Findlay and others (n 18) 112.

[89] Sarat and Clarke (n 9) 410; Laurie Levenson, 'Working Outside the Rules: the Undefined Responsibilities of Federal Prosecutors' (1999) 26 *Fordham Urban Law Journal* 553–71.

and private intersect; and where formal rules and informal other knowledges co-mingle. The elasticity of the norms of public interest are powerful not because they are meaningless but precisely because they are meaningful. They resonate within deeper societal norms alongside commitment to a justice imaginary.

This gap in the rules thereby exposes a further gap, an opening for a greater degree of interaction and communication. The possibility, however, requires deeper recognition of the mutually constitutive nature of criminal law and its public; a recognition, moreover, that is put into practice with those citizens whose direct and affected interests are engaged. What has been characterized as a struggle for control and domination of the public over the private is, as Bourdieu claims, rather 'overdetermined and ambiguous'.[90] In the chapters that follow, what members of the public – as victims of violence – might bring to the world of justice is explored. The multiplicity of voices that can be heard from the community, and the citizen interests they carry, ponder the potential – in the gap – for democratizing justice.

---

[90] Bourdieu (n 10) 851.

5. Ordinary people accessing justice

> [It's] having your rights and feeling you need to be protected by the system. If you don't feel safe and your rights aren't protected then what's the point.
> (Winona, 2010)

> They are ordinary people, after all. For a time they had entered the world of the newspaper statistic; a world where any measure you took to feel better was temporary, at best, but that is over. This is permanent. It must be.
> (Guest, 1976, 94)

FOCUSING IN

Institutional narratives on punitive or pathetic victims perform two key functions. In the first instance – as explored in the previous chapter – they cast monopoly power in mellow light. In the second, they disconnect people from their communal context and fragment rounded identities and perspectives. This chapter introduces the ordinary men and women who participated in the Justice Study and brings to the fore a little of who they are as persons. My intention is for them to author themselves and to share their 'sense of the legal'.[1] The approach may be criticized for portraying people in a rosy glow: the mythical good, innocent and deserving victim. Indeed, the 33 lay participants were not selected as representative. Nonetheless, a sketch of their social values, their interpersonal and social environments alongside local and national samples show they are not so different to other Australians.

The chapter brings more critical attention to the terms 'victim' and 'ordinary people' used thus far without definition. It also asks why and how did these particular people decide to mobilize the law in response to the incident of violence against them. For this purpose, I enlist Zemans' decision-making model of legal mobilization, introduced in Chapter 3, and consider the ways people linked their words to perceived community norms and perspectives on the availability of law to them. It is a portrayal

---

[1] Patricia Ewick and Susan Silbey, *The Common Place of Law* (U Chicago P 1998) 22.

that shows that turning to law is a move enacted with distinctly variable degrees of confidence.

ORDINARY PEOPLE

The legal consciousness and legal mobilization literature is replete with examples of ordinary people. In two classic texts, Sally Engle Merry's *Getting Justice and Getting Even* and Patricia Ewick and Susan Silbey's *The Common Place of Law*, the notion is not defined. Yet groups and group definition are central to law and society scholarship. The availability of an identifiable 'group' such as working-class Americans, the welfare poor, victims of sexual harassment, and organized labour are key examples of this feature. These are 'non-ruling communities'.[2]

The idea of 'victims' as one such grouping is both powerful and inherently unstable, given their diversity. Victims of violence are 'not a natural social group'; they 'neither share a distinctive background nor common ties of sentiment; [and] they vary greatly in their life situations'.[3] However, when research is focused on persons in a social location, for example on female victims or child victims, then definite social group identities can be used. Analysis then more easily attends to issues of social discrimination, structural oppression and the operation of power. However, the base characteristic that unites the lay participants in the Justice Study is their experience and perception of victimization. Second is the fact that the violence was reported to police. Of course, there is irony in depicting these victims as ordinary when their experience of victimization combined with their participation in the criminal justice system is decidedly not common. Notwithstanding, the concept of 'ordinary people' is an analytic and interpretive device that can overcome the confines of the 'victim construct'.

---

[2] The texts referred to here are: working class Americans (Sally Engle Merry, *Getting Justice and Getting Even* (U Chicago P 1990)), the welfare poor (Austin Sarat, 'Law is All Over: Power, Resistance, and the Legal Consciousness of the Welfare Poor' (1990) 2 *Yale Journal of Law and the Humanities* 343–79), victims of sexual harassment (Laura Nielsen, 'Situating Legal Consciousness: Experiences and Attitudes of Ordinary Citizens About Law and Street Harassment' (2000) 34 *Law and Society Review* 1055–90), organized labour (Michael McCann, *Rights at Work: Pay Equity Reform and the Politics of Legal Mobilization* (U Chicago P 1994)), and minorities (Gad Barzilai, *Communities and Law: Politics and Cultures of Legal Identities* (U Michigan P 2003)).

[3] Sarat, Ibid., 348.

The Victim Construct

The political and academic discourse on victims has tended to one-dimensional representations. They have been drawn as passive and pathetic; often as punitive and pernicious. Victims have been cast as a pawn in some wider game of social control and as political actors who have distorted criminal justice policy. In these ways victims are posed as somehow different to the wider community or as toxic within it. Representations join around victims as a problematic, the upshot of which makes exclusionary practices possible if not permissible.

A singular notion of victim is clearly limiting and narrow. Kristin Bumiller's analysis of the victim construct focuses on race discrimination in the US but is equally applicable to other victims of everyday violence. In social and legal discourse about victims, she contends, historical personality is irrelevant, and individuality and plurality of persons are actively suppressed and denied. Features that enable the victim construct are the docility of the grouping, a weak basis to group identity, and their powerlessness in network situations. Thus the social formation of victims is 'dependent on the stability of power relations', in that their relative powerlessness serves to reinforce dominant political and legal structures and discourse. The mask of *victim* is a construct both of legal reasoning and a socially fashioned abstraction, and themes of sacrifice, exclusion and distortion comprise both the 'psychology' and the 'politics' of victimhood.[4] Ironically, when victims do claim agency through public action, this frequently attracts a response that is blaming – both for not acting responsibly to avoid victimization, and for perceived vengeance or avarice.

Victimization has the effect of atomizing individuals and detaching them from their normal. Then, the social and legal constructs of victim, complainant or witness further render them as other. People's identities, their connectivity, their intents and their experiences become wedged – and judged. In the media and in popular imagination, a sacrificial victim stirs both revulsion and reverence, and 'community' is thereby bonded against disorder.[5] In the late twentieth century, the victim emerged as a

---

[4] Kristin Bumiller, *The Civil Rights Society: The Social Construction of Victims* (Johns Hopkins UP 1998) 59–71, 72–76.

[5] Alison Young, *Imagining Crime: Textual Outlaws and Criminal Conversations* (Sage 1996) 16.

political and professional construct, and as an instrument of policy.[6] People were no longer presented as multi-dimensional individuals who navigate, construct and re-construct their relationships with each other and with social institutions. Rather the victim construct obscured the historicity and plurality of legal cultures within communities.[7] The construct makes little room for differing experiences of victimization and power, given features of race, gender and age in particular.[8] Communities and the people within them are presented as at once different and the same. Returning people to their ordinariness is a way to side-step these constructs.

Constructs of Ordinary People

Since the label of victim is a construct of many features, so too is the description of people as 'ordinary'. Cultural theorists use it as a term to distinguish between those who have power, status, resources and knowledge, and those who do not. In this sense, ordinary people are construed as those other than 'professionals' or 'technicians', as voices from below or from the margins, and 'the seldom seen and rarely heard'.[9] At the same time, the boundary distinguishing the ordinary from others is permeable, and continually constructed and reconstructed.[10] Theorists are careful to acknowledge that, while the social realities of ordinary people are a construction, 'these constructs have real, lived consequences'.[11]

In the political realm, the concept is variously handled. One account has ordinary people as intentional actors who shape history. They are not simply political subjects. They rise up at extraordinary moments to defy

---

6 Paul Rock, 'Aspects of the Social Construction of Crime Victims in Australia' (2006) 1 *Victims and Offenders* 289–321; Sandra Walklate, *Imagining the Crime Victim* (Open UP 2007).

7 Barzilai (n 2); Austin Sarat and Thomas Kearns (eds), *Law in Everyday Life* (U Michigan P 1993).

8 Kimberle Crenshaw, 'Mapping the Margins: Intersectionality, Identity Politics, and Violence Against Women of Color' (1991) 43 *Stanford Law Review* 1241–99.

9 John Gilliom (2001) quoted in Nancy Thumim, 'Mediated Self-Representations: "Ordinary People" in "Communities"' in Stefan Herbrechter and Michael Higgins (eds), *Returning (to) Communities: Theory, Culture and Political Practice of the Communal* (Rodopi B.V 2006) 266.

10 Nick Couldry, *Inside Culture: Re-imagining the Method of Cultural Studies* (Sage 2000).

11 Thumim (n 9) 265.

rules and to disrupt institutions.[12] Here ordinary people mould and sculpt their own lives as sovereign personalities. Deliberative democrats thus pose ordinary people as a counter-weight to the power of elites.[13] Another account sees ordinary people claimed and valorized by rival ideologies. Creating connections with their lot serves a legitimating function. When so deployed, however, the concept is often promptly decried as oppressive and as bleaching diversity.[14] There is inherent volatility to the relationship between ordinary people and sources and institutions of power.

In domains other than criminal justice, the idea of ordinary people has been developed with active intent. In public health care, for example, the idea of 'bringing in' ordinary people as service-users is connected both to the discourse of participatory practice and of 'democratic renewal'.[15] In the cultural sphere, the idea of ordinary people acts in a bifurcated manner where members of the public are invited to participate and create representations of themselves and their 'place', and are posed as a source of accountability. As a matter of self-representation, ordinary people are said to author themselves.[16] In the cultural enterprise, previously excluded experience is re-centred.[17] Stanley Deetz talks about this as the 'amplification of voices'.[18]

Cultural theorist, Nancy Thumim captures these various meanings in four broad senses of the term: *hierarchical-pejorative*, *hierarchical-celebratory*, *customary* and *public*. In the first iteration, ordinary people

---

[12] Wayne te Brake, *Shaping History: Ordinary People in European Politics, 1500–1700* (U Cal P 1998); Frances Piven, *Challenging Authority: How Ordinary People Change America* (Roman and Littlefield Publishers 2006).

[13] John Dryzek, *Discursive Democracy: Politics, Policy, and Political Science* (CUP 1990).

[14] Sarat and Kearns (n 7).

[15] Graham Martin, '"Ordinary People Only": Knowledge, Representativeness, and the Publics of Public Participation in Healthcare' (2008) 30 *Sociology of Health & Illness* 35, 35.

[16] Cheung (2000) quoted in Thumim (n 9) 262.

[17] It is outside the scope of this chapter to expand further on the debates about ordinary people' as a construct. Nonetheless it is important to note that there is extensive critique about what biases self-representation and participation carry with them and the extent to which the ordinary people construct acts as a cynical legitimizing device. Both Thumim (n 9) and Martin (n 15) discuss these issues with regard to the cultural sphere and public health care.

[18] Stanley Deetz, *Democracy in an Age of Corporate Colonization: Developments in Communication and the Politics of Everyday Life* (State University of New York Press 1992) 53.

are beneath and a 'mass'. They are defined 'in opposition' to differentiated others: experts, special people and those above. As such, ordinary people can be 'inferior', 'mundane', and without identity. In the second meaning, ordinary people are celebrated precisely because they have been marginalized. Thumim suggests this sense 'indicates a political position, which disputes whose account of reality matters'. Here, groups of people are united across their differences before some dominant and dominating account. A third sense of ordinary people refers to people whose practices are ordinary. It acts both as a claim to commonality and as a means of including the banal and the bizarre. Finally, ordinary people are cast as citizens of democracy: *the public*. Political force is located and invoked in *the people*. For public institutions, the use of the term in this manner has dual meaning where the people are both a source of legitimacy and accountability, and are a consumer base.[19] In this book I mine all these categorizations of the term.

In summary, ordinary people are neither simple nor singular. Their identity is plural, with numerous influences on personal and group identity and deployment. Multiple, often overlapping, realities of what is ordinary jostle, just as violations of varying kinds are casually deployed and made ordinary. Ordinary people act, react, interact and connect; they ignore, de-code and re-construct; and they negotiate, manipulate, block, manage, mobilize and plan in a complex reality that is both material and imagined.

ORDINARY PEOPLE IN EVERYDAY WORLDS

From these critical constructs, who were the lay people interviewed for the research? What do they share with other ordinary Australians, and what is distinct? Are they more or less moralistic than others? Do they have greater faith in the power of the law? Are they more trusting of authority? In answering these questions I avoid creating typologies or hierarchies. Rather, how people interpret their situation and what they say of their social world are highlighted as influences on their recourse to law.

At Time 1, 33 people were interviewed. Each had experienced a violent incident from which police had laid a criminal charge against an alleged assailant. The cases had not yet gone to court. People were diverse and included senior federal government officials as well as

[19] Thumim (n 9) 262–5.

mothers drawing social security. There was a body piercer and an IT analyst, private business owners, a warehouseman and a hospital technician, a musician and a service worker among others. Within the group were doctoral and master's students, law graduates, and trade-qualified persons. People had varying levels of involvement in local activities such as sport, culture and community. Very few described themselves as active in religious or political activities although nearly half said they were very or fairly interested in politics. They were busy in their ordinary lives – taking children to school and expecting new babies, working in high-pressure policy jobs, studying hard, and going to the gym and to parties. They were trying to establish new businesses and make existing ones flourish. They referenced to many different relationships that defined and connected them. Some of these personal networks came to sustain them through the experience of violence and their journey through the justice process. Others in their social circle did not.

The demographic characteristics of interviewees were both consistent with and divergent from others in the ACT region (the Appendix has a fuller description). Most were Australian born although none was Aboriginal Australian. A small proportion hailed from countries in Europe, Africa, the Middle East, South America and Asia. However, that 27 per cent spoke a language other than English at home is evidence of a more mixed heritage that accords with local census data. Participants' socio-demographic profiles were equally diverse, though the population is generally well-off and educated. The region hosts both the federal and territory bureaucracies and four universities. However, only one in five of the lay participants described themselves as professionals; others were managers or employed in technical and trades. Most were employed (39 per cent full-time and 24 per cent part-time) and many also had a tertiary qualification as their highest level of education. Income for the lay participants was arranged in a similar distribution to that for the region. Over half said that they rented their home and a third were married.

While victims are often popularized in terms that emphasize their passivity, individuals in the study group displayed a high sense of personal agency. Over half felt that they had control over the direction their life was going and felt good about themselves all or most of the time. This strong sense of self is a shared characteristic with other Australians.[20] This characteristic may, of course, be a feature of selection

---

[20] A personal agency scale was constructed from four variables. The mean of the personal agency scale for the national sample was 3.8 (N=3465), and for the study sample it was 3.7 (N=33).

bias but the strong sense of personal agency was also reflected in the fact that 64 per cent of the lay participants reported the incident to police themselves.[21] However, a quarter felt good about themselves only 'now and then' or 'hardly ever'. They also expressed significantly higher pessimism compared to the national sample: 18 per cent agreed that it was very much like them that 'there is really no way I can solve some of the problems I have' whereas just 5 per cent of the national sample agreed that this was very much like them. These assessments perhaps reflected a grounded estimation of their circumstances and the upcoming justice processes.

ORDINARY CITIZENS

In ordinary and everyday worlds, who people are and what they do form a submerged, deep social fabric. When they come into contact with public authority these features come closer to the surface – in an easy glide or with a jolt. The nature of their relationship with those authorities becomes a question and also becomes more specific. In this process their political identity is foregrounded and their citizen identity becomes salient.

There are as many conceptions of the idea of 'citizen' as there are of ordinary people. As a status it is a term that can mark sharp boundaries between 'us' and 'them' in a manner similar to the terms victim and offender. Therefore, defining the 'us' of community membership becomes a central concern. Antony Duff answers the question by asserting 'we' are 'citizens of a particular kind of polity' 'whom its laws claim to bind'.[22] While placing citizens within normative boundaries, there is recognition too that the various visions of the citizen are plural, multiple and overlapping. As an account of their status, the notion of citizen has more import and is more robust than simply classifying people as ordinary community members.

---

[21] Half of the male assault group initiated the report, and 68 per cent of the female domestic assault group. The latter finding is compatible with an earlier study that found that 70 per cent of spouse/ex-spouse incidents attended by police and recorded by them over a three-year period within the ACT arose from contact initiated by the victim (Robyn Holder, 'Police and Domestic Violence: An Analysis of Domestic Violence Incidents Attended by Police in the ACT and Subsequent Actions' (2007) *Research Paper No.4* Australian Domestic and Family Violence Clearinghouse).

[22] Anthony Duff, 'Towards a Theory of Criminal Law?' (2010) 84(1) *Aristotelian Society Supplementary Volume* 1, 3, 5.

There is considerable political and academic debate about what citizens owe themselves, each other and the state, as well as what the state owes and can expect from its citizens. Undoubtedly posing 'citizen-as-status'[23] affects how we view people's relationship to the state and its entities. It suggests that structures and applications of power require careful calibration. It further suggests that the tone and conduct of institutional relations with citizens ought, as a default, to be respectful and abjure paternalism. This characterization can only be because of the authority inherent in understanding the foundational nature of the citizen to democratic theory.[24] Certainly there is nothing in this cast to citizen status that differentiates between persons who could be either or both victim or offender at any given moment.[25] Both are part of the public.[26]

I am interested here in the idea of the citizen as politically sovereign as it creates a sharper boundary between their interests and the interests of the state. Thus, ordinary people are citizens within communities, and are conjured in direct contrast to institutions and their power to define. This representation necessarily calls for a closer examination of values, attitudes and beliefs of the *demos* – those comprising the study sample and the wider society – as a precursor to exploring how these influence interaction with authorities.

---

23 That is citizen as *social* and *political* status, in addition to the more usual citizen-as-*legal*-status. For a thorough discussion on the various models of citizen and citizenship see Linda Bosniak, 'Citizenship Denationalized' (2000) 7 *Indiana Journal of Global Legal Studies* 447–509. Scholars such as Bosniak are concerned with citizenship as a transnational concept as well as one determined through the nation state. I focus on the citizen as a member of a particular bounded and territorial community.

24 And is particularly strongly argued by Benjamin Barber, *Strong Democracy: Participatory Politics for a New Age* (U Cal P 1984).

25 However, for a thoughtful discussion of the proposition that convicted and imprisoned offenders should be viewed as temporarily foregoing some citizenship rights see Jean Hampton, 'Retribution and the Liberal State' (1994) 5 *Journal of Contemporary Legal Issues* 117–44.

26 I acknowledge that the citizen-status of some 'subjects' (e.g., refugees, itinerant workers) and their concomitant enactment of citizenship activities are topics of deep debate (Engin Isin, 'Citizenship in Flux: The Figure of the Activist Citizen' (2009) 29 *Subjectivity* 367; Kim Rubenstein, 'Citizenship and the Centenary: Inclusion and Exclusion in 20th Century Australia' (2000) 24 *Melbourne University Law Review* 576–608).

Values, Attitudes and Beliefs

Values, attitudes and beliefs are the 'psychological infrastructure' underpinning social action as well as peoples' relationships to authority. Foregrounding these features reveals their agency, 'both moral and otherwise' and their capability to choose 'to cooperate overtly [with authorities] and defy covertly'.[27] From this standpoint, we understand that a decision to turn to the law is not simply a feature of circumstance, in which people act like automatons. To explore this infrastructure the lay participants were asked questions, drawn from three different national surveys,[28] about their personal values, their trust in society's institutions and certain of their attitudes towards law and justice. Because of the very large N difference between the surveys I describe general patterns rather than specific values.

In a series of large-scale studies examining the micro foundations of Australian democracy, two key dimensions to personal values were identified. A security dimension comprised strength, order and social and economic status. A harmony dimension focused on 'the quality of relationships, knowledge, understanding and human dignity'.[29] As Valerie Braithwaite argues, the two value systems point to different, although not mutually exclusive, bases for considering people's orientation towards others as well as towards authority.[30] One orients to exchange and security, while the other to commitment and the communal. The surveys found that Australians tend towards the latter, as did the lay participants.[31] People's civic ideas and their level of involvement in community

---

[27] Valerie Braithwaite, *Defiance in Taxation and Governance: Resisting and Dismissing Authority in a Democracy* (Edward Elgar Publishing 2009) 15, 18.

[28] When examining the comparisons between the local sample and all three of the national studies I expected the means to be roughly equal because the samples come from the same population. I would expect large differences between sample means to occur very infrequently. On this basis I have drawn conclusions observable from the means.

[29] Braithwaite (n 27) 122.

[30] Valerie Braithwaite, 'Security and Harmony Value Orientations and their Roles in Attitude Formation and Change' (2009) 20 *Psychological Inquiry* 162–7.

[31] The mean of the harmony scale for the national sample was 5.8 (N=3523), and for the study sample it was 6.4 (N=33). The mean of the security scale for the national sample was 4.4 (N=3523), and for the study sample it was 4.0 (N=33). Derived from a seven-point Likert scale where 1 = reject and 7 = accept as of utmost importance. Given the greater number of women than men in the Justice Study, there may be a gender influence at work. The national survey

and political affairs provided further insight into the way in which they orient themselves within the wider community and towards others, as well as how they orient towards authority. Australians and the study sample shared a conception of citizenship that emphasized self-reliance.[32] Both groups expressed a high degree of trust in the public services in their area (being public schools, emergency services, neighbours),[33] but their trust in authorities (being local and federal government and law courts) was not strong. In the Justice Study this pattern of trust in community institutions was broadly similar for domestic and non-domestic assault victims, although the former had stronger trust in those communal institutions commonly associated with the relational such as public schools and neighbours. The non-domestic assault group had a stronger sense of trust in law courts, hospitals and charities.

Law and justice questions put to the lay participants showed that domestic and non-domestic assault victims displayed strong adherence to the idea of rules, with a strong majority agreeing with statements that: 'obeying the law is the right thing to do', 'I feel a moral obligation to obey the law', and 'I may not like all the laws and rules we have in place, but obeying them is a part of life we must accept'. These beliefs were shared with other Australians surveyed[34] and shared also by Dutch

---

comprised 47 per cent men and 51 per cent women which made it more equal than the balance in the Justice Study (Valerie Braithwaite, *The Community Hopes, Fears and Actions Survey: goals and measures* Working Paper No.2 (Centre for Tax System Integrity The Australian National University 2001)).

[32] Two scales factored from seven variables. The mean of the self-reliant citizenship scale for the national sample was 4.1 (N=3535), and for the study sample it was 4.5 (N=33). The mean of the involved citizenship scale for the national sample was 3.5 (N=3535), and for the study sample it was 3.5 (N=33). Derived from a five-point Likert scale where 1 = strongly disagree and 5 = strongly agree.

[33] The mean of the trust in authorities scale for the national sample was 2.2 (N=3544), and for the study sample it was 2.3 (N=33). The mean of the trust in public services scale for the national sample was 3.4 (N=3544), and for the study sample it was 3.0 (N=33). Derived from a four-point Likert scale where 1 = do not trust them at all and 4 = trust them a lot (reverse coded).

[34] The national sample asked confidence, legitimacy and performance questions primarily in relation to police. Therefore the scales developed for the current study are different to those reported by Murphy and her colleagues (Murphy and others 2010a, 2010b). For the national sample, the mean of the obligation to obey scale was 4.3 (N=1173), and for the study sample it was 4.6 (N=33). Derived from a five-point Likert scale where 1 = strongly disagree and 5 = strongly agree.

victims surveyed by Wemmers.[35] However, 'confidence in justice' for both local and the Australian samples was moderate.[36] The study sample was quite uncertain about their local justice system. A substantial proportion could neither agree nor disagree that the justice system reflected the needs of the community (42 per cent) or that they had confidence in the justice system (49 per cent). A slight majority (52 per cent) agreed/strongly agreed that they 'sometimes question the laws we are asked to obey'. The sense that the justice system is not fair for all was also reasonably strong in the local and Australian samples. Furthermore, in terms of preparedness to comply with and accept authority, there was a three-way split on the question that 'people should accept the decisions of police even if they think they are wrong', although 42 per cent disagreed/strongly disagreed that 'disobeying the law was sometimes justified' (27 per cent agreed).

Australians' cynicism about the application of our laws and justice is generally well established, and shared by comparable societies.[37] A majority (70 per cent) believe that the criminal courts have regard for defendants' rights whereas just 47 per cent agree the same for victims' rights, and only a slight majority agrees that criminal courts deal with matters fairly.[38] But Australians' commitment to the 'moral credibility' embedded within legal arrangements is also well established.[39] The views of the local lay sample accord with this paradoxical stance – although this ambivalence was much more pronounced for women than men. In the national sample, responses by men and women were similar on confidence in justice and for their critical orientation to authority. People's beliefs about our laws and justice also relates to their opinion on the sentencing applied by courts. Here too there was similarity between

---

[35] Jo-Anne Wemmers, *Victims in the Criminal Justice System* (Kugler Publications 1996) 182–3.

[36] The mean of the confidence in justice scale for the national sample was 3.2 (N=1125), and for the study sample it was 3.0 (N=33).

[37] For the US, see Tom Tyler, *Why People Obey the Law* (Princeton UP 1990/2006) and, in relation to Canada, see Julian Roberts, 'Public Confidence in Criminal Justice in Canada: A Comparative and Contextual Analysis' (2007) 49 *Canadian Journal of Criminology and Criminal Justice* 153–84.

[38] Lyn Roberts and David Indermaur, *What Australians Think About Crime and Justice: Results from the 2007 Survey of Social Attitudes* Research and Public Policy Series 101 (Australian Institute of Criminology 2009) 3.

[39] Paul Robinson, 'Why Does the Criminal Law Care What the Layperson Thinks is Just? Coercive Versus Normative Crime Control' (2000) 86 *Virginia Law Review* 1839, 1865.

the local and national samples. Nearly two-thirds agreed that the sentences handed down by courts are too lenient/much too lenient; but about a quarter of the local sample and a third of the national sample indicated that sentencing was 'about right'.[40]

Interrelationship of Elements

The picture of the ordinary people in this study is thus broadly consistent with national characteristics in that they have a strong sense of personal agency and a moral pathway mapped between their personal values and their stated beliefs. Their personal value set orients them towards communal trust norms and self-reliance. They have a strong moral and normative commitment to the rule of law, alongside less robust confidence in the fairness and efficacy of the legal system, and a belief that sentencing by courts for offences in general is too lenient. They are more trusting of society's helping responses than they are trusting of authorities. With this portrayal, it is tempting to view the victim participants in the Justice Study as 'ideal'.[41] The main point, however, is that they are not so different to other ordinary people in Australia.

Values and beliefs form a latent structure within the social world. They are interrelated and inform assessments of experience. They shape peoples' inclinations and orientations, and influence expectations. Beliefs cluster in particular circumstances, but all contribute to judgments about justice (see Figure 5.1). The importance of prior values and beliefs on the procedural justice judgments was also found by Wemmers for Dutch victims of crime.

Human actions arise from a complex interaction of personal and social factors and differing identities, and not solely from the calculation of cost-benefit or the avoidance of threat. Indeed, an individual's 'ethical

---

[40] The Justice Study sample appeared slightly less punitive than the national sample in that 21 per cent said the sentences are much too lenient as opposed to 34 per cent in the national sample. However, the study sample is too small to regard this difference as reliable. In the national sample there was a tendency for victims to be more punitive than those who have not been victimized (74 per cent of victims answering a little too lenient and much too lenient versus 67 per cent of non-victims), but this tendency is not very strong.

[41] The 'ideal victim' is a classic depiction of Nils Christie ('The Ideal Victim' in Ezat Fattah (ed), *From Crime Policy to Victim Policy: Reorienting the Justice System* (Macmillan 1986)). It is particularly relevant to representations of 'good' and 'bad' victims and the function these constructs serve justice agencies.

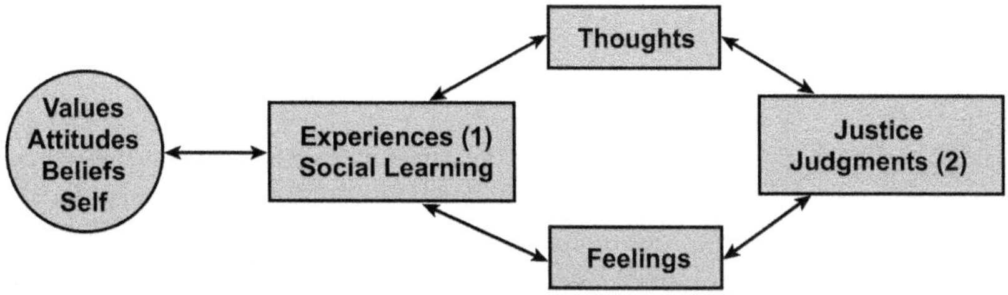

Notes: (1) Where 'experiences' includes elements including the victimization and its context, considerations about the offender and others, as well as experiences of justice process.
(2) Where 'judgments' relate to the institutions of justice as well as to the idea of justice itself.

Source: Adapted from Tyler et al. (1997) 7 and Braithwaite (2009) 17.

Figure 5.1 Conceptual model of interrelationship of latent factors in justice judgments

identity' may be prompted through engagement with authorities.[42] This can be seen, for example, in the civic duty reasoning people often give when reporting crime to authorities as discussed in Chapter 3. However, in people's everyday worlds, institutions move 'between states of irrelevance and relevance'.[43] As such, assessments made from a position of some social distance may be subject to rapid reappraisal when the authority is approached as in the extraordinary circumstances presented by violence.[44]

---

[42] Nathan Harris, 'Shame, Ethical Identity and Conformity: Lessons from Research on the Psychology of Social Influence' in Susanne Karstedt and others (eds) *Emotions, Crime and Justice* (Hart Publishing 2011), Ch 9. Although Harris' focus is on those who commit crime, his notion remains relevant for persons as victims of crime. The literature discussed in Chapter 3 points to a similar triggering of 'ethical identity' when deciding whether to report a crime and whether to cooperate with authorities.

[43] Braithwaite (n 27) 254.

[44] Richard McAdams presents the idea that law provides a 'focal point' for the 'coordination' of behaviour ('A Focal Point Theory of Expressive Law' (2000) 86 *Virginia Law Review* 1649–729). This idea of the focal point also accommodates the suggestion (posed by Frances Zemans, 'Legal Mobilization: The Neglected Role of the Law in the Political System' (1983) 77 *The American Political Science Review* 690–703) that citizens use an event (or series of events) that gives rise to some adjustment or decision around which to consider other criteria to the possibility of mobilizing law.

ORDINARY PEOPLE IN EXTRAORDINARY CIRCUMSTANCES

Having sketched the lay participants as similar to other ordinary Australians, this section now shifts to present them as extraordinary in the following ways. First, the incident of violence sets them apart even though for some the abuse was unfortunately regular. Secondly, the mobilization of justice resources after victimization is uncommon.

The Incident and its Effects

All of the lay participants had been victims of violence for which another person had been charged with a criminal offence. At the first interview (from which the data in this chapter are drawn), the case had yet to proceed through the justice system. All of the six men had been victims of acquaintance or stranger assault,[45] and all of the 27 women had been victims of a partner or ex-partner. All described a range of experiences with abuse and violence. The incidents of non-domestic assault took place either in social or neighbourhood settings.

> He was the ex-boyfriend of a person in a group of friends. He made a scene, smashed a glass and left. Then I walked to the door to make sure he had left. I saw another friend leave and go up to this man to confront him to say 'you can't do that'. She pushed him on the shoulder. I pushed her aside and he hit me instead. (Bailey)

> His body language was like he wanted to fight. I couldn't get away from him. After he punched me, I grabbed him and took him to the ground. He yelled to let him go. I did and then he stood up and punched my friend full in the face. (Finn)

The incidents of domestic assault commonly comprised part of a pattern of abuse that took place in intimate relationships, some of which were long standing. Some incidents were unexpected or arose from particular circumstances.

> He'd belittle me to such an extent – everything was wrong. He'd beat me but then be the nicest person. He was really controlling on everything I bought or did. He was that possessive. Said I was ugly and useless and he wanted full control. (Molly)

---

[45] Two were victims of neighbors known casually or by sight.

> He'd never done this [hit me] before. He was just really down but he flew at me and was insulting and abusive. I sat down. He was hitting me on either side of the face. (Ursula)

The incidents of non-domestic assault were described predominately as physical assaults while the incidents of domestic assault were accompanied by a high degree of verbal abuse. The domestic assault victims described stronger emotional after-effects than did the non-domestic assault victims, while the latter described the physical effects in strong terms.

> I was spitting blood out. (Edward)
>
> My ear was hurting. I put my hand up and there was blood. (Finn)
>
> He's been harassing, stalking, nasty. It just never stops. (Quinn)

A majority of the non-domestic assault victims said that they were angry at the time of the incident whereas the domestic assault victims emphasized their distress and fear. A small majority also felt humiliation. Overall a majority assessed the incident they experienced as very or extremely serious, although victims of domestic assault were twice as likely as victims of non-domestic assault to make such an assessment.

Of the 27 domestic assault victims, just over half described the assailant as husband, de facto partner or boyfriend, and a third as ex-husband, ex-de facto partner or ex-boyfriend. Seven had had that relationship for over ten years, for nine the relationship was between five and ten years, and ten for under three years; 22 women indicated that they did not want the relationship to continue. Nearly all of the domestic assault victims described experiences of violence from the same assailant prior to the most recent incident.[46] Of these, 13 said that it had happened quite a few/many times before, 14 described the abuse as becoming very/pretty serious, and 15 that their situation was becoming very/pretty bad.

Study Participants as a Sample of Victims in the ACT

Most victims do not report, but a majority of the lay participants initiated the call to police at the time or after the incident. They were also extraordinary because they formed part of an even smaller proportion for

---

[46] Three of the non-domestic assault victims described experiencing violence at other times from other assailants. These experiences were not part of this study.

whom the report actually resulted in a matter being charged, prosecuted and resolved in court action. In a representative year 2007–08, just over 26,000 individual victims reported a wide range of offences to police in the ACT. Of these, less than 10 per cent were victims of offences against the person (homicide, assault, sexual assault, other offences against the person, robbery). Of the 26,000 victims of crime, most were male and a third were female.[47] Males were also the majority of victims of assault. The vast majority of all offences reported to police in the region were recorded by them as 'not cleared', with a tiny proportion cleared by way of arrest and as charged and before the court. For 2007–08, just 20 per cent (n=453) of assault matters were subject to arrest with 1 per cent (n=27) recorded as charged before the court. Thus the study sample of 33 is distinctive of the small overall proportion of victims of violence for whom the matter reaches court.

As a sub-set of inter-personal assault, police attended nearly 3,000 incidents of domestic and family violence in 2007–08.[48] Of these, 84 per cent involved female victims with males making 83 per cent of offenders. Approximately half of incidents attended by police were recorded as offences and half of those resulted in a person being apprehended. Of the formal resolutions to these apprehensions, 94 per cent were formally charged. The most common offence type leading to formal charges was assault. Also in the representative year 2007–08, 435 defendants appeared before the court for family violence offences. Of the adult defendants, 88 per cent were male.[49]

The 27 female participants arose from the 800-plus annual crisis visits conducted by a community-based victim agency within the ACT, the Domestic Violence Crisis Service (DVCS).[50] While the service assists

---

[47] Kiah McGregor and others, *ACT Victims of Crime Referral Project: Final Report* Technical and Background Paper No.55 (Australian Institute of Criminology 2013) 21.

[48] The dataset for domestic and family violence discussed is not the same as for 'all crime' data notwithstanding both derived from ACT Policing. Police in ACT record a range of incidents as 'family violence'. A sub-category describes 'spouse/ex-spouse' (or domestic violence and assault). Using ACT Policing data, Holder (n 21) has described the key differences in characteristics between the 'spouse/ex-spouse' sub-category within the 'all family violence category'.

[49] Tracy Cussen and Matthew Lyneham, 'ACT Family Violence Intervention Program Review' Technical and Background Papers No.52 (Australian Institute of Criminology 2012).

[50] Domestic Violence Crisis Service (DVCS undated), *Annual Reports 1988–2008* DVCS Canberra, 44. The service receives nearly 9,000 calls per annum on its helpline.

people subjected to violence as well as people using violence, the overwhelming proportion of clients are females subjected to violence. A client evaluation conducted by the service in the representative year 2007–08 was responded to by 66 persons, of whom a majority were female. Of this sample, 73 per cent had contact with the police in the year in question with 40 per cent seeing criminal charges arise from the incident.

CONTEMPLATING LEGAL MOBILIZATION

If victims of violence largely do not turn to the law after victimization, then why did the people interviewed in this research do so? Decision-making comprises several factors. As Zemans argues, the possibility of a resolution or the attainment of an outcome for the incident is just 'one among many reasons to invoke the law'.[51] For those in the Justice Study, their daily life was busy and full. Life was patterned by habit and punctuated by interactions of various kinds. These continuities framed peoples' victimization experience and also the long months to the unfolding justice process.

As a precursive frame to the report to police, this section describes the ways in which people understood what had happened to them. The meanings they ascribed to the incident are informed by their orientation to the perpetrator of the violence and the attributions they made to explain his conduct. However, other people in the victim's world acted as facilitators to legitimate pathways to law enforcement within a specific social and cultural milieu. Legal consciousness theory discussed in Chapter 3 illuminates this mutually constitutive relationship between private and public elements to an assessment that the incident is potentially justiciable. Throughout, I touch on how differently these issues appear to work in relational terms. Finally, I sketch how the evocation of justice was moderated by participants' assessments and expectations.

Making Meaning of the Event

The lay participants deployed a number of interpretive frames to assemble meaning and from which to construct possible lines of action. Self-assessment is, without doubt, no neutral exercise. It is woven with community values, infected by personal doubt, and influenced by third

---

[51] Zemans (n 44) 994.

party views.[52] An incident or event thus carries potential for either action or inaction.

The 'ambivalent invocation' of victimhood was present for both men and women.[53] The men, however, were much more tentative and ambivalent in commenting about their actions. Young men hear polarized social messages about their involvement in violence as well as mixed messages about their representation as victims.[54] In this environment the male participants more readily verbalized the criteria they considered for their engagement of police. That is, clear attribution of the incident to the violent person, a sense of blamelessness on their part, the absence of any provocation, and assessed seriousness. For a couple of the men the fact that police were on the scene and witnessed the incident lent an immediate reliability to assessments of what and who was 'in the wrong'. For example, Bailey said:

---

52 Studies have examined the characteristics and nature of the social context that contributes to the 'collective efficacy' of neighbourhoods in enforcing collective norms and informal social controls (Jeffrey Morenoff and others, 'Neighborhood Inequality, Collective Efficacy, and the Spatial Dynamics of Urban Violence' (2001) 39 *Criminology* 517–58; Robert Sampson and others, 'Neighborhoods and Violent Crime: A Multilevel Study of Collective Efficacy' (1997) 277 *Science* 918–24). A Dutch study confirmed the importance of social cohesiveness and socio-economic disadvantage of the neighbourhood as factors affecting reporting (Heike Goudriaan and others, 'Neighbourhood Characteristics and Reporting Crime Effects of Social Cohesion, Confidence in Police Effectiveness and Socio-Economic Disadvantage' (2006) 46 *British Journal of Criminology* 719–42). The normative influence of the social network is also clearly influential on female victims of violence reporting to police (Catherine Kaukinen, 'The Help-Seeking Decisions of Violent-Crime Victims: An Examination of the Direct and Conditional Effects of Gender and the Victim-Offender Relationship' (2002) 17 *Journal of Interpersonal Violence* 432–56 and 'The Help-Seeking Strategies of Female Violent-Crime Victims: The Direct and Conditional Effects of Race and the Victim-Offender Relationship' (2004) 19 *Journal of Interpersonal Violence* 967–90).

53 Bumiller (n 4) 99.

54 Joe Clare and Frank Morgan, 'Factors Affecting Perceived Criminality: Evidence from Victims of Assault' (2009) *Trends and Issues in Crime and Justice* (AIC); Veronika Burcar and Malin Åkerström, 'Negotiating a Victim Identity: Young Men as Victims of Violence' (2009) 10 *Journal of Scandinavian Studies in Criminology and Crime Prevention* 37–54; Tim Newburn and Elizabeth Stanko, 'When Men are Victims: The Failure of Victimology' in Newburn and Stanko (eds), *Just Men Doing Business: Men, Masculinities and Crime* (Routledge 1994) 153–65.

> The incident took place directly opposite a police van. They intervened. I pushed him away and then the cops came. They told me to sit down. He resisted police and had drunk far too much. They took him into custody. They had seen everything. They dispersed the crowd.

The men were also explicit in asserting their blamelessness. Charlie's comment typifies this point. He further sets out another criterion – that of initiation – that would have diminished his assessment of being the innocent party.

> I hadn't invited the violence upon myself. It had just happened. I'm not sure what happened. If I had somehow started it I'd feel more like taking responsibility and accept my losses. But I hadn't.

That the violence apparently came from nowhere contributed to a sense of blamelessness for the men. For Finn, the assault was 'unwarranted and random'. In contrast, these validating criteria were largely absent from the accounts of women as victims of domestic assault. Instead, a stronger sense of social support was evident, perhaps as one outcome from repeated government and community assertions over previous decades that domestic violence is a crime. Aimee's comment encapsulated this combination of the breached personal, community and legal norm with the identification of the entity appropriate to deal with it. She said, 'I knew [it] was illegal, a crime. It was obvious to me … I just knew that this was not on and that the best way of dealing with it was to go to the police.'

For both men and women the idea that the less relational distance between victim and assailant brings less law was only part of the story. Other factors came into play. David, assaulted by a neighbour, referred both to his desire to change his previous cultural milieu as well as his concern for others as influencing his report to police. He said:

> As a kid I was raised not to 'dog' and not go to the cops. But now I haven't offended for four years or more and am trying to work and was worried about my girlfriend. I don't want them to look closely at me so I'm cautious about what to tell them and whether to get help from them.

Alex was also assaulted by a neighbour and suffered retribution following his report to police. He said:

> I think the biggest issue I had was actually talking to police because of how this is viewed by others. Others think this is 'dobbing'. Maybe this is something the judge can say when sentencing: 'people have the right to ask for help from police'. Because I talked to police I had repercussions.

> Like-minded people to [the assailant] see police as different. I see police as protectors of society. They see police as those who come and lock you up, as authority. When the protection order was served, people drove by and said 'dog'. When I was down the street people yelled out and I tried to defend myself and I got a black eye. In this type of neighbourhood there are repercussions to talking to police. In Sydney you get your house burned down.

Notwithstanding their stronger sense that they had community support for turning to the police about domestic violence, a number of the women referred to differing levels of validation they received from family and friends. Two comments represent the extremes experienced. Zola said, 'my sister said I deserved it. I didn't like that'. Winona received a different response. She 'knew' she 'didn't want any more contact with him [the assailant] but I was not sure about telling police. I wasn't sure what his reaction would be'. However, a friend encouraged her to contact police.

For all the participants, family and friends were the most likely source of help after victimization but considerable nuance was expressed about how this worked at a micro level. For example, Charlie deciphered the complex messages and information he received in the following way:

> I had a cut above my eye so the level of injury also mattered. It was more serious. My friends and family are all fine and thought it was the right thing to do to tell police. My nearest and dearest were upset that it had happened at all. That was tempered by their view that I was out at 4 am and alcohol was involved. My father thought I'd been careless. My friend had his brother assaulted and his jaw broken and all our friends knew. I saw what they went through. The general view is that it was the right thing to do.

Overall, the Justice Study people felt social support for their perception of the incident with 70 per cent agreeing with the statement that 'the community saw incidents such as happened to me as serious'. Event seriousness is certainly not posed as determining action but the lay participants frequently remarked that it was the perceived seriousness of the incident either to themselves and/or to others that served as a motivator. Cathy's comments encompassed her child and unborn baby. 'It happened in front of [our son]' she said, 'and I was hit in the stomach and was afraid for the baby. I was not having [our son] grow up thinking it's ok'. In counterpoint, Roslyn (who did not initiate the contact with police herself) said that she would call police in the future if her partner 'was physically violent to me or threatened me somehow that I perceived there was a grave danger'.

The emotional response to the incident was different between the two sub-groups. Distress and fear were particularly salient for women victims of domestic assault, whereas anger was the dominant emotion for male victims of non-domestic assault. A number of women felt their situation was worsening and the violence escalating. For example, Deanna 'was very fearful for my life' and Eliza commented that she 'was extremely terrified of him'. The emotional landscape was vastly different for the non-domestic assault victims. The men tended to express affront and a couple referred to the incident as an exemplar of the problem of violence in social settings. Bailey, for example, indicated this was a motivation to his report to police. He said: 'fighting in general shouldn't be supported' and reporting to police was 'a way of preventing it'. He felt that 'there's a huge lack of young people not getting this message'. These emotional and cognitive responses informed the assignment of attribution to the violent person and contributed to 'an exculpation continuum'.[55]

Making Meaning in a Social Context

How individuals ascribe meaning to an event does not result only from the circumstances. The social milieu is also influential. Third parties act as important validators and facilitators of interpretation and action.[56] Those in the Justice Study turned primarily to friends and family for assistance. In these networks, social norms and contacts are highly influential, but are also a form of advice seeking without deliberate intent. For example, Winona did not tell her parents what happened but she 'called another friend and she got me to go [to police]'. Bailey said 'later that night a lawyer friend and I were having a drink. He advised me to go over and make a statement to police. I felt supported to do that'.

Both domestic and non-domestic assault victims used these conversations to test out their interpretation of the events and to gain information about the types of responses they might anticipate from the justice system. The concept of social validation is important to the

[55] Philip Tetlock and others, 'People as Intuitive Prosecutors: The Impact of Social Control Goals on Attributions of Responsibility' (2006) 43 *Journal of Experimental Social Psychology* 195, 197.

[56] A Special Issue of *Law and Society Review* (1976) provides a number of classic texts on the role of third parties in legal mobilization. In particular, see Jack Ladinsky, 'The Traffic in Legal Services: Lawyer-Seeking Behavior and the Channeling of Clients' 207–23; Raymond Marks, 'Some Research Perspectives for Looking at Legal Need and Legal Services Delivery Systems: Old Forms or New' 191–205.

interpretive exercise and works to assess the calibration of one's views with trusted and respected others as the following examples show.

> Later I discussed it with a lawyer colleague at work. They talked to me about the system. (Edward)
>
> My best friend's partner is a police officer and he talked to me about it. (Nada)
>
> In my current job I … was very across the issues. I knew the justice system was pretty strong. (Aimee)

Not all these conversations were supportive of the victim or of decisions to report incidents. Some individuals recognized that their decision to turn to police went against the practices of their social sub-group. These nuances were evidenced in participants' reflections on how third parties may perceive incidents such as theirs. As a formal third party, police have been shown to be disinterested or discourteous to domestic assault victims and other victims.[57] However, in the Justice Study police were viewed as a sympathetic source of assistance. Interestingly, domestic assault victims were more likely than non-domestic assault victims to agree that 'police see incidents such as happened to me as serious', whereas the reverse was true with the statement that 'police understand how it feels to be a victim of violence'. Both groups were more ambiguous about agreeing that 'the community sees incidents such as happened to me as serious'. The strong marketing in Australia of messages encouraging women to come forward and seek help for domestic violence may have been influential. Perhaps also influential was knowledge of the ACT's pro-arrest and pro-prosecution approach to domestic violence.[58]

However, turning to informal or formal sources of help does not translate into certainty. Asked a series of questions probing their expectations of the reception and possible outcome of their mobilization of

---

[57] For domestic assault victims, see Kathleen Ferraro, 'Policing Woman Battering' (1989) 36 *Social Problems* 61–74; and for other victims, see Steven Brandl and Frank Horvath, 'Crime-Victim Evaluation of Police Investigative Performance' (1991) 19 *Journal of Criminal Justice* 293–305.

[58] The ACT Family Violence Intervention Program and its policies are described in Robyn Holder and Jane Caruana, *Criminal Justice Intervention in Family Violence in the ACT 1998–2006* (VoCC 2006). Assertive local criminal justice policies have been shown to have an effect (Meghan Novisky and Robert Peralta, 'When Women Tell: Intimate Partner Violence and the Factors Related to Police Notification' (2015) 21 *Violence Against Women* 65–86).

legal resources, participants revealed moderated and grounded perspectives. Both domestic and non-domestic assault victims overwhelmingly agreed with the statement: 'I expect the justice system to be fair'. Just over half of the participants also agreed they expected 'to have my say at court about the case', that the prosecution lawyers 'will ask me what I want to see happen to the case', and that 'the justice system [would] be able to stop the violence'. However, these positive expectations were driven by domestic assault victims. Only a third of non-domestic assault victims expected the justice system would be able to stop the violence, and 17 per cent expected to have a say at court.

In summary, this section reveals a group of people operating with a complex set of social messages to their mobilization of law. Their immediate social circle was mostly supportive but others were not. Perceptions and expectations of institutional support were strong for domestic assault victims which suggests that localities can effectively incentivize decision-making. Overall, the salience of law conceived as 'part of a reciprocal process in which the meanings given by individuals to their world, and law and legal institutions as part of that world, become repeated, patterned and stabilized' did emerge through people's various interactions and conversations.[59] Thus both consciousness and mobilization of law were deeply socially embedded and constitutive. A picture of these ordinary people as rationally calculating individuals attracted by the certainty of the law as a tool is unsettled. The more contingent representation goes to Frances Zemans' comment that a resolution or the attainment of an outcome for a problem is just 'one among many reasons to invoke the law'.[60] What now do the participants say of these many reasons?

A JUSTICE IMAGINARY

It is striking that the vast majority of lay participants *expected* the justice system to be fair, even when a majority also generally agreed that the justice system is not fair to all. It is an expectation that has been found elsewhere.[61] The orientation to and views of citizens about different

---

[59] Patricia Ewick and Susan Silbey, 'Conformity, Contestation, and Resistance: An Account of Legal Consciousness' (1992) 26 *University of New England Law Review* 731, 741.

[60] Zemans (n 44) 994.

[61] Paula Barata, 'Abused Women's Perspectives on the Criminal Justice System's Response to Domestic Violence' (2007) 31 *Psychology of Women*

aspects of criminal justice – often characterized in terms of 'confidence' – have been extensively examined largely through population surveys. However, these fail to capture the nuance of situated perspective. As discussed in Chapter 2, the notion of *fairness* performs a unique set of functions to perceptions of justice. It is firmly embedded within everyday ideas of justice. As Sarat and Kearns argue, these are the 'taken-for-granted assumptions of shared values and common identities' of liberalism.[62] Thus what is imagined about a set of social institutions infuses meaning into situations and interactions, influences interpretation and acts to open and to close pathways. Justice, in this manner, is an *imaginary* that is both stable as an ideal and unstable as a civic resource.

To illuminate this richer prior thinking, I built a representation of the participants as a 'citizen evaluator' from responses to two key questions asked of the lay participants at their first interview. These questions relied on a broad perspective. People were asked: 'prior to the incident [in which you were the victim], if someone had asked you what you thought about the justice system in our community, what might you have said?', and second, 'when you think about the idea of justice, what sorts of things come to mind for you?' Responses showed that, for many, the formal legal world barely registered until it was propelled to relevance for them. Yvette said she 'probably wouldn't have had any thoughts about it because I've never had anything to do with it'. Prior to her present experience, Quinn commented that she 'would have said I assume the justice system did what it was supposed to do and that I believed in it'. Others drew on their exposure to the legal world as jurors, students, and as litigants or parties. Still others had prior experience as victims in other situations or as offenders or as both; 14 of the women had previously reported a domestic abuse incident to police. Three men mentioned previous violence victimization. Two of the men and two of the women also referenced past histories as children with welfare and, as adolescents, with criminal justice authorities. Nonetheless, the ostensibly disinterested interpretive mode of citizen appraisal facilitated participant comment, and enabled them to place themselves in a different social and political space other than as victim.

Quarterly 202–15; Margaret Bell and others, 'Battered Women's Perceptions of Civil and Criminal Court Helpfulness: The Role of Court Outcome and Process' (2011) 17 *Violence Against Women* 71–88.

62 Austin Sarat and Thomas R Kearns (eds), *Law in the Domains of Culture* (U Michigan P 1998) 2.

Thinking about the Idea and Institutions of Justice

Overall, people's evaluative narratives clustered into four themes: *symbolic* acknowledgment; assessments of *efficacy*; the *governance functions* of justice; and the system's *normative performance*. Symbolic representations acknowledged (e.g.) 'the legal scales of justice' (Edward), and 'police and the court system' (David).

The efficacy assessment was, perhaps not surprisingly, readily mentioned. Many opinions were critical, such as from David, who said 'it's too soft, very liberal. Magistrates are useless. Cops are OK and understand crime and what should happen but Magistrates just don't follow through'. Ursula had been on a jury years ago and 'came out of there thinking it sucks'; while Lorraine thought 'they're probably not very good'. Olivia connected her view on efficacy to civic inputs by saying that 'we do the best we can with the resources we have'. Relativity also informed Winona's belief that 'if it's really big then they [the justice system] help. If it's small, it's not important to them'. Other views were moderated with direct experience. Asked about her prior view of justice, Roslyn (for example) said that, 'I have the belief that it's there for our benefit. I just had no idea how long and convoluted it would be using it for myself'.

Some people had positive assessments of efficacy. Nada thought that 'it was adequate so far as I knew about it'. Teresa, born outside Australia, thought that the system was efficient and not corrupt. She 'always had a high opinion of the Australian system in general'. In her home country, she said:

> The system is quite good but the size of the population affects the capability of the system to address all the issues. I think the number of police and the system can cope better here with demand [in Australia]. It was all more efficient – even the tax system. Processing works better.

Comments on the governance functions of justice touched on its role and purpose for the polity. Zola said that justice was 'common-sense that I put it in the hands of the public'. For Charlie, it was about 'adherence to the law'. Ursula claimed that:

> Well to me it's just like rules – you have to have rules to keep people in check so they don't go running amok and doing strange things. They're here to protect people – hopefully.

Observation on the governance functions of justice also referenced its rectificatory purpose. Aimee said that it was about 'rightful outcome, truth, safety, protection'. Quinn's idea of justice embodied common understandings of deservingness. She thought it was 'just the guilty will be charged and innocent will come through. People pay for their mistakes or that they've done wrong'. Bailey said that his idea of justice 'would be fitting retribution; basically making sure that people who do wrong are corrected in their ways and giving remedies to those who are affected'.

The rights-protecting function of justice was acknowledged by some. Winona, for example, said that justice was 'having your rights and feeling you need to be protected by the system. If you don't feel safe and your rights aren't protected then what's the point?' Connecting the governance function to its normative appeal, Olivia said justice was:

> Ensuring a fair and equal chance for everyone to live their life in a fair and equal way and for everyone to live the lifestyle they choose without fear and regardless of background. Justice is about a support network, about community and laws for a cohesive community.

The normative theme reflected upon the extent to which the justice system calibrated to perceived practices, values and priorities of the community at large. How the ideal of fairness worked proved a common refrain. To Xenia, for example, justice was about 'fairness and professional[ism]. [It's] looking after the victim and a fair outcome'. Whereas Molly said simply, 'it's unfair'. Polly claimed that 'they do what they think is best in their eyes but it might not be best in actuality […] half of it was very fair and the other half is downright toxic'. Nada was indignant that 'criminals have got more rights than victims … I don't have the right to be treated like a human being. Where are my basic human rights?' Other normative criteria prioritized the protection of people over property. Said Bailey:

> I think it does serve a purpose to the best of its ability but it is lacking enforcement or is misdirected. There's a huge undertaking on traffic infringements and disproportionate to tackling minor crimes but violence in the city at night is a greater risk to social conduct.

In his comments, Finn took a long view and said that 'in historical accounts justice was blind and swift but these days it can take a long time and doesn't really get any results'. Other normative reflections encompassed consistency. Svetlana commented that justice was about 'not going from one extreme to the other on certain matters'. However, she felt that 'there are too many differences between the judges and it depends who you get and the mood they're in. It can also come down to the lawyer'.

These citizen appraisals worked as stocks of knowledge that rendered the law as both available to and distant from their everyday life. People's general and particular stories revealed schematic complexity about what the justice system did or was to them in their community. Legal liberalism suggests that law has 'encoded' ideals of fairness and equal treatment in ordinary people.[63] While these codes were indeed powerful, they were not accepted uncritically. The perspective of the law in action was it as unstable, uncertain and ambiguous. At the same time, the justice system was acknowledged to play social roles with a number of purposes, in which the ideal of fairness was deeply embedded as well as imperfectly executed.

CONCLUDING DISCUSSION

Constructing meaning is not a simple exercise. It comprises both rapid situational appraisal along with information gathering and interpersonal reflection. Here meaning-making included components that were situational, interpersonal, social, civic and juridical (see Table 5.1). Some components were more salient for the domestic assault victims and others for the non-domestic assault victims. Similarly, meanings drew on perceptions of availability and relevance.

Drawing on this mix of elements and soliciting an intervention from legal authorities constitutes an act of agency. For victims, it is agency that is bounded as well as burdened. As an activity it may be construed as 'with the law' as it imagines consensus forged around ideals of fairness and equal treatment. However, as Ewick and Silbey caution, these are schemas that are unsettled. This group of people expected a fair system and felt social legitimation of their action; but at the same time, other more concrete of their expectations were remarkably low, or 'realistic' as has been observed of victims in England.[64] People additionally drew on ideas 'against the law' in critical comment about its working. The encoding that law is said to work on ordinary people therefore accommodates a context of conditional factors and relational dynamics to capture the unstable, ambiguous and contradictory effects of consciousness. As Michael McCann contends, legal consciousness may help structure meaning or imagination, but it does not dictate a particular

63 Susan Silbey, 'After Legal Consciousness' (2005) 1 *Annual Review of Law and Society* 323, 337.

64 Joanna Shapland, Jon Willmore and Peter Duff, *Victims in the Criminal Justice System* (Gower 1985) 45.

Table 5.1 Victim meaning-making informing legal mobilization

Situational	Perceived seriousness Attribution to violent person Victim blamelessness Absence of provocation
Social	Relevant and available communal norm breached Salient public policy discourse Social legitimacy to legal mobilization Concern for others
Interpersonal	Validation by social supports Relevant and applicable information from social networks
Civic	Symbolic imagery Perceived efficacy Governance relevance Normative salience
Juridical	Perceived wrongfulness Accountability Victim, offender, community trilogy Multiple justice goals

course of action. As he suggests, law merely creates a 'structural opportunity'.[65] Both the incident of violence, as well as public pronouncements about the availability of protective law, generates separate and distinct opportunities for ordinary people that could be said to lubricate the *potential* for action. People may recognize, from their status both as persons in need and as citizens, the unique opportunity created through legal mobilization to enable the law itself to 'step up' and do the work they imagine it is there to do. They also recognize, however, that they are stepping into uncertainty. The next chapter considers how people's mixed expectations interacted with the goals they sought from justice.

65 McCann (n 2) 239.

6. Exploring justice goals*

[It] was mean and nasty and he shouldn't have done it. (Zola, 2010)

What is ... central to the idea of justice is that we can have a strong sense of injustice on many different grounds, and yet not agree on one particular ground as being the dominant reason for the diagnosis of injustice. (Sen, 2009, 2)

Those who experience violence infrequently access justice institutions. However, when people do mobilize law in response to violent victimization they speak of justice in a variety of ways. As an imaginary, justice acts as a lure for the law. It is also a concrete assortment of entities; it is processes and activities as well as an authority with specific civic purpose and effect. As ordinary citizens and, following the violence as victims, people carry with them a bundle of paradoxes and contradictions that expect fairness as well as a degree of ineptitude. The *potential* of the law is embodied in it as a structural opportunity. Within their reading of their social and civic world, ordinary people imagine it is just possible their ideas of justice may be realized.

This chapter explores more of the specific contextual motivations and objectives victims have for engaging with justice. Drawing on the key conceptions of justice outlined in Chapter 2 – justice as normative guide, as duty, as accountability, as fairness, as relational and as contextual – I argue these illuminate different grounds to ideas about justice. The different grounds then give rise to multiple justice goals and serve 'the ultimate goal of achieving justice'.[1] The different objectives people articulate combine deontological and consequential reasoning, and

* Aspects of Chapter 6 appeared in Robyn Holder and Kathleen Daly, 'Sequencing Justice: A Longitudinal Study of Justice Goals of Domestic Violence Victims' (2017) *British Journal of Criminology*, OUP (online). Figure 6.1 was first published in the Sage publication, *Journal of Mixed Methods Research*, Robyn Holder (2016) 'Untangling the Meanings of Justice: A Longitudinal Mixed Methods Study'. Reproduced with permission.

[1] Dena Gromet and John Darley, 'Punishment and Beyond: Achieving Justice through the Satisfaction of Multiple Justice Goals' (2009) 43 *Law and Soc Rev* 1, 29.

expand to encompass the interests of themselves as victim, the offender and their community of others. These three are a justice trilogy. The longitudinal prospective panel provides rich and unique data. Over the course of three interviews the multiple objectives are sequenced within the architecture of criminal justice.[2] At Time 1 after police had attended and before the case had gone to court, people indicated what justice goals they wanted in terms of verdict, sentence and application of principle. Then, at Time 2 after the case had been assessed by the prosecution and decided by the criminal court, people were asked for a retrospective evaluation of the decisions. Finally, at Time 3 some six to eight months after the court, people were asked to reflect on whether justice had been done. These outcomes are indicators of substantive justice.

I start with some more emotional and relational features to the context in which people expressed their objectives, and then move to consider the specific reasoning they gave at their first interview for their mobilization of law. I particularly attend to the question of victims 'getting what they want'. Peoples' narratives speak to the complex and sometimes contradictory perspectives they have of justice.

EMOTION AND CONTEXT

Emotion is a key driver to human action. There is a clear relationship between emotion and justice, especially injustice.[3] Some studies have found a correlation between the post-traumatic impacts of the incident on the victim with feelings of revenge, while others have unsettled this punitive picture.[4] The assumed equation of 'just deserts' with punitiveness

---

[2] Robyn Holder and Kathleen Daly, 'Sequencing Justice: A Longitudinal Study of Justice Goals of Domestic Violence Victims' (2017) *British Journal of Criminology*, explore the sequencing concept more fully in relation to the women victims of domestic assault.

[3] Gerold Mikula, 'On the Experience of Injustice' (1993) 4 *Euro Rv of Soc Psych* 223–44.

[4] Ulrich Orth and others, 'Feelings of Revenge, Retaliation Motive, and Posttraumatic Stress Reactions in Crime Victims' (2006) 21 *Journal of Interpersonal Violence* 229–43, found that feelings of revenge correlated with intrusion and hyperarousal. Other empirical work finds little correlation (Joanna Shapland, 'Victims, the Criminal Justice System and Compensation' (1984) 24 *The British Journal of Criminology* 131–49; Heather Strang, *Repair or Revenge: Victims and Restorative Justice* (Clarendon Press 2002); Jonathan Doak and David Mahoney, 'The Venegeful Victim? Assessing the Attitudes of Victims

has also been questioned.[5] But how, if at all, did the after-effects of the incident and the emotions of the situation edge the preferences and viewpoints about justice for those in the present study?

Emotion was certainly present for the lay participants at the time of the violent incident while they displayed a strong sense of personal agency at both Time 1 and at Time 2. Nearly three-quarters felt strongly that 'what happens to me in the future mostly depends on me'. A majority felt they had control over the direction their life was taking, and disagreed that they felt helpless in dealing with the problems of life. Furthermore, a majority felt good about themselves all or most of the time. However, overall emotional reactions to the incident were complex and related to others as well as to the violent person. For example, Finn said he remembered thinking '"how dare he hit me?" Basically because I had my daughter's birthday and I felt very indignant'. Aimee's emotional reaction also encompassed others. She said, 'I didn't think about any other course of action [than calling police]. His son was witness to it and so my maternal instincts came forward. I wanted to protect him'. People's emotional orientation towards the violent person showed fluidity over time. At Time 1, anger, fear, confusion and sadness were the most common feelings expressed by people towards the violent person at the time of the incident. These feelings moderated substantially by Time 2. At this occasion, while feelings subsided, anger remained dominant among other emotions and dominant for both groups of victims. Anger is especially associated with the experience of injustice.[6] Fear was dominant for domestic assault victims at the first interview but this also had moderated substantially by Time 2.

For both groups, these feelings about the violent person were neither narrow nor one-dimensional. At Time 1 they factored along two dimensions. One reflected warm feelings of love, empathy and forgiveness. The other reflected more emotional distance from the violent person and included fear, confusion, sadness and pity. These scales both measured moderately and did not shift noticeably at the Time 2 interview. Of

---

Participating in Restorative Youth Conferencing' (2006) 13 *International Review of Victimology* 157–77).

[5] Gromet and Darley (n 1); John Darley and Dena Gromet, 'The Psychology of Punishment: Intuition and Reason' in Ramona Bobocel and others (eds), *The Psychology of Justice and Legitimacy: The Ontario Symposium* (11th Volume, Taylor and Francis 2010) 229–50.

[6] Gerold Mikula and others, 'The Role of Injustice in the Elicitation of Differential Emotional Reactions' (1998) 24 *Personality & Social Psychology Bulletin* 769–83.

course, the domestic assault and non-domestic assault victims had different relationships with the violent person. At Time 1, five domestic assault victims indicated that they wanted a relationship with the violent person to continue. At Time 2 four of these people maintained this intention. Unsurprisingly, there was a strong and significant relationship between this desire and warm feelings toward the violent person.[7]

Another emotional realm for lay participants was their view about the violent person's conduct. Both domestic and non-domestic assault victims had a very strong perception, at Time 1 and Time 2, that the violent person 'knew what he was doing' when committing the violence. The ascription of intentionality to the violent person strengthened slightly by Time 2. There was a strong and significant relationship (r_s = 0.575 p<0.01) between the sense that the violent person 'knew what he was doing' and feelings of emotional distance from that person. Also at Time 2, there was a significant negative relationship between the sense that the violent person knew what he was doing and perceptions that the person did not mean to hurt and felt sorry for what he had done.[8] The strength of the intentionality assessment could be an artefact of the sample but is consistent with other studies. Laboratory research, for example, has found that the extent to which people ascribe intentionality to an offender's motivations is important to assessments of culpability and is influential on interests in retribution.[9] In essence, emotion bonds to the experience of an injustice; and emotional distance informs but is not causative of the attribution of intentionality. Finally, only a small portion of the participants indicated agreement with statements that the violent person was 'influenced by other people', or 'did not mean to hurt me' or was 'provoked by me'. At Time 2, a majority believed that the violent person 'blamed' them for the incident. The sense of blame was felt most strongly by domestic assault victims.

[7] Spearman's correlation coefficient at Time 1 was r_s = 0.67 (p<0.01) and at Time 2 was r_s = 0.69 (p<0.01).

[8] 'Did not mean to hurt me' had a correlation coefficient at Time 2 of r_s = –0.5 (p<0.05) and 'feels sorry' correlated at r_s = –0.418 (p<0.05).

[9] Philip Tetlock and others, 'People as Intuitive Prosecutors: The Impact of Social Control Goals on Attributions of Responsibility' (2006) 43 *Journal of Experimental Social Psychology* 195–209; Kevin Carlsmith, 'The Roles of Retribution and Utility in Determining Punishment' (2006) 42 *Journal of Experimental Social Psychology* 437–51; John Darley and Thane Pittman, 'The Psychology of Compensatory and Retributive Justice' (2003) 7 *Personality and Social Psychology Review* 324–36.

Under half of this group thought that the violent person felt a degree of remorse for or felt sorry about and shame for what he had done.

However, a focus on the broad structure of emotion variables is a contour sketch of victims' relational landscape. The emotional context could not account for the intricate reasoning people gave about their decision-making and engagements with formal authority. The next sections explore the different reasons people gave for their mobilization of law, and the concrete outcome preferences they expressed. These preferences then enable reflection on the extent to which 'getting what they want' was influential on people's justice appraisals.

MOTIVATIONS AND GOALS

Victim decision-making about legal mobilization combines instrumental and non-instrumental reasoning (see Chapter 3). There is an extensive literature canvassing the constraints, barriers and restrictions to ordinary people's access to law and justice.[10] There are 'incentives' as well as costs to reporting, but research consistently shows that victims believe they ought to report, that it is somehow part of their civic responsibility.[11] A further common characteristic to the decision is that it is a subject-based assessment of priority located within perspectives drawn from people's social and cultural environment. Given that the study group's prior thinking was largely negative about the institutions of justice and that this view is widely held, the question why they turned to the police and the legal system on this occasion is a pointed one. The participants were neither ill-informed nor inexperienced in accessing forms of support more generally available in their community. But turning to the law was, for them, neither simple nor clear-cut. As Teresa said, she 'felt a mix of emotions'. She 'had already kept a logbook of what happened' and,

> wanted [police] to take my statement and make a report. But I didn't know what they were going to do. When the sergeant came out and said he would

---

[10] See, e.g.: Heather Genn, *Paths to Justice: What People Do and Think About Going to Law* (Hart 1999); Eva Buzawa and Carl Buzawa, *Domestic Violence: The Criminal Justice Response* (Sage 2003).

[11] Richard Felson and others, 'Reasons for Reporting and Not Reporting Domestic Violence to the Police' (2002) 40 *Criminology* 617, 619; Joanna Shapland, Jon Willmore and Peter Duff, *Victims in the Criminal Justice System* (Gower 1985) 15; Jan van Dijk and others, 'Criminal Victimisation in International Perspective: Key Findings from the 2004–2005 ICVS and EU ICS' (WODC 2007).

> be arrested I felt a mix of emotions and I had to tell myself it wasn't me. I wanted a clear decision, that it was wrong and it wasn't the right thing to do. I wanted him to know he had done wrong and to stop.

Teresa and most others gave multiple reasons for calling for police assistance. For the group as a whole these reasons clustered. Top of the list and mentioned most frequently as a reason to involve police was a desire for safety and protection. Next, and related, was to stop the violence. Then, and equally strong, was that reporting was for their community of others: their children, the wider public, and other future victims. Following this reason was belief that it was a police function to receive reports of crime and that a response to the wrongdoing was warranted. After this, people said they needed help for themselves as a victim and that reporting to police was also to get help for the assailant.

In elaborating on their reasons, many participants tended to evaluate the nature of the incident as warranting a particular set of responses most likely forthcoming from police. Police were viewed as a trusted help agency that had both legitimacy and authority to deal with the issue, a view evidenced in the following observations:

> I wanted them to fix it up, for the stats about what's happening. It's just what you do if you are growing up and you're a kid and you're in trouble. You're told to go to them. (Edward)

> The police would have to do something. A neighbour he would have just sworn at. (Molly)

Others' reasoning about turning to the law encompassed longer-term goals as well as the immediate purpose. Cathy said she 'wanted him arrested', and 'just wanted to be safe at the time'. Ari said that he 'knew [police would] calm the situation and put an end to it [the violence]'. Others had different longer term and specific justice goals. Edward, assaulted by three men when he went to get his car, said his goals were for 'justice, retribution'. He said that 'they've done something wrong so something has to happen'. He wanted 'to make sure they're punished'. Olivia 'just wanted him [her ex-partner] to stop doing it'. She went on to say that she wanted police to 'identify the support services and make him go to hospital or get counselling and make him aware of the consequences of what he was doing'.

In recalling their initial motivation some participants spoke of reasons in a layered way. Another reflection from Teresa encapsulates this fluidity. She said that she wanted 'to be able to move on with [her] life'. In addition, she 'wanted him to know he was doing the wrong thing and to stop. I thought police would tell him that. I didn't really have in mind to have him arrested. I wanted justice, to leave me in peace.' Teresa went on to acknowledge a wider social context to her decision by claiming 'this is why police step in – to say these are the rules we live by and this is what we are going to do. If there is a breach of the law then there has to be a consequence'. Her comments reveal the way in which an immediate priority for her own safety and an end to the violence are accompanied by other objectives for the violent person and for her community of others. Legal mobilization has self-regarding motivations as well as other-regarding motivations; reasons are individual and communal.

OUTCOME PREFERENCES

To these motivations can be added victims' more specific interest that the justice agencies take particular actions. That is, that the court makes a finding or gives a verdict, that it imposes (or not) a sanction for the behaviour, and that particular justice principle(s) be applied by the court to their case. Most research about desired outcomes is laboratory-based in which disinterested respondents are asked to make a judgment. The Justice Study is unique in asking victims their prospective preferences *before* the case went to court. This section describes these preferences at Time 1 and the narration given for them. Then, the section gives people's retrospective reflection at Time 2 on the decisions and analyses the interplay of private and public reasoning. The section then describes final retrospective reflection and assessment offered at the Time 3 interviews.

Time 1 – Looking Back, Looking Forward – The First Interview (N=33)

The lay participants were interviewed a first time after the police intervention and the police decision to charge a person with an offence, but before the matter had gone to court. The time lapse between the actual incident and the first interview varied between two weeks and two months.

At this first interview a slight majority confirmed that they had wanted police to arrest the violent person and take him away, with 18 per cent saying they were unsure what they wanted. No demographic or incident variables correlated with this preference. However, nearly all non-domestic assault victims said they had wanted police to arrest, whereas 44 per cent of domestic assault victims did so. Of this latter group, one-fifth was unsure what they had wanted, and another 11 per cent had wanted the violent person taken away but not arrested.[12] Five women said that they asked for charges to be dropped. Of those who did so, one said she felt her husband was mentally unwell, another because she felt shared culpability for the incident, another because she felt the arrest was sufficient to produce changes in behaviour, and two because of their emotional attachment to and concern for the violent person. The ambivalence shown by domestic assault victims towards formal external intervention is well researched.[13] Further nuance arising from these individual cases is discussed later in Box 6.1 (p.145).

For the group as a whole, a strong overall majority (85 per cent N=28) indicated that they had not asked the police or prosecution to drop the charges arising from the incident notwithstanding mixed views about arrest. Of those who did not ask to have the charges dropped, the most common concern was for accountability and from a normative perspective. For example, Winona commented that she 'wouldn't drop it because he [the assailant] needs to learn he shouldn't touch females'. As a non-domestic assault victim, Charlie said he wanted charges to proceed 'because of the nature of the event'. He went on to say that he did not 'believe [in] punching people on the head and getting away with it. If I thought I got into a fight of my own accord I would have a different view and there were injuries sustained'. Variants to this theme argued that 'truth' should be known and wrong behaviour highlighted. Said Svetlana, 'he should know better, know what's right and wrong'. The next most common reason for not dropping the charges was for protection and stopping the violence. Teresa said that the abuse from her ex-partner had

---

[12] This study did not set out to examine gender differences in conceptions of justice. It did aim to examine differences and similarities as they may relate to offence type. Distinguishing the differential influence of gender and of offence type on victims' justice judgments is an important area for future research. The influence of personal characteristics is a contested area. For example, Scott and his colleagues noted significant gender differences in distributive justice norms (John Scott and others, 'Just Deserts: An Experimental Study of Distributive Justice Norms' (2001) 45 *American Journal of Political Science* 749–67). Brockner and his colleagues (2000) also noted that the interactive relationship between procedural and distributive justice was more pronounced among those with more interdependent forms of self-construal. They argued that the nature of the interpersonal and social culture of respondents needed also to be better explored (J Brockner and others, 'Culture and Procedural Justice: The Influence of Power Distance on Reactions to Voice' (2000) 37 *Journal of Experimental Social Psychology* 300–315).

[13] Carolyn Hoyle, *Negotiating Domestic Violence* (Clarendon Press 1998).

'been going on for a while'. Turning to police was her 'last resort to stop him'. She had 'tried counselling, AVO [Apprehended Violence Order] and he has not accepted the boundaries. This is all I have left'.

Looking ahead to the justice process before them, people were also asked about their preferences on the court outcome. They were in a real-world situation and had to think about and confront this question. Therefore the nature of outcome was asked in different ways: what decision they wanted the court to make, what sentence outcome they would prefer, and what principles of justice they thought were important to apply to their case.

On the first query about the finding, people were overwhelmingly in favour of the court making a guilty verdict. Equal proportions of domestic and non-domestic assault victims strongly preferred this verdict. For most the reason for the preference was simple. Asked why this choice, Charlie said, 'because they were [guilty]'. Some research suggests that firm views as this are consistent with the *a priori* viewpoint that led to the initial engagement.[14] It is also consistent with the problem-judgment element of Zemans' decision-making framework. In addition, there was a strong and significant positive correlation between the verdict preference and the attribution of intentionality to the violent person ($r_s = 0.57$ $p<0.01$), and with more distanced feelings held by victims towards the offenders.[15] The preference for a guilty verdict also had a significant relationship with the scale measuring adherence to self-reliant citizenship ($r_s = 0.52$ $p<0.01$), and strong relationships to the harmony scale ($r_s = 0.42$ $p<0.05$), and to the measure demonstrating a commitment to laws ($r_s = 0.43$ $p<0.05$).

After stating a preference for a guilty finding, the participants indicated their preference for a sentence outcome from a menu of 17 options drawn from the jurisdiction's sentencing legislation. They could choose more than one option as 'essential, the highest priority'. For the group as a whole, strong preferences clustered on sentence outcomes that drew on the authority of the court to constrain the violent person's conduct, were rehabilitative of that person, and protective of the victim and community. Least favoured was the imposition of a fine or for the violent person to perform some sort of service. Neither domestic nor non-domestic assault victims displayed a strong interest in receiving a written or a verbal apology from the offender at this stage. Then, when asked to specify their

---

[14] Robert Folger and others, 'Elaborating Procedural Fairness: Justice Becomes Both Simpler and More Complex' (1996) 22 *Personality and Social Psychology Bulletin* 435–41.

[15] A result that is in line with the findings of Darley and Pittman (n 9).

first and second priority out of these sentence preferences, people's views sharpened. Of primary importance was that the violent person had some type of treatment: for drugs and alcohol, violence rehabilitation or mental health. Next was to have a custodial sentence of some type imposed: weekend detention, a suspended sentence or full-time custody.[16] Combined sentence choices fitted with the multiple goals previously expressed. Bailey, for example, commented that he did not think the violent person 'should go unpunished because he did have a short term impact on me'. He went on to say that,

> You do wrong, you get punished – that's how our society works. I think something should be done to get rid of violence. I don't like it. I'm not a violent person. This may be done through rehabilitation. I don't feel a personal need for protection but if these things happen more and more then the society might need protection. There's nothing to restore [with him]. He can't give me the week back where I looked bad. I think denouncing it will help deter it amongst the community in general.

Finally, people were asked to indicate which justice principle or set of principles they would like a magistrate or judge to apply to their case: rehabilitation, specific deterrence, general deterrence, denunciation, punishment, restoration, incapacitation, victim protection and community protection. The wording of these items was kept simple. The principle of punishment, for example, was to 'do something to punish/discipline/penalise/chastise the person', and the restoration principle was to 'do something to recognise the harm caused and to help restore all parties'. Of all justice principles, participants' thought rehabilitation, specific deterrence and victim protection were of the utmost importance to their case. The rehabilitation principle was largely driven by the domestic assault sub-group. The principle of next priority – specific deterrence – was of strong interest to the non-domestic assault sub-group.

Asked what was important to them about the particular justice principle they wanted applied to their case and responses again clustered around the desire for accountability. Comments emphasized that there be a consequence to the behaviour, that the person 'learn a lesson' but that the wrongfulness of the behaviour also be recognized. For Xenia the 'most important' principle was 'to rehabilitate the person'. She said that

---

[16] In the UK longitudinal study, when asked at their first interview, 40 per cent of the victims whose offender was subsequently sentenced had wanted a custodial order (Shapland and others (n 11) 72).

rehabilitation should include that the violent person 'see what they've done is wrong and to change'. She also said that 'protecting the victim is important and letting the community and the person know it is not acceptable'. Edward was 'out of pocket' as a result of injuries he had incurred. But he spoke of the interests of others in giving reasons for his sentence preferences. He preferred the punishment principle be applied in his case but wanted a rehabilitative sentence. The reason, he said, was that it was 'better for [offenders] to give something back to the community'. He commented that it was 'better to do this than sending them to gaol. It's the same message but it doesn't cost as much. As it's a lower offence it may help rehabilitate. The costs [of prison] are significant, thousands of dollars'. Participants saw their sentence preferences imbued with wider social meanings such as Edward's concerns about the cost of incarceration. Their combinations of sentence preference related to the justice trilogy of victim, violent person and their community of others.

Overall, people's outcome preferences were consistent in both concrete and abstract terms. There was no statistical correlation between the stated outcome preferences at the first interview and any demographic variable although those with closer relationships to the violent person, albeit strained, exhibited a stronger inclination towards outcomes that were protective of themselves as victim. In summary, interviewed after police had attended and before the matter had reached court, the lay participants wanted arrest and had a strong preference that the court would come to make a guilty finding. They joined this preference with a desire for accountability and for reinforcement of a normative standard of behaviour. They wanted sentence outcomes that were protective, rehabilitative and which drew on the authority of the court; and they wanted the principles of rehabilitation, specific deterrence and victim protection applied to their case. Outcome preferences were consistent with people's stated motivations for legal mobilization: safety, stopping the violence, and protecting others. As Gromet and Darley suggest, people have a number of aims and preferences to the 'ultimate main goal of achieving justice'.

Time 2 – Assessments and Reflections – The Second Interview (N=26)

The Time 2 interview was conducted with the same, albeit slightly smaller, group (N=21 women, N=5 men) and after the case had finished at court. Finalization could have been a guilty verdict following a plea, or the charges being dismissed, or a verdict reached after a contested trial.

By this stage, the majority of cases had indeed resulted in a guilty plea being entered in the Magistrates' Court. The time lapse between the first interview and the second varied considerably. The shortest time between first and second interview (that is, to court finalization) was four months. The longest was 27 months. The case that took the longest involved a contested trial at a higher court.

At the second interview, two more participants indicated that they had asked police or prosecution to drop the charges raising the number from five to seven. All of these – as on the first occasion – were domestic assault victims. The reasons women gave were varied. Three had reconciled or were concerned about the possibility of a gaol sentence, and two were worried about the length of time the justice process took. Aimee and her partner 'were reconciling and the length of time the court case was taking was causing a lot of stress'. She also went on to say that 'the police told me if I did [withdraw] it they would not be as helpful next time it happened'. A further two others mentioned direct pressure placed on them. Finoula said the violent person 'talked me into' asking for charges to be dropped and Polly that she was intimidated by both the violent person and the court. She said:

> I definitely didn't want to testify. I was frightened what would happen from people he knows. I thought there'd be retaliation. I didn't think the system would protect me. I had my tyres slashed. I was wondering what might happen.

However, when asked specifically what they had wanted prosecution to do, all non-domestic assault victims and most domestic assault victims wanted prosecution. Of the combined victim group, most (81 per cent) said they preferred all or some charges to be prosecuted. Both Karla and Edward emphasized 'the deterrent effect' of proceeding. Karla said that her ex-partner 'did the action' and she felt that 'if he suffered the consequences maybe he won't do it again. It was a serious thing he did'. Edward also said, 'why withdraw it? They've done all this work so why stop it?'

At this point in the study, all but four cases had been resolved by way of a guilty plea.[17] A majority of both domestic and non-domestic assault victims at this second interview remained in favour of this outcome. Two

---

[17] Guilty pleas also formed the dominant outcome for cases in the longitudinal UK study (Shapland and others, Ibid., 70).

women had preferred a not guilty verdict at Time 1 but had now changed their minds. Roslyn was one of these. At her Time 2 interview she said she now wanted her partner to 'be accountable for what he did'. She did not want 'to be afraid in my own home' and said she wanted to be 'true to myself'. Aimee also now preferred the verdict simply 'because he was guilty'.

The reasons people gave at Time 2 for prosecution and for the guilty verdict reiterated a strong desire for accountability. They wanted the violent person to accept responsibility for his actions and the consequences. Finn, a non-domestic assault victim, said simply, 'I believe something had to be done about what happened'. Others were clear that they wanted a meaningful consequence. Another proportion indicated that prosecution of the assault recognized wrongfulness, seriousness and the degree of harm caused, and that accountability and responsibility were desirable. Taken together, these interests go to the manner in which justice equates with accountability.[18] For another portion of people, particularly the domestic assault victims, the idea of the violent person 'getting help' after prosecution was influential, as was concern for their children within their community of others.

The nature of the sentence provided further definition to the meaning of the outcome for participants. At the Time 2 interview most offenders had received a good behaviour bond (N=11) or a good behaviour bond plus supervision (N=7). Two cases resulted in a term of custody, four were dismissed and two had some other sentence. Non-custodial sentences were also dominant in the longitudinal UK study where most cases resulted in the imposition of a fine by the court.[19] The Justice Study participants thus received their preferred verdict but not their preferred sentence outcome. Despite this, a majority (60 per cent) said that they felt the sentence was 'about right'. Two women indicated they felt the sentence was too tough. Birgit favoured the guilty verdict, but did not feel that the eight-month term of imprisonment given to her ex-partner actually helped him. She maintained a preference for court orders to keep

---

[18] Robert Folger and Russell Cropanzano, 'Fairness Theory: Justice as Accountability' in Jerald Greenberg and Russell Cropanzano (eds), *Advances in Organizational Justice* (Stanford UP 2001) 1–55.

[19] Of those cases for which a result was identified, most were sentenced with a fine (plus compensation order) (N=106), a term of custody (N=62), were discharged or bound over (N=13) or a supervision order (N=9) (Shapland and others (n 11) 73).

the violent person away from her and for his alcohol treatment. She did, however, want her child to have a relationship with his father. Roslyn also felt the sentence was too tough. She wished to remain with her partner and shared a business with him. While she came to favour the guilty verdict, she felt that a message of condemnation from the magistrate would have adequately indicated to the violent person that the 'bad behaviour' had been noted and had to change.

A third of participants commented that they felt the sentence was 'too lenient'. In the main they expressed concern that the violent person would not learn a sufficient 'lesson' or not get the assistance needed to change his wrongful behaviour. Two of the non-domestic assault victims had experienced an assault in their neighbourhood. David felt that the violent person had 'gotten away with' the assault against him. Finn felt that the good behaviour bond was not a sufficiently strong 'lesson' to the assailant about the wrongfulness of violence and the harm it causes. Of the domestic assault victims who felt the sentence was too lenient, none wanted a continuing relationship with the violent person. Of those who had preferred a custodial sentence their comments about leniency focused on the violent person. Karla wanted her ex-partner to have 'time to think about it and to learn from what he'd done'. Instead he received a bond. Winona had indicated an early preference for a court order to keep the violent person away but, upon his conviction, had preferred a custodial sentence 'because they are harsher, he deserves it'. Although at her first interview she had not wanted any apology or contact, the offender had in fact apologized to her in writing. In response Winona now commented that she would 'prefer face-to-face' apology. However, the court recorded a suspended sentence against the offender with supervision and community service. Nada felt her ex-partner's behaviour had been very serious. She felt that a bond neither addressed his problems nor provided a means for him to serve the community. While she had expressed a preference for a custodial sentence at the first interview, at the second she said she would have preferred drug and alcohol and violence rehabilitation programmes and community service. Janelle had also stated her preference for a full-time custodial but, upon conviction, the sentence was deferred with the violent person subject to regular drug and alcohol testing. While she felt this was too lenient, she also indicated that rehabilitative sentences such as drug and alcohol and violence programmes were preferable. In her reasons about these preferences, Janelle layered concerns for rehabilitation, protection and deterrence. She said her ex-partner needed 'to get off the pot'. It was, she said, 'the biggest problem and a big part of why he did the things he did'. At the same time, she said he needed 'to control his anger as well and stay away from me so it doesn't happen again'. In sum, therefore, most comments on leniency went to concerns that sentence was insufficient to enable the offender to change his behaviour.

Other of the domestic assault victims had other reasons for their disappointment with the sentence. Zola was already financially disadvantaged and suffered further the cost of property damage done during the incident. She indicated at the outset that her preferred sentence was that the violent person be ordered to pay the costs and to keep away from her. At the second interview the case had finalized at court with the violent person being sentenced to a bond. Zola maintained her preference for a court order for the costs. She added that the property damaged had been of sentimental value to her and that breaking it 'was mean and nasty and he shouldn't have done it'. Imogene had indicated a preference for a drug and alcohol rehabilitation programme but, upon conviction, said she preferred that her ex-partner be sentenced to a violence rehabilitation programme. She said that he needed violence rehabilitation 'for his sake and others'. She went on to say, 'I believe in this more than punishment. But public shaming is the only thing that would work with him at the moment. He couldn't give a stuff except for others knowing'. Instead, the court ordered a good behaviour bond and did not record a conviction.

On the surface of it, most participants 'got what they wanted' from the court, especially the guilty plea. If outcome favourability is, in part, 'personally beneficial', in that a personal goal(s) is achieved,[20] then, given their desire for offender accountability, the people in the Justice Study were vindicated. They expressed satisfaction with the court outcome and thought that it was fair. However, when asked directly, just under half agreed it was what they wanted, was what they expected or what they as a victim deserved (see Table 6.1). The variation in assessment suggests that people apply different criteria in their thinking about a 'right' outcome other than preference. Outcome preferences are different to outcome favourability. To their outcome preferences the lay participants applied different criteria that related to the objects in the justice trilogy of victim, offender and community.

[20] Patricia Krehbiel and Russell Cropanzano, 'Procedural Justice, Outcome Favourability and Emotion' (2000) 13 *Social Justice Research* 339, 340–41.

Table 6.1 Victims' assessments of court outcome at Time 2 (N=26)

Assessment statement	Agreed/strongly agreed per cent
The outcome I received was fair	69
I was satisfied with the outcome	62
I received the outcome I wanted	46
I received the outcome I expected	42
I received the outcome I deserved	38

For most of those who were interviewed twice, their cases were resolved at court by way of a guilty plea. Four did not (see Box 6.1). In three cases the prosecution offered no evidence and the charges were dismissed at court (one non-domestic assault and two domestic assaults); and one non-domestic assault resulted in an acquittal.

In summary, at the Time 2 interview after the case had finalized at court, most wanted the charges to have been prosecuted although a small number of domestic assault victims did not. The majority of all victims maintained a preference for the guilty verdict and reiterated giving offender accountability as the main reason and that there be consequences to his violent behaviour. Most cases did result in the violent person admitting or being found guilty, and a majority of these resulted in the court sentencing the offender to a bond to be of good behaviour. A majority of victims felt that the sentence was about right even when it was not what they had wanted. Victims made a distinction between assessments of satisfaction with and the fairness of the outcome, and getting what they wanted or what they (as a victim) deserved. Their reasoning about the outcomes reflected deontological thinking about right and wrong, as well as thinking what should happen in consequence of the behaviour. Their reasoning encompassed the offender and the wider community, and to these victims attached preferences for composite sentences. Outcome preferences could not, therefore, be reduced to something of singular and personal benefit. Overall, there was a remarkable degree of stability across time between preferences, outcomes and assessments on those outcomes. Finally, the lay participants did not see their recourse to law or their engagement with the criminal justice system as divorced from the communal and the civic. Only a couple of people viewed theirs as a private dispute.

BOX 6.1 CASES THAT DID NOT RESOLVE AT COURT BY WAY OF A GUILTY VERDICT OR FINDING

Case 1 – At the first interview this domestic assault victim stated a preference for the matter to be dismissed. By the second interview the violent person had entered a guilty plea and was sentenced to a good behaviour bond. The victim indicated at this stage that she preferred this guilty verdict. She indicated satisfaction with the outcome and agreed that it was what she wanted. She was neutral on whether the outcome was fair. She agreed that she was 'satisfied with the outcome and that justice was done'. She and the violent person continued in their relationship, with a child in common.

Case 2 – At the first interview this domestic assault victim stated a preference for the matter to be withdrawn and dismissed. By the second interview the violent person had entered a guilty plea and was sentenced to a good behaviour bond. The victim maintained her preference at the second interview that the case should have been withdrawn and dismissed. She nonetheless strongly agreed that she was satisfied with the outcome, and agreed that it was fair and what she wanted. She agreed that she was 'satisfied with the outcome and that justice was done'.

Case 3 – At the first interview the non-domestic assault victim stated a preference for a guilty verdict. By the second interview the prosecution had offered no evidence and the case was dismissed at court. At this stage, the victim maintained his preference that the violent person should have been found guilty. He indicated that he neither agreed nor disagreed that he was satisfied with the outcome but agreed that it was fair. He disagreed that the outcome was what he wanted. He did not agree with the statement that he was 'satisfied with the outcome and that justice was done'.

Case 4 – The non-domestic assault victim stated his preference for a guilty finding at the first interview. The violent person was acquitted at court. At the second interview, the victim maintained his preference for a guilty verdict. He voiced strong dissatisfaction with the outcome, that it was fair, or what he wanted. He strongly disagreed with the statement that he was 'satisfied with the outcome and that justice was done'.

Time 3 – Final Reflections – The Third Interview (N=19)

The third interview was conducted about six months after the finalization of the matter at court. Of the original 33 study participants, 19 were interviewed on the final occasion, comprising five non-domestic assault victims and 14 domestic assault victims. On this occasion, just under half of the group indicated that they were 'somewhat' satisfied overall with how the justice system handled their case, and another third indicated that they were extremely or very satisfied overall. There was a strong and significant correlation between overall satisfaction, and a feeling that their interests as a victim of violence were looked after (r_s = 0.83 $p<0.01$). A strong and significant correlation was also found between overall satisfaction and the view that, in a similar situation in the future, the victim would like the justice system to deal with it in a similar way (r_s = 0.65 $p<0.01$). However, when asked how well they felt their interests as a victim of violence were actually looked after people's views were decidedly mixed. While 42 per cent felt they were definitely/maybe looked after enough, 42 per cent felt that they were definitely/maybe not, and 16 per cent were unsure.

At Time 3, a greater proportion of participants shifted from unqualified satisfaction with the outcome and agreement that 'justice was done' at Time 2, to more qualified satisfaction. All who shifted were domestic assault victims. Looking behind these data through individual narratives provides some insights about why there was a shift. The narratives again show the importance of understanding not only multiple justice goals of victims, but the different objects to which they attached these goals. Ursula was one of those whose views shifted. She had been somewhat satisfied with the outcome at Time 1 when her husband had been charged with an offence. At that point however, she said that her husband's mental health condition meant his case was not appropriate for the criminal justice system. But she had also wanted some form of compulsion to ensure his engagement with mental health services. Six months later at Time 2, the court had indeed dismissed the charges – rightly in Ursula's view – and she remained somewhat satisfied with the justice system response to the case. However, at her final interview at Time 3, Ursula was much more uncertain about the outcomes arrived at. She could not agree that justice was done. On this occasion, perhaps for the first time, she felt able to reflect on her own interests rather than her concern for her husband's mental health. 'Supposedly he didn't know what he was doing', she said. 'He got the outcome for him but I haven't. I'm no safer than I was then'.

Like Ursula, Xenia remained married and living with the violent person at Time 3. She indicated that her dissatisfaction stemmed from the emotional, personal, family and financial toll the case generated. The matter had finalized with a guilty plea to some of the charges, with others withdrawn by the prosecution and the matter resulting in the conviction not being recorded but with a good behaviour bond. She had expressed great difficulty in communicating with the prosecutor while also voicing ambivalence about her personal situation. Her financial security was entwined with that of her husband and she wanted a stable family for her children. With this entanglement she was 'not sure what justice I wanted'. She said, 'I just wanted it to go away. At the end of the day they eventually listened. I can only guess it was from all the letters I wrote'.

At the same time, Xenia remained wary of her husband and felt he had shuffled off a sense of responsibility for his conduct.

Others were satisfied that there had been a result but questioned its appropriateness. Winona was 'just unsure' whether justice was done. She compared unfavourably the result in her situation with others by saying 'it could have been done better and the punishment didn't fit what happened. Other similar cases got more punishment'. Deanna also had mixed feelings. She said, 'On one hand, I was content to see [the defendant] being convicted and sentenced but on another, I felt the sentence was a tad too light and the case was not finalised as thoroughly as I would have hoped.'

In summary, the particularities of cases highlight complex views about substantive outcomes. The dominance of goals related to the offender and the community at the second interview softened at the third interview. On this last occasion people spoke with a sense that goals for themselves as victims were somehow lost or unattended. Therefore, the dilution of attention to victim-related goals may lie behind the ambivalence voiced in final reflections. Goals for the offender and for community – here about rehabilitation and deterrence – may have been partially satisfied. However, when justice is articulated as a composite concept, it is the missing elements that underpin dissatisfaction. Nonetheless, and perhaps paradoxically, 74 per cent of people who participated in all three interviews said at Time 3 that they would seek help from the justice system if something similar happened to them in the future. There is clearly something to the logic of institutional fit with people's instrumental motivations in mobilizing the law, especially law enforcement.

MULTIPLE AND LAYERED GOALS FOR JUSTICE

This chapter has highlighted an informationally rich depiction of people's justice goals. At their first and second interviews the lay participants gave more than one reason for mobilizing the law and in reasoning their preferences. These were instrumental (stop the violence) but also ethical (protect others). Both men and women frequently drew on public policy concerns in giving robustness to their reasons, saying that violence against women is wrong and violence in public is a problem. The incident happened to them as an individual and was private to differing degrees. In their narratives, however, this private interest was co-determined with wider public discourse and public norms. Thus the idea of offender accountability emerged as critical to their thinking about justice just as it is a core function for the justice system. Offender accountability acted as motivation for engaging with legal authorities, as justification for the appropriateness of public authority to their situation, and as a threshold to thinking about other more particular justice goals. Indeed, people made a clear distinction between the guilty verdict – which they equated with accountability – and the sentence – which they considered to be a consequence of the wrongful behaviour and something to influence the offender's future conduct. Outcome-oriented justice therefore comprised both retributive and utilitarian elements. For these victims accountability did not equate with punitiveness. Their particular interest in the accountability of the violent person was underpinned by a more general position that accountability is but one point to both law and justice. It is a first order preference.

The detail of people's narratives shows them directing the good of justice in three ways: towards themselves as the subject victim, and to other objects of value being offender and their community of others. This trilogy of justice interests attracts diverse and multiple goals. A layered conceptualization of justice goals ripples outwards from the experience of an injustice (see Figure 6.1).

The fine-grained analysis in this chapter shows people's views about the offender are nuanced, particularly and obviously for domestic assault victims, but not only for them. Greater social distance between victim and offender tends to greater harshness.[21] However, this notion requires more attention to the dynamic nature of attitude formation, to the particulars of circumstance, and to the motivational norms at play. Further, a close or intimate relationship is not a requirement for the victim thinking about the offender. Rather, a connection is forged not just in prior association but through the incident and responses to it. The connection has an emotional element but not only that. There was a strong perspective in both groups of victims in the Justice Study that the offender knew what he was doing. This assessment of intentionality is important to offence attribution as well as to perceived wrongdoing. However, it was also critically important in generating people's turn to a public criminal response. These victims prioritized the principles of rehabilitation, specific deterrence and protection. There was little interest in expelling, through incarceration, the offender from the community. Even with feelings of fear and anger and a sense that the offender blamed them for what had happened, both domestic and non-domestic assault victims wanted outcomes that sought to address the causes of the

---

21 Donald Black, *Towards a General Theory of Social Control* (Academic Press 1984).

Note: First published in the Sage publication *Journal of Mixed Methods Research*, Robyn Holder, 'Untangling the meanings of justice: A longitudinal mixed methods study' (2016). Reproduced with permission.

Figure 6.1 Justice outcomes for victims: different objects of value, multiple goals and reasons

behaviour and to constrain future violence. In taking up the opportunity provided by law, people tended to accept overarching public goals to justice while at the same time maintaining focus on individual interests. These were not either/or choices; rather, they were mutually reinforcing.

When asked to think about justice – in the abstract as well as in their particular circumstances – people necessarily thought expansively and considered others' concerns.[22] Their justice trilogy looked to the victim,

---

[22] Linda Skitka, 'Of Different Minds: An Accessible Identity Model of Justice Reasoning' (2003) 7 *Personality and Social Psychology Review* 286–97.

the offender and the community. Their priorities were consistent in both concrete and abstract terms at different points in the justice process and remained stable over time. Yet what was particularly striking was the almost complete silence – even with open and supplementary questions – about what might be owed them, or what they might be entitled to as a victim. Put another way, it appears the concern for others can overwhelm concerns for oneself. Therefore, underneath 'surviving contrary positions' to assessments of justice, may lie partial ordering of priorities.[23] In that ordering, attention to others may supersede attention to oneself. The longitudinal method made transparent people's intrinsic capacities for reasoning as well as this ordering and contrariness. Their reasoning unfolded through their interactions with the researcher and through the steps of the criminal justice process; it was sequenced just as the process proceeded in a sequence.

The next chapter takes another approach to unpacking what people think is fair and just. It looks more closely at how participants perceived their treatment by authorities, and considers further the interactive relationship between this experience and the outcomes.

---

[23] Amartya Sen, *The Idea of Justice* (Harvard UP 2009) 394–400.

7. Experiencing justice*

> [They] treated me like a normal person, not sorry for me or anything, like I had a right to be there. (Janelle, 2011)

> Justice is fundamentally an interpersonal construct, one that would be unnecessary if people lived in isolation from others. (Skitka, 2003, 293)

After victimization, ordinary people invest varied meanings in the idea of justice and seek multiple goals when mobilizing law. There is remarkable stability and consistency over time and process to what they say they want from justice. The trilogy of interests underlying their goals reflects relational, social and civic concerns.

These goals, objectives and outcomes are one way of approaching justice, another are the assessments that people make about their experiences and interactions with justice institutions. Prior to becoming involved in the criminal justice system and from a disinterested stance, described in Chapter 5 as 'citizen-evaluators', the lay participants drew on themes of symbolic acknowledgment, assessments of efficacy, the governance functions of justice, and the system's normative performance to imagine justice. What happens to these ideas when they then actually experience it? Just as their pre-existing thinking was not fixed and narrow, neither do people as victims have a single and simple encounter with the criminal justice system. It is a long and complex process made up of a number of parts. As a journey, it tests and changes the understanding that ordinary people have of justice to themselves and to others. In these circumstances, the idea of justice becomes slippery and unstable.

* Portions of Chapter 7 including Figures 7.1, 7.2 and 7.3 first appeared in Robyn Holder, 'Satisfied? Exploring Victims' Justice Judgements' (2015) in the edited collection from Dean Wilson and Stuart Ross, *Crime, Victims and Policy: International Contexts, Local Experiences* reproduced with permission by Palgrave Macmillan.

THEORIZING ON JUSTICE JUDGMENTS

Debates on the social psychology of justice have attempted to pin down this slipperiness. Since the 1960s two paradigms of distributive and procedural justice have dominated. Distributive justice argues that people in conflict will agree that a settlement is fair and just using different criteria of deservingness, equity, need, or merit.[1] The first two criteria are commonly referenced in assessments about the fairness of criminal justice. In distributive justice theory, people are said to prioritize what they get of a valued resource. A just process thereby becomes something that maximizes a just outcome to the individual and their group.[2] The metaphor of *homo economicus* for this mode of thinking assumes humans are selfish beings who rationally calculate the costs and benefits of the attainment of goals. In the second paradigm of procedural justice is embedded a metaphor of *homo socialis*. Here human behaviour is assumed to rest on relational concerns. Procedural justice attends to 'people's need for status, standing, and to belonging' as key drivers in justice judgments.[3] It cares less about the steps that maximize gain and more about how the processes demonstrate the individual's value to the group and validate social identity.[4] The fairness of the procedures used by the decision-maker and the fairness with which they treat the person(s) subject to the decision are central concerns in procedural justice.

The two approaches are useful to unpack and to leverage understanding about what ordinary people think is fair and just. No predominance is ascribed to either the focus on outcome or that on treatment; nor

---

[1] The classic texts on these criteria are Peter Blau, 'Justice in Social Exchange' (1964) 34 *Sociological Inquiry* 193–206; Morton Deutsch, *Distributive Justice: A Social-Psychological Perspective* (Yale UP 1985); and Elaine Walster, William Walster and Ellen Berscheid, *Equity Theory and Research* (Allyn and Bacon 1978).

[2] John Thibaut and Laurens Walker, *Procedural Justice: A Psychological Analysis* (LEA Pub 1975).

[3] Linda Skitka and others, 'Knitting Together an Elephant: An Integrative Approach to Understanding the Psychology of Justice Reasoning' in Ramona Bobocel and others (eds), *The Psychology of Justice and Legitimacy: The Ontario Symposium* (11th Volume, Taylor and Francis 2010) 2.

[4] E Allan Lind and Tom Tyler, *The Social Psychology of Procedural Justice* (Plenum 1988); Tom Tyler, *Why People Obey the Law* (Princeton UP 1990) and Tom Tyler and Steven Blader, 'The Group Engagement Model: Procedural Justice, Social Identity, and Cooperative Behavior' (2003) 7 *Personality and Social Psychology Review* 349–61.

is one shown to be more or less important than the other. Rather, in this chapter I examine people's assessments as constructions that integrate variables identified as important from both theories. These constructions are active, dynamic and interactive. They *unfold* within criminal justice and within their wider social context.

VICTIMS IN THE JUSTICE PROCESS

As a process, criminal justice is at once simple and complex. It is a series of locations and moments in which citizens interact with professional agents. A system perspective considers the whole as a sum of parts. Equally, however, each of these parts creates opportunities for interaction. The different exchanges will be experienced positively or negatively; one exchange may cancel out the benefits of an earlier positive one or redeem the overall engagement. The different moments produce possibilities for an expansive conception of justice to grow. Thus, I lay the groundwork in this chapter to later consider 'the interdependence of sites within a larger system' in which deliberation might take place.[5]

It would be wrong, however, to either over- or under-state the enormity and intrusion of this engagement. Over time the intensity of the experience of violence victimization dissipated for the lay participants as the activities constituting their ordinary lives continued. Some moved house (even towns), some changed jobs and others graduated. For most, life maintained its regular routines. At the same time, each person had interactions with institutions that were way outside their everyday life. Each person came to the realization that, to varying degrees, they were not central to a process that had evolved from their individual experience. Participants came to feel detached from the system.

> It took so long I have very little faith in it. For something so straightforward it took so long – over a year – just ridiculous. (Holly)

> The communication was a bit lacking at times. It would go a while without anything. It would have been nice to feel a bit more in touch. (Bailey)

As victims, people's most intense interaction with the system is at the beginning as so few cases end up in court or trial. Depending on the circumstances, victims can feel a strong connection with investigating

---

[5] Jane Mansbridge and others, 'A Systemic Approach to Deliberative Democracy' in John Parkinson and Jane Mansbridge (eds), *Deliberative Systems* (CUP 2012) 1.

police. These are the moments of telling; that is, in response to questioning, a narrative of what happened begins to emerge. There will be accompanying feelings of relief, embarrassment, uncertainty, shame and anxiety. Victims may say things without realizing the consequences; or say things they think are vital which are unnoticed or ignored. They may or may not be asked what they want to see happen; may or may not be told when or if a person is arrested and on what charge; and may or may not be told what is to happen next. These steps can take place quickly in the space of 24 hours, or they can take weeks or months. In England this initial contact can be 'less than 10 minutes' to 'over 12 hours', and likely dissipate significantly over coming weeks.[6]

The laying of a criminal charge against an alleged offender by police generates processes potentially involving both the prosecution and the court. To the outsider victim these offender-focused processes are almost all but invisible, and the institutions themselves opaque. As often as not, they may not even be told what is happening.[7] Both police and prosecution processes require basic information about the charge and the alleged offender. Information about the victim may accompany the charge but usually does not. Within the prosecutor's office, the evidence prepared by police is reviewed and critical decisions made about proceeding or not, and on what charge(s). A prosecutor may or may not seek to contact or liaise with a victim. It is more likely she has contact with the defendant's lawyer and the investigating officer. The confusion ordinary people generally feel when they learn that the prosecutor is not 'their' lawyer can quickly turn to anger and frustration at what is commonly experienced as obfuscation if not rudeness and discourtesy.

Once the charge enters the court system, it will proceed through a step-by-step process of appearances, mentions, case management and – infrequently – a trial.[8] Because of the high rate of guilty pleas, victims as witnesses in a trial are rare. The occasion afforded to submit a written or verbal VIS after conviction is also rarely taken up. Mainly victims are not told of its availability and matters are not 'stood over' in order to solicit

---

[6] Joanna Shapland, Jon Willmore and Peter Duff, *Victims in the Criminal Justice System* (Gower 1985) 26, 33.

[7] Ibid., 49.

[8] The majority of criminal offences that enter the court system in Australia result in a guilty plea and do not proceed to contested trial. See Australian Bureau of Statistics, *Criminal Courts 2011–2012* Cat 4513.0 ABS 2013.

or produce one.[9] For ordinary people exposed to a steady diet of flash television programmes showing portrayals of (usually) empathetic interaction with victims, dynamic justice practitioners and rapid dénouement, the mannered, long and complex reality is a shock. Any sense that they as victims (or citizens) matter collides rather quickly with this reality. The experiences of ordinary people – in all their diversity and victimized by a range of personal and property crimes – with the institutions of justice have been found almost universally wanting across common law countries.[10]

CONSIDERING VICTIM EXPERIENCES WITH JUSTICE

The experiences of victims are often reduced in particular ways: either that dissatisfaction with justice is about its outcomes, most notably sentence leniency; and/or that dissatisfaction with justice is about how as victims they were treated, most notably by exclusion and discourtesy. Very few studies go behind these narrow assessments of dissatisfaction, though some recent research has sought to examine victim experience through a procedural justice lens.[11] Most studies are limited by the singular, retrospective capture of experience at one point in time. Since the 1990s, exceptions have focused on restorative justice and on victim roles and perspectives within its diverse applications.[12] Although immensely influential, this work has been constrained by its focus on the

[9] Tracey Booth, '"Cooling Out" Victims of Crime: Managing Victim Participation in the Sentencing Process in a Superior Sentencing Court' (2012) 45 *Australian and New Zealand Journal of Criminology* 214–30.

[10] See for example, with regard to Australia, Bree Cook and others, *Victims' Needs, Victims' Rights* Research and Public Policy Series No.19 (AIC 1999); the UK see Matthew Hall, *Victims of Crime: Policy and Practice in Criminal Justice* (Willan 2009) and Shapland and others (n 6); the US see Robert Elias, *Victims of the System* (Transaction Books 1983) and for Canada see Kent Roach, *Due Process and Victims' Rights* (U Toronto P 1999).

[11] Jo-Anne Wemmers, 'The Meaning of Justice for Victims' in Shlomo Shoham, Paul Knepper and Martin Kett (eds), *International Handbook of Victimology* (CRC Press 2010) 27–43.

[12] There are multitudinous texts on restorative justice. Classic tomes are John Braithwaite, *Crime, Shame and Reintegration* (CUP 1989) and Howard Zehr, *Changing Lenses: A New Focus for Criminal Justice* (Herald Press 1990). See also Elmar Weitekamp and Hans-Jürgen Kerner (eds), *Restorative Justice: Theoretical Foundations* (2nd ed, Taylor and Francis 2011).

beginning or end of the criminal justice process; that is, on restorative justice as a diversion from court or its place in or after sentencing.[13]

Notwithstanding these debates, there remains consistency on the core criticisms offered that is irrespective of offence type or victim type.[14] Victims, it is agreed, feel alienated and excluded. What may be a studiously neutral stance adopted by justice professionals, is instead experienced as disrespect and discourtesy, especially where information is absent or withheld. Victims, as well as members of the public,[15] are disquieted that, on the one hand, the system is unwieldy, devoted to hearing its own voices and takes an inordinately long time; and on the other, that it treats ordinary people (as witnesses, accused, or victim) as widgets in a grinding industrial machine. Moreover, these perceived inadequacies seem to translate into inappropriate or inadequate decision-making, especially with regard to sentencing; which is associated with failure to involve or hear from victims adequately or at all. The system is viewed as weighted towards the accused. This person has rights and representation, it is said, but victims have neither. Indeed, throughout the long process from police to prosecution and court, to community corrections, prison and to parole (assuming an offender goes through it all), people as victims largely sink or swim by themselves. Victims consistently say there is a lack of support, assistance and advocacy for them.[16]

---

[13] Heather Strang, *Repair or Revenge: Victims and Restorative Justice* (Clarendon Press 2002); Jo-Anne Wemmers and Katie Cyr, 'Victims' Perspective on Restorative Justice: How Much Involvement are Victims Looking For?' (2004) 11 *International Review of Victimology* 259–74; Mark Umbreit, Robert Coates and Boris Kalanj, *Victim Meets Offender: The Impact of Restorative Justice and Mediation* (Criminal Justice Press 1994).

[14] There are seminal texts on, for example, the experience of domestic violence victims: see Eva Buzawa and Carl Buzawa, *Domestic Violence: The Criminal Justice Response* (Sage 2003); on sexual assault: Jennifer Temkin and Barbara Krahé, *Sexual Assault and the Justice Gap* (Hart 2008); on child victims: Julia Morgan and Lucia Zedner, *Child Victims: Crime, Impact and Criminal Justice* (OUP 1992); on residential burglary: Mike Maguire and Trevor Bennett, *Burglary in a Dwelling: The Offence, the Offender, and the Victim* (Heinemann 1982); and on homicide: Paul Rock, *After Homicide: Practical and Political Responses to Bereavement* (OUP 1998).

[15] Lyn Roberts and David Indermaur, *What Australians Think About Crime and Justice: Results from the 2007 Survey of Social Attitudes*, Research and Public Policy Series 101 (Australian Institute of Criminology 2009).

[16] For discussion of these experiences in the ACT see Robyn Holder, *The Quality of Justice: Operation of the* Victims of Crime Act 1994 *in the ACT 1996–2007* (VoCC 2008).

These core criticisms all informed the Justice Study: to what extent were people given the opportunity to express their views and were these considered? Did they agree with and understand decisions reached? Were people treated with respect and provided with information? These questions cohere around victim interests in recognition and respect, and with inclusion and participation. In detail (see Appendix) the interview and survey questions drew heavily from procedural and distributive justice literature.

SATISFACTION WITH JUSTICE

It was not possible, however, to get away from 'satisfaction' as a measure. Common as it is, satisfaction is a 'simplistic criteria for [a] dependent variable'.[17] It provides a paucity of explanation. It is still less a full picture of complex interactions over time, and consistently delivers ambiguous findings.[18] Nonetheless, for the Justice Study, satisfaction was pressed into service as a measure around which to organize and explore different experiences. It is with peoples' qualitative narrative that the chapter gets behind the numbers.

At Times 1, 2 and 3 the lay participants were asked, 'generally speaking, how satisfied were you with the [police or prosecution or court or justice system overall] handling of your case?' The question anchored to four different entities and thus is not a direct comparison. However, it does provide a means to reflect different interactions at different times. Using only the 19 people who were interviewed on all three occasions, satisfaction with police was high at Time 1 but then victim satisfaction plummeted and did not recover (see Figure 7.1). There was significant difference between overall satisfaction with police, and overall satisfaction with regard to prosecution, court and the justice system overall.

What might account for these shifts in opinion and assessment by victims?[19] Australians generally report higher levels of trust in police

---

[17] Leslie Sebba, *Third Parties: Victims and the Criminal Justice System* (Ohio SUP 1996) 87.

[18] Malini Laxminarayan and others, 'Victim Satisfaction with Criminal Justice: A Systematic Review' (2013) 8 *Victims and Offenders* 119.

[19] There are mixed findings from other countries on victim satisfaction with justice personnel. Early US research also noted a more positive orientation of victims towards police than towards prosecutors, judges and other justice personnel (Brian Forst and Jolene Heron, 'The Criminal Justice Response to Victim Harm' *Research in Brief* (US Department of Justice 1985) and Deborah

Note: Figure first appeared in Robyn Holder, 'Satisfied? Exploring victims' justice judgements' (2015) in the edited collection from Dean Wilson and Stuart Ross, *Crime, Victims and Policy: International Contexts, Local Experiences*, reproduced with permission by Palgrave Macmillan.

Figure 7.1 Victims' percentage overall satisfaction with justice agencies at Time 1, Time 2 and Time 3 (N=19)

than in courts.[20] Explaining this fact may, in part, relate to understanding the initiation of contact with police. Members of the public who

---

Kelly, 'Victims' Perceptions of Criminal Justice' (1984) 11 *Pepperdine Law Review* 15–22). However, the British Crime Survey has showed that victim/witnesses were more likely to be satisfied 'with other parts of the criminal justice system' than their 'dealings with police'. This analysis also showed that people who had been victims of crime or witnesses in the past 12 months were less likely than were non-victims to express confidence in the criminal justice system (Dominic Smith, *Public Confidence in the Criminal Justice System: Findings from the British Crime Survey 2002/03 to 2007/08* Research Series 16/10 (Ministry of Justice 2010) 2, 10). In the longitudinal UK study, victim satisfaction with police was found to diminish over time (Shapland and others (n 6)). In Australia, however, people who had contact with courts in the previous twelve months (undifferentiated between victims and non-victims) had higher levels of confidence and were less likely to support harsher sentencing (Roberts and Indermaur (n 15) 3).

[20] In Valerie Braithwaite's Australian dataset, 35 per cent of people expressed 'a lot' of trust and 45 per cent 'a fair bit' in police. For law courts the percentages were 9 per cent and 39 per cent. A Canadian study suggests that the difference in viewpoint may be due to the crime control mandate of police more closely aligning with public priority and perception, and less with the due process focus of criminal courts (Julian Roberts, 'Public Confidence in Criminal Justice in

have sought law enforcement place a stronger emphasis on performance as opposed to procedural fairness.[21] That is, the authority is being invited to do or to perform a function unique to it. The immediacy of the problem faced by the individual, the availability and salience of police, and their perceived and actual effectiveness are important criteria to those seeking help. Therefore, citizens view police as a distinct emergency or help agency. However, the institutions of the justice system proper – prosecution and courts – are clearly viewed in a different light to law enforcement.

MEASURING EXPERIENCES OF JUSTICE

If judgements about justice are heavily contextualized, what components matter? To begin exploring this question, repeat quantitative measures were developed from survey questions about outcome and treatment (see Appendix). These were asked at Time 1 and Time 2 and in relation to all three justice entities – police, prosecution and court. Ultimately four conceptually coherent and meaningful scaled measures were derived from the data. The number of respondents is small so the measures can only be regarded as exploratory. However, each recorded high reliability scores. The scales represent dimensions to people's experiences of justice and can be described as justice assessment measures. These were:

1. *Outcome acceptance* (agree with decision, accept the decision, received honest explanation for decision, understand the decision, decision was fair, and decision was expected).
2. *Quality of interpersonal treatment* (I was treated with respect, I was treated with dignity, fair treatment of me, respect my rights, helpful, and I was treated as victim).

Canada: A Comparative and Contextual Analysis' (2007) 49 *Canadian Journal of Criminology and Criminal Justice* 153–84).

[21] Kristina Murphy, 'Public Satisfaction with Police: The Importance of Procedural Justice and Police Performance in Police-Citizen Encounters' (2009) 42 *Australian and New Zealand Journal of Criminology* 159–78; Lyn Hinds and Kristina Murphy, 'Public Satisfaction with Police: Using Procedural Justice to Improve Police Legitimacy' (2007) 40 *Australian and New Zealand Journal of Criminology* 27–42; William Wells, 'Type of Contact and Evaluations of Police Officers: The Effects of Procedural Justice across Three Types of Police-Citizen Contacts' (2007) 35 *Journal of Criminal Justice* 612–21.

3. *Influential victim voice* (opportunity to express views, able to influence decision, views considered before decision, decision deserved, and decision wanted).
4. *Respect offender rights* (treated the violent person with respect, and respect offender rights).

Outcome acceptance can be described as a quasi-distributive measure. At Time 1, and in relation to the experience with police, it predicted 40.3 per cent of variance. The scale incorporates items measuring victims' sense of the fairness of the decision made by the authority as well as perspective that the decision was expected. The items describing *interpersonal treatment*, such as respect and dignity, are commonly found in the procedural justice literature. However, the *quality* of that treatment is emphasized with the inclusion of items that acknowledge aspects of the person's status. That is, 'my rights were respected' and 'I was treated as the victim of the incident/matter'.[22] The quality of interpersonal treatment scale explained 13 per cent of variance. The items in the third scale are also found in procedural justice studies and accounted for 8.4 per cent of variance. This scale is described as *influential victim voice* because of the way in which the expressive and participatory items cohered with assessments on the outcome decision – that it was an outcome the victim deserved and the outcome the victim wanted. The fourth scale, *respect offender rights*, may seem unusual. Concern for the treatment and rights of the offender is not generally asked in victim studies.[23] However, given the importance ascribed by victims to offender-related objectives discussed in the previous chapter, this particular measure is perhaps not so surprising. Nonetheless, it represented a small 6 per cent of shared variance. The mean of each of the scales (using only those cases who completed an interview at Time 1 and Time 2, N=26) allows comparison of interactions across the measures (see Figure 7.2). That is, whether and

---

[22] In the circumstances of the Justice Study, this statement was intended to reveal the extent to which people felt believed or disbelieved by authorities. Respondents understood and responded to the statement in this manner. Thus, a positive response indicated people's perception that authorities believed they were a victim and treated them as such.

[23] The study by Wemmers and Cyr (n 13) illuminating victim concerns for young offenders stands outside this claim. Restorative justice researchers have generally noticed victim concerns for the rehabilitation of offenders, especially young offenders. See also Kees Van den Bos and Allan Lind, 'The Psychology of Own Versus Others' Treatment: Self-oriented and Other-oriented Effects on Perceptions of Procedural Justice' (2001) *Personality and Social Psychology Bulletin* 1324–33.

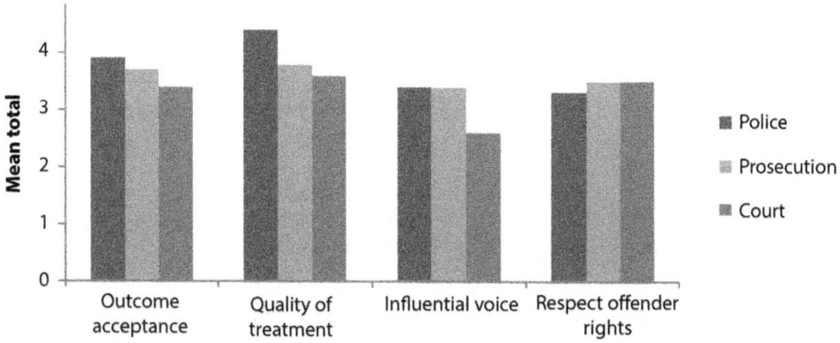

Note: Figure first appeared in Robyn Holder, 'Satisfied? Exploring victims' justice judgements' (2015) in the edited collection from Dean Wilson and Stuart Ross, *Crime, Victims and Policy: International Contexts, Local Experiences*, reproduced with permission by Palgrave Macmillan. Scale: 1 = strongly disagree; 5 = strongly agree.

Figure 7.2 Victims' assessment of police, prosecution and courts at Time 1 and Time 2 (N=26)

how people distribute their views and experiences across police, prosecution and court.

People made strong and positive assessments of the quality of interpersonal treatment they received from police. This was significantly different to the assessments made of the quality of interpersonal treatment experienced from prosecution and from court. The difference between prosecution and court on the quality of their interpersonal treatment of the victim is not significant. People had a negative assessment of the strength of their *influential voice* with regard to the court. The assessment was significantly lower than for police and prosecution. The difference between police and prosecution, however, was not significant. Finally, there was no statistical significance in assessments of police, prosecution and court with regard to the scales measuring victims' assessed *outcome acceptance* or victims' perspective on justice entities' *respect for offender rights*.

But how did these justice assessment measures relate to 'satisfaction'? There was a strong and significant correlation of satisfaction with the quality of interpersonal treatment for each entity, especially for prosecution.[24] The

---

24 The interpersonal treatment scale presented a strong and significant correlation to overall satisfaction with police ($r_s = 0.6$ $p<0.01$), court ($r_s = 0.64$ $p<0.01$) and prosecution ($r_s = 0.76$ $p<0.01$).

same was found with outcome acceptance and satisfaction. The victims' influential voice scale only correlated in a strong and significant manner with satisfaction with prosecution and with the court. Of interest was the strength of the relationships between the scales. For all three justice entities, the stronger the influential voice, the more accepting are victims of the outcomes reached by each agency.

AN INTEGRATED JUSTICE JUDGMENT

Both the longitudinal English and Dutch studies made similar findings. While it is not possible to make direct comparisons and the studies use different analytic strategies, both found that the quality of treatment from justice professionals mattered a good deal to victims. Both noticed how victims' positive assessments declined from the initial police handling, and, although assessment differed in relation to prosecutors and the courts in each study, they clearly varied depending on the justice entity. Shapland and her colleagues attribute this, in part, because victims were 'forgotten in the business of processing the defendant as quickly as possible'.[25] Both studies also noticed how little victims were kept informed about the progress of the case including the outcome at court, observations that made it difficult to assess the relative importance of the substantive outcome. For the Dutch victims, fair treatment included having 'an opportunity to express their wishes' and to have those taken 'into consideration'.[26] In both countries, people as victims and witnesses did not have a single and static assessment to make of their engagement with justice authorities.

Identifying and quantifying the underlying dimensions of the experiences of victims with different justice agencies from all three studies creates a more complex picture of justice than distributive and procedural justice theories suggest. Rather than being separate or in tension, there is arguably a strong and interactive relationship between assessments of the outcome and of procedural aspects in overall justice judgments. Indeed, they are perhaps better understood as dimensions of an integrated, normative conception of justice.[27] The elements identified in the Justice

---

25 Shapland and others (n 6) 59.

26 Jo-Anne Wemmers, *Victims in the Criminal Justice System* (Kugler Publications 1996) 148.

27 Joel Brockner and Batia Wiesenfeld, 'An Integrative Framework For Explaining Reactions To Decisions: Interactive Effects Of Outcomes And Procedures' (1996) 120 *Psychological Bulletin* 189–208; Russell Cropanzo and

Study affirm these arguments for an integrated conception of justice judgments that is captured in Figure 7.3.

Note: Figure first appeared in Robyn Holder, 'Satisfied? Exploring victims' justice judgments' (2015) in the edited collection from Dean Wilson and Stuart Ross, *Crime, Victims and Policy: International Contexts, Local Experiences*, reproduced with permission by Palgrave Macmillan.

Figure 7.3 Integrated components to victims' justice judgments

---

Maureen Ambrose, 'Procedural and Distributive Justice are More similar Than You Think: A Monistic Perspective and a Research Agenda' in Jerald Greenberg and Russell Cropanzano (eds), *Advances in Organizational Justice* (Stanford UP 2001) 119–51; Robert Folger and others, 'Elaborating Procedural Fairness: Justice Becomes Both Simpler And More Complex' (1996) 22 *Personality and Social Psychology Bulletin* 435–41; Robert Folger and Russell Cropanzano, 'Fairness Theory: Justice as Accountability' in Greenberg and Cropanzano, Ibid.; Neil Hauenstein and others, 'A Meta-Analysis of the Relationship between Procedural Justice and Distributive Justice: Implications for Justice Research' (2001) 13 *Employee Responsibilities and Rights Journal* 39–56; E Allan Lind, 'Fairness Heuristic Theory: Justice Judgments as Pivotal Cognitions in Organizational Relations' in Greenberg and Cropanzano, Ibid.; Kees Van den Bos and others, 'Procedural and Distributive Justice: What is Fair Depends More on What Comes First Than on What Comes Next' (1997) 72 *Journal of Personality and Social Psychology* 95–104.

This notion of integration remains insufficient, however. Reasoning about justice in the real world is not about 'competing conceptions'.[28] Justice judgments are context sensitive as well as malleable and fluid.[29] Thus, rather than ascribe 'single motives or simple frames' at singular moments to human behaviour, people are 'both flexible and complex' in their thinking about justice. The narration that people in the Justice Study provided as context to their assessments highlights important social and political concerns.

DISCURSIVE UNDERPINNINGS TO JUSTICE JUDGMENTS

The comments provided by the lay participants about the police, prosecutors and the court allow further exploration of their evaluations of interpersonal treatment, outcome acceptance, and their influential voice. These show what is important within integrated assessments, and why. In this section a number of themes were found to underlie evaluations (see Table 7.1) and are fleshed out in the remainder of this chapter.

The Quality of Interpersonal Treatment

The importance of interpersonal treatment of citizens by authorities has a long research history. That people are treated with respect and dignity, and that the authority is fair and unbiased in its treatment of citizens are important to people in a range of settings.[30] The quality of interpersonal treatment for those in the Justice Study was strong across all three entities though experienced differently. The vast majority of people (96 per cent) felt that police treatment of them was fair, whereas the figures were 58 per cent and 62 per cent respectively for prosecution and the court. The distribution was similar, though lower, for Dutch victims

---

[28] Skitka and others (n 3) 2.

[29] Susan Clayton and Susan Opotow, 'Justice and Identity: Changing Perspectives on What is Fair' (2003) 7 *Personality and Social Psychology Review* 298–310.

[30] Adding a note of caution, Robert MacCoun discusses how procedural justice may manipulate and exploit people in vulnerable positions to those in power ('Voice, Control, and Belonging: The Double-Edged Sword of Procedural Fairness' (2005) *Ann Rev Law Soc Sci* 171–201).

Table 7.1 Themes underlying victims' distributive and procedural justice evaluations

Quality of interpersonal treatment	Outcome acceptance	Influential voice
Recognition of standing	Relationship to offender-related concerns	Uniqueness of being known and 'knowing'
Equality of treatment	Relationship to victim-related concerns	Demonstrations of respect and recognition
Information as reciprocity and recognition	Normative and governance concerns	Constitutive of a dialogue with justice officials
Interaction as respect		Connection with 'properness' of decision-making
		Giving and receiving information as a powerful transaction

Source: Robyn Holder, 'Satisfied? Exploring victims' justice judgements' (2015) in the edited collection from Dean Wilson and Stuart Ross, *Crime, Victims and Policy: International Contexts, Local Experiences*, reproduced with permission by Palgrave Macmillan.

where the figures were respectively 79 per cent, 19 per cent and 42 per cent.[31]

As discussed earlier, theorists suggest two main reasons for the differences. One relates to the manner in which fair processes generate fair outcomes, and the other argues for attention to the 'effects of values associated with group membership' and the ways in which group procedures work. Both arguments emphasize that fair, respectful and unbiased treatment of individuals by authorities generates cooperation and compliance.

Compliance with laws is a general social good but may be less relevant to understanding the importance of fair treatment to victims. Indeed, the longitudinal Dutch study found victims rather less compliant than non-victims. Wemmers found that personal morality of the individual and their perceived obligations to obey the law were influential on compliance, but not deterrence or peer disapproval.[32] The idea of cooperation is more relevant for victims, especially at the decision-making stage of

31 Wemmers (n 26) 125.
32 Ibid., 174, 185.

prosecution. However, both compliance and cooperation reflect a state-centric perspective on the relationship between citizens and authorities. A citizen-centric perspective invites consideration of a different set of issues. One possibility is simply that victims value 'customer service' and feel valued 'as a person' when they are treated well by authorities.[33] Another is that the quality of treatment carries a social and political message, and is a reflection of the justice system's recognition of the citizen-status of persons 'over whom it claims authority'.[34] Analysis of victim narratives reveal a number of themes that help explore these possibilities. These are recognition of their standing in the justice process; equality of treatment; information as a demonstration of reciprocity; and interaction as respect.

Recognition of standing

Being valued as a person was important to people, but so too were perceptions that the incident, the case and the victim was taken seriously. Police, said Karla, 'never made me feel like a stupid woman'. But the nuances and differing qualities of the experience of interpersonal treatment signalled more than a service-based assessment. The quality of treatment the lay participants received was experienced expansively and as constituting forms of recognition by authorities. It was a reflection – positive as well as negative – of the person's particular or unique status as a victim and the meaning of that status in the public sphere of criminal justice. Janelle, for example, said that authorities 'treated me like a normal person, not sorry for me or anything; like I had a right to be there'. Edward, on the other hand, was offended that he was treated like 'just another' victim. The connection between respect and recognition was particularly acute for people whose relationship with authorities was unstable. For Deanna, born outside Australia, the experience initially 'won my confidence in the justice system. At first I was paranoid because I am not a citizen and [I wondered] would they be biased'. Indeed, she went on to say, 'I thought they were fair. The law applies to everyone in the community.' For Birgit, whose life history involved childhood care arrangements with welfare authorities as well as prior offending as an adolescent, the meaning of her positive treatment was clear. She said, 'it matters what happened to me'. Respectful recognition also went directly

---

33 Irina Elliott and others, 'Procedural Justice in Contacts with the Police: The Perspective of Victims of Crime' (2012) 13 *Police Practice and Research: an International Journal* 437–49.

34 Anthony Duff, 'Towards a Theory of Criminal Law?' (2010) 84(1) *Aristotelian Society Supplementary Volume* 1, 3.

to the specificity of their individual standing. Xenia, for example, said, 'it's about me, not them'. At her final interview she went further to say, 'no one cares what I want. They are only after what they want ... who's interest is the law in?' For some, this sense of their unique role expanded to claims for particular advocacy or representation. 'I needed someone just for me,' was Ursula's comment. In sum, status is more than a victim category and more than personhood, just as the notion of 'standing' is more than a legal term.

Equality of treatment

Others drew strong connections between recognition and respect, and equal treatment. David, who also had a prior history of non-violent offending, felt he was not of equal worth to others in the community (in his words, like a 'little old lady'). At his second interview he described how he had wanted to change his life but 'felt discriminated against'. The criminal case against his assailant was, he said, 'a waste of time and effort ... we all waited around, I gave evidence but they brought up my old mental health history and that I wasn't a competent witness'. David reckoned, if he 'had been a little old lady they would have put a more experienced lawyer on it. Because I was an ex-offender, live in public housing and am a young man there was no effort in it'. He felt that the system had been fairer to him as an accused than when he was a victim. At his third interview David again emphasized how it was 'much harder as a victim, I guarantee you that'. He understood that it was not possible to 'be completely fair to everyone' but that getting 'torn to pieces' on the witness stand was 'ridiculous'. 'Before', he said 'I thought I had a choice to be a responsible citizen but now I see it's also how they see you.'

In a different way, Ursula came to feel unequally treated in relation to her husband who had been charged with a violence offence in relation to her. She had pushed strongly for her husband's mental health issues to be taken into account and was relieved that the charges were eventually dismissed. But at her third and final interview she noticed that her own interests had been unattended. She said 'you get into issues where you get into human rights. Mine get put to one side but his get thought about'. In the end she said, 'justice is about fairness to everyone'. Finn's perspective was that police and prosecution just 'swept it under the carpet' as the person who assaulted him was a juvenile. He said, 'they didn't seem to care [about me]'. He claimed that 'everyone in the situation should be heard'. Nada reflected that 'maybe they [authorities] have a mentality that victims are like second-class citizens. Maybe they think victims aren't serious and they don't take it seriously'. Her observation went directly to her citizen status and the consequent obligation for equal treatment.

Concern for equitable treatment from authorities also encompassed the offender and was, in the main, commented upon as a positive. While the offender rights scale did not correlate strongly with victims' overall satisfaction, a majority agreed that prosecution and the courts treated the violent person with respect and with respect for his rights. Some directly related their assessment of fairness to this point. Zola strongly agreed, at her second interview after the case had finalized, that justice had been done. Asked why she thought this she said it was 'the fact that they're all neutral – prosecutors and judges – and they respected both our rights. They didn't eliminate his rights to help me. In that way justice was fair'. However, when asked about fairness to themselves as victims, the assessment generally reversed.

Information as reciprocity and recognition

Respectful treatment was also more than equality, fairness and standing. People saw respect discharged practically in part through the provision of information. The transaction was experienced differently by victims depending on the justice organization. A majority agreed that police gave them information about what was happening in their case, but not so prosecution or the court. Edward commented negatively on 'the lack of information'. He said, 'it was frustrating. You just didn't know even how to chase the case, chase the police officer. It's all just difficult really. I had to do the chasing'. For many, the case status updates, information about their rights and responsibilities and the sources of support offered and given all pointed to their unique importance in a very particular space. Charlie's positive comment that 'they made time to see me and tell me' signalled to him that he was important enough for authorities to do so. Deanna received a different message. She said she 'was never even sent a subpoena' and 'felt like a ball being tossed about'. For Imogene, the significance of the information gulf carried negative inferences about the equity of status. She said:

> Definitely not enough information is given. [He] was far more thoroughly briefed on what was to happen than I was. That's a huge hole. It says that the system doesn't take the situation seriously enough. It's just another job without taking into consideration that people's lives are considered.

Both men and women commented that, without the victim advocates, they might never have known what was going on. Edward observed that he 'had to do all the chasing' and that it was 'no wonder that victims just give up'.

Interaction as respect

To the absence of information was added the absence of meaningful (or any) interaction with authorities. Interaction indicated the possibility of dialogue – 'the ability to participate in a face-to-face way' as Karla put it. Without the interaction it was 'like I wasn't relevant to anything'. When interaction did take place, people noted its quality in both positive and negative terms. Polly felt she was made to 'feel like a child who didn't know what was good for me'. For her, the interactions were occasions of disrespect. She recounted a prosecuting official saying to her, 'there are women like you all the time and we just carry on'. She said, 'I didn't like he said I had to do this and I had to do that'. Charlie, on the other hand, said that even though 'justice might not have been served on the perpetrator [because it was dismissed] … I was certainly included'.

If interaction signalled something important about the particular status and standing of the person, it also marked something of the citizen's wider interests. Charlie felt that being included was 'the positive'. He felt he 'was treated as a member of the community. The circumstances of the incident could have been swept away. They followed it as much as they could'. Nada's concluding comments in her final interview emphasized that 'part of justice is seeing the effort for justice they put in and the impact of that'. Her reflection says something of her interest in observing the normative and actual performance of public institutions charged with very particular responsibilities. It was their participation in the distinctive criminal justice journey that took Nada, Charlie and the others, as citizen-victims, to this point.

Outcome Acceptance

As a composite scale and single measure, victim acceptance of the outcome reached by each of the justice entities was strong. Understandably, there was a strong and significant correlation of outcome acceptance with overall satisfaction in relation to police ($r_s = 0.48$ $p<0.01$), prosecution ($r_s = 0.58$ $p<0.01$),[35] and the court ($r_s = 0.65$ $p<0.01$). While the outcomes were

[35] There were no correlations between the overall satisfaction with prosecution handling or the scale measuring outcome preference, and any contextual

clearly important, people's reflections at their Time 2 and Time 3 interviews after the case had finalized at court offered a number of different themes operating within their assessments. These were concerned with what the offender 'got' and the impact on him; what the victim 'got'; and the normative and wider governance implications of the outcome.

Thinking about offender-related outcomes

Comment about the outcomes the violent person received comprised the largest cluster for the study participants. These grouped into two key sub-themes: the nature and appropriateness of the interventions (the arrest decision, the prosecution and the court outcomes), and the perceived or hoped-for impact of the various decisions on the violent person.

Yvette, Karla, Svetlana, Bailey and Deanna observed the simple fact of a decision. Yvette felt the dismissal of the case against her husband was 'right'. Karla thought the plea of guilty by her husband meant 'it is an ownership of his actions rather than it being forced upon him'. For Svetlana, 'he did what he did and got something for it'. Bailey said that the conviction meant 'something happened ... there was an outcome'. Similarly, Deanna said, 'I'm very glad he's convicted.' To her it was modest indication that justice was done but also 'a personal victory'.

Participants also offered both positive and negative comments on the nature and appropriateness for the violent person of the various interventions. Xenia had wanted authorities to look at the situation 'holistically'. The decision to proceed with some charges and not the assault charge 'was a good outcome for what happened' she said. Finoula and Aimee were also positive about the provision of mandated on-going engagement by probation authorities with the offenders in their cases. Finoula was pleased that her ex-partner was 'going to get the counselling'. Aimee felt that the 'monitoring of [my] partner's counselling activities is helping keep him to his promises'. Janelle, on the other hand, felt that the 12-month good behaviour bond for her ex-partner was 'a crock'. She said, 'I would have preferred weekend detention or lock-up. He's gotten away with so much, for example, his past driving offences. I feel he's gotten away with it and won't learn anything from it.' Birgit was pleased that the court did not 'just let him out on bail' and 'the time inside [prison] is good'. She said, 'I'm thinking the judge looked back over our history and the previous bail and stuff and the judge thought "right, you're not getting this".' However, she also thought that an eight-month

---

variables related to the relationship with the offender, emotional after-effects or continuing physical abuse.

term of imprisonment was 'too long' and that it 'should maybe be four months'. What was an appropriate outcome for the offender was, for these victims, something that needed to reflect what was particular about the offender and his behaviour.

The question of appropriateness bled into people's thinking about the perceived or hoped-for impact of the various decisions on the offender. Comments on this sub-theme echoed people's interest that legal mobilization should have some effect. Typically, the observations revolved around the violent person himself having an opportunity to reflect; to 'see what he's done' said Svetlana. Zola was unhappy with the sentence arrived at by the court but nonetheless said that 'it has made him [my ex] stop and think'. Finoula also said that her ex-partner 'has to stop and think about what he is doing now'. He has, she said, 'to deal with his stuff'. The process for Holly had been long drawn out and she expressed mixed feelings. She felt the time her ex-partner spent on remand was an 'opportunity to de-tox and that's been good for him'. But she also wanted the 'punishment to fit the crime. Two years [in custody] is massive. If they really did give a crap about rehabilitation for him then the outcome of going to gaol isn't right'. Finn also felt that the good behaviour bond ordered by the court was insufficient for the young offender in his case to 'deal with' his issues. He said that 'it's finished and all over in the eyes of the court' but the young person 'needs to face the fact if he is going to keep being a criminal or is he going to do something different'. At his final interview Finn also positioned his comments in a wider frame of reference. 'If you're hungry and steal a chocolate bar you're likely to get worse', he said. 'Stealing is bad but it isn't life threatening or hurting'. In victims' view, the opportunity created by criminal justice was not only for the offender, but also for the wider community – 'anyone else' or 'us' in the words of Finoula and Birgit. Emphasizing the wider implications of safety, Birgit felt that the custodial sentence given to her ex-partner gave her and their son some 'time out for us'. At her final interview Finoula reflected that the outcome had 'planted a seed in [my ex-partner's] mind not to do this to anyone else'. She hoped 'he's learned from it', but soberly reflected, 'I don't think so'. In sum, victims reflected a primary interest that accountability should have a consequential effect on the offender.

Thinking on victim-related outcomes

The lay participants also made comment about what they as victims 'got' (or did not get) through the outcomes. In keeping with the weight placed on stopping the violence as an initiating motivation, many of the domestic assault victims emphasized the safety implications of the outcome. Olivia said that the outcome had stopped some of 'the extreme stuff'. However, she said that 'while it recognized what he'd done and was a kind of win … I still sleep with [my daughter] with the phone and the keys and with the door locked'. On the other hand, for Genevieve the conviction made her 'feel safer'. Finoula also said she felt safer because the authorities 'wouldn't let [my ex] near me'. Nada's ex-partner was 'banned from the ACT'. She felt this 'was good for me and good to get him out of the environment he was in'. Janelle said that the conviction of her ex-partner 'made me realize a lot more what he was really like … I wondered what I was doing with him in the first place. The justice system opened my eyes'. Teresa had 'just wanted peace' and got it.

Others commented on something missing for them. Although Karla said that the system 'protected me from verbal bullying and assault' she also wanted something more. She thought that the non-recorded conviction of her husband was 'probably not what I hoped for'. Instead she 'would have liked and still would like a true recognition of the pain and angst he caused me through the experience'. Edward felt that justice had been done to the offender but not towards himself. He said, 'the costs [of my injury] are significant – thousands of dollars. I was in the wrong place, now I'm out of pocket'. While the court made a reparation order in his favour, he was left to chase payment himself. Holly was disgruntled that her ex-partner 'wasn't punished for what he did to us.' Rather, the court had 'punished [him] for missing an appointment [with his probation officer]'. Generally, protection objectives were secured but not other victim-related objectives.

Thinking on normative outcomes

Many emphasized the normative implications of the outcomes. It was 'the right thing' and emblematic of their concern about the wrongfulness of the violence. The good behaviour bond imposed by the court told Lorraine that her ex-partner 'couldn't do it'. For Deanna, the criminal justice system 'finally let him know that what he did was wrong'. She said that she had 'warned him lots of times that it wasn't right. He didn't listen … now it's the court telling him it's not acceptable'. Teresa said something similar in commenting that 'the thing I most wanted was that he be shown what he did was wrong. That he was convicted and sentenced told him that'. Charlie and Bailey both reflected on the importance of consequence to wrong behaviour. Charlie had been 'not too fussed' that the case against his offender had been dismissed at court. 'There was no great injury or emotional pain', he said. He thought that he 'might care more if there was but there wasn't'. However, at his final interview he did not agree that justice had been done 'because I think there needed to be consequences on his actions'. Bailey felt that the outcome 'was "fit" for the actual incident'. He felt that his case 'was reasonably minor' but 'was noted and went through a due process'. At his final interview he went further, to comment:

> I think the outcome was appropriate to what happened. It wasn't that serious so didn't need a heavy-handed response. I imagine it's the same as others like it. I don't think he was mistreated and I wasn't underdone. He got his punishment and I didn't require any reparation.

Comments like this from Bailey deployed both a private and a public frame to normative concerns. Similarly, Deanna reiterated that 'the law applies to everyone in the community'. At her final interview, Finoula emphasized that her ex-partner 'can't just go bashing people because he thinks he can. It's about consequences to actions. The justice system is there to remind people of this'. For Aimee, the 'strength of the legal system' had 'helped to draw a line at unacceptable behaviour'. These comments were emblematic of *homo moralis* as a metaphor for human behaviour, a conception that directs attention away from wants and desires and towards 'ought'.[36] It is particularly relevant when people feel the harm or wrong was intentional and undeserved, and when it has, in their eyes, wider civic implications.

Influential Victim Voice

The idea of 'voice' is central to procedural justice. In victim-relevant studies, voice has been explored in a number of ways: as contributing to confidence levels, in regulating anti-social behaviour, in mediation, and through VIS.[37] Wemmers has explained the different emphases Dutch victims placed on their assessments of police and of prosecution, particularly in relation to key issues of notification and restitution, in that

---

[36] Skitka and others (n 3) 2.

[37] The references here are for confidence levels: Ben Bradford, 'Voice, Neutrality and Respect: Use of Victim Support Services, Procedural Fairness and Confidence in the Criminal Justice System' (2011) 11 *Criminology and Criminal Justice* 345–66; regulating anti-social behaviour: Susan Bright and Chara Bakalis, 'Anti-Social Behaviour: Local Authority Responsibility and the Voice of the Victim' (2003) 62 *The Cambridge Law Journal* 305–34; mediation: Jo-Anne Wemmers and Katie Cyr, 'What Fairness Means to Crime Victims: a Social Psychological Perspective on Victim-Offender Mediation' (2006) 47 *Applied Psychology in Criminal Justice* 102–28; and through VIS: Paul Cassell, 'In Defense of Victim Impact Statements' (2008) 6 *Ohio State Journal of Criminal Law* 611–48.

the former represents an instrumental function and the latter a normative one.[38] Her point underscores seeing that victims value their voice being meaningful in different ways with different justice agencies.

Over the course of the three interviews with the lay participants, multiple different meanings emerged out of the notion of 'having a say' with all three justice agencies – police, prosecution and court. Phrases such as 'being able to talk' and 'being consulted' were frequent. These spoke to 'involvement' but the phrasing hid more nuanced interests that were about the uniqueness of being known and 'knowing'; were demonstrations of respect and recognition; were constitutive of a dialogue between themselves and the justice entity; went to a concern that decision-making itself be full and 'proper'; and which saw the giving and receiving of information as a powerful transaction (as well as being powerful in itself).

Knowing and being known

Knowing and being known were ideas that expressed a sense that people knew something that was useful and particular; that their views were important and their experience valuable. Finn said he had 'heard from people around here'. These networks had told him that the young offender had 'been able to shrug and walk out' of court. About her ex-partner, Birgit said, 'we should have a say – we know the violent person better than the judge'. More importantly, knowing something was being known. This idea asserted the centrality of people's real life. 'This is someone's life they're dealing with', said Roslyn about the prosecution decisions. There was a sense that their centre of gravity was being pulled somewhere else – '[It's] about me, not them. It was weird', said Xenia – and that expressing opinions and wants re-focused back on their known and lived reality – the real world not the institutional world.

Respect and recognition

Respect and recognition were embedded within this claim for their lives. Within these concepts was a very real stress on individual dignity – '[they] kept me up-to-date. It really helped', said Svetlana. But not having one's voice heard and understood was equally experienced as a demonstration of disrespect and as a lack of recognition. Deanna said that she was 'kept in the dark about the changes and updates, like I did not have a right to know'. Said Finn:

---

[38] Wemmers (n 26) 135.

> I don't expect them to be over for a cup of tea every day but contact once every so often and to know what is happening with dates and things and what is the case made up of. I really didn't know. I kept the card for ages but there was no point. I don't think they really care that much.

Voice as dialogue

Voice as dialogue was linked to these first two points. Victims perceived their own voice as not echoing in the dark as it did for Xenia: the prosecution, she said, 'never called to respond' to her questions. Rather, as Roslyn said, there was an expectation that she would 'be asked questions about what [I] wanted in the future'. At her final interview, Olivia said she would have 'liked more input, to be more involved and get more information'. Dialogue was not undirected communication but sought understanding and 'answers' (Charlie). Many, like Teresa, were 'never contacted by the prosecution or the court'. She said, 'I would have liked them to contact me. The DVCS [victim advocates] gave information but if I had questions I don't know if they would have been able to answer. For example, I asked why he had not entered a plea and the DVCS couldn't tell me. I would have thought the DPP could tell me why'. Teresa's comments acknowledge that dialogue is in part about an exchange on the technical detail of decision-making and not superficial.

Proper decision-making

Comments such as this from Teresa suggested a link between what victims perceived as the properness of the decisions and judicial decision-making, and victim dialogue. Nada said, 'the magistrate needs to hear from the victim to make a proper decision. There is a lot lost between what happens and reading something off a paper'. Properness was about the decision-maker being fully informed – 'it shouldn't be done in isolation' said Roslyn. 'There should be an interview of sorts'. Hearing the whole story also meant that the decision-maker would see the 'many shades of grey' said Teresa; it would mean that 'everything' would be 'taken into account and ... the best interests of everyone thought about', commented Xenia. A proper decision not only drew on a range of information, but information from those such as the victim who were directly affected.

The power of information

The power of information was obvious to victims: 'If you know something then you don't feel further victimized', said Roslyn. Victims 'needed lots of information', but most often, however, 'had to ask all over the place' for it (Edward). These reflections marked a shift from the subject 'victim' back towards the more critically informed citizen. Winona commented that 'it would be good to get more technical information about what happens in the justice system and a bit more detail on my case and why'. A similar desire to be and perform as a citizen-victim underlay Polly's observation that she didn't 'know what the procedures are or what is expected of me. I would expect someone to let me know'. This call from victims for more information is ubiquitous. Here it is voiced by a directly-affected citizen demanding answers from authorities.

The complexity inherent in voice has been simplified to its expressive nature.[39] As expression within the criminal justice system, the victim's voice is characterized as subjective,[40] designed to emote and, in consequence, to have therapeutic benefits.[41] However, the diverse meanings in this section instead suggest people's recognition of the unique character of the decision-making spaces with which they are engaged. That is, spaces designed to address a convergence of different concerns for victims, offenders, and communities. It is in consideration of all these concerns that victims felt they could, or even should, contribute. For the lay participants, the variables on voice did in fact cluster with their preferred decision or outcome. Theirs is clearly an interest in a voice that *influences*. It is one of the underlying dimensions to people's experience of justice, and carried a strong relationship with their overall satisfaction with each of the justice institutions.

CONCLUDING DISCUSSION

Victims' observations and reflections revealed how important the specificity of context to procedural and distributive justice judgments is. As a

---

[39] Julian Roberts and Edna Erez, 'Communication in Sentencing: Exploring the Expressive Function of Victim Impact Statements' (2004) 10 *International Review of Victimology* 223–44.

[40] Ian Edwards, 'An Ambiguous Participant: The Crime Victim and Criminal Justice Decision-Making' (2004) 44 *British Journal of Criminology* 967, 976.

[41] Antony Pemberton and Sandra Reynaers, 'The Controversial Nature of Victim Participation: Therapeutic Benefits in Victim Impact Statements' in Edna Erez and others (eds), *Therapeutic Jurisprudence and Victim Participation in Justice: International Perspectives* (Carolina Academic Press 2011). Discussing international criminal responses to mass atrocities, Eric Stover also comments on the tendency to 'valorise "therapeutic value"' to victims in testifying at court (Eric Stover, *The Witnesses: War Crimes and the Promise of Justice in The Hague* (U Penn P 2011) 131).

simple measure 'satisfaction' usefully illuminated this point and showed that victims experience each justice institution differently. Satisfaction with police was significantly higher than satisfaction with prosecution, court and with the justice system overall. However, as a measure of the long and complex interaction that citizens have with the justice process, satisfaction was parsimonious. Getting at the contingent nature of justice required real world justice research which identified that, underlying victims' judgements about justice, were dimensions of outcome acceptance, the quality of interpersonal treatment, influential victim voice, and respect for offenders' rights.

These dimensions embedded within justice judgments fluctuated in importance but were all present in victims' assessments about police, prosecution and the court. For all three justice agencies, the strongest positive correlation with overall satisfaction was with outcome acceptance and the quality of the interpersonal treatment. But the elements bled into each other. Outcome acceptance and interpersonal treatment correlated strongly. The influential victim voice connected strongly with outcome acceptance for all three agencies. While the elements can be separated, they are clearly not separate. Rather, they form dimensions of an integrated conception of justice that is supple in the real world of criminal justice. They do not require fixing to any single understanding of human behaviour.

Moreover, participant narration showed the nuances within these dimensions of justice were highly particularized. The emphases placed on the quality of their interpersonal treatment embraced recognition of their unique standing and circumstances, as well as respect for their personhood. Respect and recognition were demonstrated through the manner in which information was or was not provided to people by authorities. Victims experienced information both as a power resource and as reciprocity. They also understood interaction with authorities as dialogue. The strong expectation for fairness in criminal justice that people articulated at their first interview emerged here in concerns for equitable and fair treatment from authorities for themselves as well as for the violent person.

Justice as the attainment of outcomes linked with the trilogy of interests participants articulated at the commencement of their engagement with authorities: victim, offender and their community of others. Over time, these reflections sharpened to focus primarily on the nature, appropriateness and impact of the outcomes on the violent person, and the consequence of these to themselves as a victim and a person. In an echo of their pre-existing citizen evaluations about justice, there was reflection on the extent to which the outcome calibrated with the normative and governance functions of justice. Given these multiple concerns, it is perhaps inevitable, as Sen has argued, that the resolutions the lay participants experienced were partial and incomplete. As with outcomes, procedural justice variables did a lot to leverage understanding of how victims experienced authority. People understood themselves as 'knowers' who added to the quality and meaningfulness of decision-making. To be heard was to be recognized as someone with distinctive and important insight into particular circumstances *and* with input that was more generally important. The desire for an influential voice suggests that institutional efforts to become customer friendly miss the mark. As Ursula said, 'they all listen but you are no further ahead'. Common perceptions of voice as simply expressive need to be re-thought.

The key conceptions of justice developed in Chapter 2 all emerged here in relation to experience, assessment and reflection: that of justice as a normative guide, as duty or obligation, as accountability, as fairness, as relational, and as contextual. Also highlighted was that these conceptions reverberate through the series of engagements that victims have with justice decision-makers. Each interaction provides opportunities for ideas about justice to be articulated, made transparent and enacted. Many of these opportunities were badly handled and lost for those in the Justice Study as in other research. The significance and implications of these losses are developed in the next chapter. This explores what participation in criminal justice looks like to victims of violence and what this may mean to the realization of justice.

8. Participating in justice*

> I'm a little undecided [whether justice was done] because I don't know what happened in the end ... There was no discussion. I just think they have no regard for the victim. Maybe they have a mentality that victims are like second-class citizens. Maybe they think victims aren't serious and they don't take it seriously. (Nada, 2011)

> The normative legitimacy of a democratic decision depends on the degree to which those affected by it have been included in the decision-making process and have had the opportunity to influence the outcomes. (Young, 2000, 5–6)

Justice is a complex, dynamic and nuanced conception that *unfolds*. If this constitutes the idea of justice in the real world, how can it be made, seen, experienced, performed and validated – in the real world? For hard-pressed systems dealing with multiple constituencies and competing demands, achieving thick and rich justice such as this can seem like impossibility. For ordinary citizens made vulnerable through violence and unprepared for the industrial dimensions of contemporary criminal justice, just coming through unscathed can be an optimistic objective. This chapter considers how demanding and citizen-centric expectations for justice can possibly be met through a lens of citizen participation.

Our thinking about justice originates from a multitude of claims and concerns (injustices) and, as discussed in preceding chapters, many evaluative arguments flow from these. Those from citizen-victims remain hidden if no opportunities for disclosure and discussion are made. As Sen has argued, a 'realisation-focused understanding' of justice, given its plural grounding, cannot be done in isolation. It is 'inescapably discursive'.[1] Interviewing people on three occasions showed this scope for involvement, interaction and dialogue, as well as revealing its boundaries. A starting point to explore this scope is to deepen understanding of the

* Portions of Chapter 8 and a different version of Table 8.2 first appeared in Robyn Holder and Kathleen Daly, 'Sequencing Justice: A Longitudinal Study of Justice Goals of Domestic Violence Victims' (2017), *British Journal of Criminology*, OUP (online). Reproduced with permission.

[1] Amartya Sen, *The Idea of Justice* (Harvard UP 2009) 10, 337.

notion of the influential victim voice identified in the previous chapter. That is, to explore voice not solely as expression but as participatory. This step necessarily requires some greater attention to the notion of 'participation', its various modes and applications. Under participation's rubric, voice becomes more clearly and strongly a practice of citizenship. As citizenship practice, participation is located in diverse communicative opportunities that facilitate the exchange of information, conversation, observation, and direct and indirect engagement in a discursive and deliberative process. For citizen-victims engaged in the criminal justice process, I show that it is through these participatory practices that the multiplicity of justice goals and orientations they articulated can be sequenced.

The notion of voice and the activities of participation sharpen focus on victims' primary status as citizen. To explore this, I draw on the literature dealing with citizen participation in other areas of public life and consider what it might say to citizen participation in justice, specifically the citizen-victim. One core rationale to citizen participation is that individuals ought to be involved in and able to influence decisions that affect their multiple interests. This particular assertion is foundational in democracy theory.[2] However, the closest that democratic theory is ordinarily allowed to get to criminal justice is to claim it as a critical pillar in the architecture of liberal societies. Yet it is somehow outside the messy exercise and practice of democratic engagement. An argument of this book is that, through inclusive participatory practices, this democratic deficit in criminal justice can be addressed. To do this, I first expand on the predominant notion of citizenship-as-status, touched on in Chapters 2 and 5, in order to develop a dynamic conception of citizenship-as-practice. Whereas the former encompasses a legal and political identity that is bound by the laws of the polity, the latter provides for a more fluid as well as diverse set of actions and interactions.

CITIZENSHIP PRACTICE

Presenting victims of crime as *citizens first* necessarily gives pause on the significance and meaning of the status, and then asks what being a citizen *does*. Citizens enact their status in various vertical and horizontal

---

[2] Jane Mansbridge and others, 'The Place of Self-Interest and the Role of Power in Deliberative Democracy' (2010) 18 *The Journal of Political Philosophy* 64–100.

engagements. Formal vertical engagements, such as an electoral vote, are commonly deliberate, conscious and confined. As activities directed outward and horizontally, myriad informal actions are taken on a day-to-day basis as people go about their business. Taken together, these are the warp and weave of civic and political endeavour. While the terms 'citizen' and 'citizenship' are often merged, the latter serves a strong 'integrative function' in the discourse. It is what people are said to *do* as citizens. As a practice, citizenship does a number of things. First, it facilitates recognition and accommodation. Secondly, citizenship connotes social and political practices that constitute a thick depiction of people in their communal setting.[3] It is this thickness that ordinary people lose under the thin mantle of 'victim'.

In their various relationships to public and private authorities, citizens do not, however, have one identity or speak with one voice. Citizens can empower and oppress.[4] The political community to which citizens belong is comprised of many publics with complex and shifting identifications. Individually and collectively, citizens are polyvocal and voice their interests from and within a range of different contexts.[5] Within debates about uses of the term, one account of citizens values transparency, consultation, accountability, and individual empowerment and choice. This works well with a dual conception of the citizen-victim as consumer. Another account gives prominence to normative concerns in a 'citizen-facing agenda' that is located in public policy challenges.[6] That is, those challenges – such as achieving justice – that are declared concerns of all members of the polity. This plurality of voice and interest

---

[3] Will Kymlicka and Wayne Norman, 'Return of the Citizen: A Survey of Recent Work on Citizenship Theory' (1994) 104 *Ethics* 352, 373.

[4] Engin Isin, *Being Political: Genealogies of Citizenship* (U Minnesota P 2002).

[5] Kenneth Gergen and Mary Gergen, 'Polyvocal Organizing: An Exploration' in Chris Steyaert and Bart van Looy (eds), *Relational Practices, Participative Organizing* (Volume 7, Emerald Group Publishing 2010) 261–73.

[6] Livingstone and her colleagues' further critique particularized notions of the citizen as vulnerable and disempowered. They say that to focus on the vulnerable and marginalized within 'citizen interests' actually serves to marginalize people further as a numerical minority, and to exclude the majority of the population from the broad concept of 'citizen interest' (Sonia Livingstone and others, 'Citizens, Consumers and the Citizen-Consumer: Articulating the Citizen Interest in Media and Communications Regulation' (2007) 1 *Discourse and Communication* 63, 79–81 and 83).

is sometimes posed as problematic in conceptions of democratic citizenship. Responding to this, political philosopher Chantal Mouffe suggests that:

> … what is at stake is to make the fact that we belong to different communities of values, language, culture, and others compatible with our common belonging to a political community whose rules we have to accept.[7]

I place the idea of *making* the political community at the heart of notions of citizenship along with Mouffe's recognition that citizens are responsible or irresponsible, good or bad, active or inactive, and more commonly all of these at different times. In the various practices of making the citizen body, competing versions of 'the common good' agitate for ascendancy in particular and general situations. These versions connect to wider bodies of political theory ranging from the atomism of libertarians to the duty orientation of republicans and to the agonism of radical democrats. While these referents are an over-simplification I mean only to connect discussion about citizenship to bodies of theory, largely ignored in studies on victims and justice, which focus on the relationship between people and the state. Within this wider body of work, there is agreement that citizenship is lateral between citizens as well as vertical with the state and its institutions. Thus the citizenry are in 'continuous re-enactment' and citizenship 'aims at constructing "we"'.[8] This *practice* of citizenship is a democratic one. It is enacted in various participatory modes and arenas, does not assume arrival at a single point of 'the good', and cannot presume an end to disagreement or its domestication.[9] Whether the citizenry are oriented towards cooperation or contestation, their private and communal interests enmesh through their many activities and engagements. Participation is constitutive of democracy.

Although the roles of citizen and the activities of citizenship are most commonly claimed in relation to governmental and civic affairs, they have a long history in law and society scholarship. Writing nearly 30 years ago on legal mobilization as political participation, political scientist Frances Zemans described the legal system as 'quintessentially democratic'. 'Unlike other governmental structures', she wrote, 'the legal system is structured precisely to promote individual rather than collective

---

[7] Chantal Mouffe, 'Citizenship and Political Identity' (1992) 61 *October* 28, 30.

[8] Ibid., 30–31.

[9] Stephen Macedo (ed), *Deliberative Politics: Essays on Democracy and Disagreement* (OUP 1999).

action'.[10] As we have seen, law creates a structural opportunity for the citizenry to engage directly in a public space on issues of direct concern to them. More recently, citizen participation in criminal justice – in juries, restorative conferences, panels and in adjudication – has been described as a form of 'collaborative governance' in which those who join are 'load-bearing'.[11] Arguably, citizen participation in courts acts to buttress community confidence and hence institutional legitimacy.[12] Criminal justice entities – comprising a system – offer a series of spaces as opportunities for participation.

CITIZEN PARTICIPATION IN PUBLIC POLICY

To see what citizen participation in criminal justice might look like, we need to know how it works in other areas of public policy, to trace the historic arc of the idea, and identify some key areas of debate. First, it is noticeable how firmly the notion of participation is yoked to that of citizen. Sherry Arnstein's influential work conceptualizing a ladder of participatory levels cemented the connection. Her analysis emerged out of the 1960s and carried the zest of critical social movements of the time – civil rights and Black Power, feminism and student activism. It is perhaps not surprising therefore that she claims 'citizen participation is a categorical term for citizen power'.[13] Ian Edwards, writing at the beginning of the twenty-first century on criminal justice, captured the managerialist flavour of the age where citizens are consumers and clients to be folded gently into institutional priorities.[14] These book-ended descriptions point to citizen participation as saying something about the interface between ordinary people and entities – be they agencies of the state, public services, community organizations, political parties and even social movements. It also says something about the nature of that interface and asks what is at stake in that particular space.

---

[10] Frances Zemans, 'Legal Mobilization: The Neglected Role of the Law in the Political System' (1983) 77 *The Amer Pol Sci Rev* 690, 692–3.

[11] Albert Dzur, *Punishment, Participatory Democracy and the Jury* (OUP 2012) 162.

[12] Marijke Malsch, *Democracy in the Courts: Lay Participation in European Criminal Justice Systems* (Routledge 2009).

[13] Sherry Arnstein, 'A Ladder of Citizen Participation' (1969) 35 *Journal of the American Institute of Planners* 216–24.

[14] Ian Edwards, 'An Ambiguous Participant: The Crime Victim and Criminal Justice Decision-Making' (2004) 44 *British Journal of Criminology* 967–82.

Conceptions of Citizen Participation

Participation is a potent term used in many different contexts.[15] It is generally conceived as a means to shape the type, scope and nature of developments, policies and services to communities, but also as a means to challenge, subvert, direct and prioritize who gets what, when and how. From its social movement roots, citizen participation has always been about the 'have not's' and 'power-holders'. Participation is a means of redistributing power and resources, and has valorized citizen control, for example, in urban planning and poverty reduction. Citizen participation is also conceived as a process whereby those with a stake or interest can be identified and engaged to deconstruct and work through complex or wicked problems, and thereby arrive at acceptable or just decisions.

In social care settings, much of the contemporary discourse is emancipatory and focuses on the autonomy, inclusion and empowerment of service users.[16] Citizen participation in public health, for example, is active involvement with *and* being in control of assessing, planning, implementing and evaluating their own *and* collective health care.[17] Citizen or user participation in social care settings has emerged in recent decades to challenge experts, clinicians and providers around issues of identity, the nature and definition of the problem, the solutions on offer and the power to decide.[18] Users of services have also been characterized as consumers.[19] In this guise, participation is informed both by market-oriented ideology and user advocacy.[20] It imagines the individual actor as rationally choosing. Here, citizen users make their voices known through these choices and through their wallets. In this transactional conception, consumers are also taxpayers whose contributions are tied to their

---

[15] Andrea Cornwall, 'Unpacking "Participation": Models, Meanings and Practices' (2008) 43 *Community Development Journal* 269–83.

[16] Peter Beresford, 'User Involvement in Research and Evaluation: Liberation or Regulation' (2002) 1 *Social Policy and Society* 95–105.

[17] Caroline Mullen and others, 'The Democratic Potential of Public Participation: Healthcare Governance in England' (2011) 20 *Social and Legal Studies* 21–38.

[18] Sarah Carr, 'Participation, Power, Conflict and Change: Theorising Dynamics of Service User Participation in the Social Care System of England and Wales' (2007) 27 *Critical Social Policy* 266–76.

[19] Hugh McLaughlin, 'What's in a Name: "client", "patient", "customer", "consumer", "expert by experience", "service user" – what's next?' (2009) 39 *British Journal of Social Work* 1101–17.

[20] Catherine Bochel and others, 'Marginalised or Enabled Voices? "User Participation" in Policy and Practice' (2008) 7 *Social Policy and Society* 201–10.

utilization of specific resources. Participation in this conception is through consultation and feedback.

In whatever setting, there is general consensus that an engaged citizenry is better than a passive one.[21] And – in the reverse – that powerlessness and alienation are problems for democratic institutions. Further, there is recognition that citizens participate when something is at stake that they care about or that is important to them, and that conditions exist to enable, facilitate or legitimate their involvement. At the same time, citizens are seen to act from different identity and social spaces and to seek a range of outcomes. This broad understanding of citizen participation recognizes a mix of selfish and selfless motivation that is both instrumental and ethical. The participation of citizens in matters that affect them ranges from 'having a say', to controlling and directing the outcome.

In summary, there are different paradigms to participation (see Table 8.1 below) but in all of these the status of *citizen* is foundational. Deploying the term as a primary identification for persons as victims can work in two ways. It can provide a frame and a platform to incorporate established participation models. These then sharpen recognition that citizen participation is not a simple proposition, and that citizens occupy multiple roles. Second, it can provide stability to the relationship between persons as diverse individuals in a relation with state authority.

Within the citizen participation literature, specificity and context obviously matter a lot. The different conceptions of participation can work discretely in specific spheres and modes. However, working from the premise that citizens have multiple identities, live and act in diverse spaces, and have myriad interests that are individual and communal, civic and personal, political and social, then these paradigms of participation also overlap and interact. The question of where power lies remains of central concern; and with this, further questions about who is defining the problem(s) as well as the solution(s). These points work to illuminate the purpose of participation. That is, in what ways and with what effects is the political community of citizens enacted and made?

---

[21] Renée Irvine and John Stansbury, 'Citizen Participation in Decision-Making: Is it Worth the Effort?' (2004) 64 *Public Administration Review* 55–65.

Table 8.1 Paradigms of citizen participation

Population	Identity(ies)	Political character	Participatory sphere	Philosophy	Mode	Purpose of participation
Social movement (e.g., urban planning, environ-mental, poverty reduction, development)	Collective identity is primary Rights-based	Democratic Bottom-up	Interest-based	Redistribution of power and resources Citizen control Rights-based	Collective action Policy setting Decision-making	Redistribution of power, resources and control
Social care users (e.g., disability, HIV, mental health)	Personal identity is primary Rights-based	Emancipatory/ liberatory Bottom-up	Social welfare Social care Person-centric User-led	Empowerment Inclusion Autonomy Independence Rights-based	Collective action Individual choice Service planning Participation in decisions where affected	Redistribution of power, resources and control
Consumers Producers (e.g., health users, taxpayers, agriculture, development)	User/ producer identity is primary Consumption/ production based	New Right market orientation Top-down	System-centric Provider-led	Managerial Instrumental	Individual choice Individual involvement Consultation Feedback	Efficiency Effectiveness Economy Productivity
Citizens	Multiple identities Rights-based	Democratic Bottom-up	Multiple locations Plural interests	Accountability Inclusion Equity Equality Fair distribution of power and resources Representation	Mass action Collective action Individual action Mixed mode Participation in decisions where affected	Fair distribution of power and resources Fair inclusion

Citizen Participation in Justice

Different legal systems have long sustained various formal mechanisms for citizen participation in adjudication.[22] However and despite low levels of public confidence in them, justice systems in many countries have

[22] Malsch (n 12).

stood resolutely against the citizen participation trend. For the citizen-victim the barriers to participation are structural and normative.[23] Chapter 4 dealt with the history behind this exclusion and its contemporary justifications. In response to agitation, a range of reforms have been allowed on the margins of criminal justice. Restorative justice conferences and victim–offender mediation have been presented as forms of 'civic engagement' with social change implications.[24] Victim impact statements have been offered as expressive moments through which emotional, physical, social and material impacts are mediated,[25] and therapeutic justice initiatives purport to heal participants.[26] Reforms such as these arguably over-claim therapeutic and other benefits,[27] while initiatives aimed at the provision of information and of service have been 'relatively non-contentious'.[28] The idea of participatory rights – on a continuum from consultation to representation – remains controversial[29] while in the domains of international criminal justice and post-conflict justice the controversies are less about *whether* and more about *how* people can be encouraged to participate.[30] Reforms at the margin of domestic criminal justice systems have not challenged the fundamental distribution and structure of power to the same extent.

This constraint is noticeable in Ian Edwards' well-known characterization of victim participation in common law systems. His focus was on the legal settlement and contains two purposes for participation – getting the disposition (the substantive outcome) or not. At the non-dispositive

---

[23] Jonathan Doak, 'Victims' Rights in Criminal Trials: Prospects for Participation' (2005) 32 *Journal of Law and Society* 294–316.

[24] Albert Dzur, 'Civic Implications of Restorative Justice Theory: Citizen Participation and Criminal Justice Policy' (2003) 36 *Policy Sciences* 279–306.

[25] Antony Pemberton and Sandra Reynaer, 'The Controversial Nature of Victim Participation: Therapeutic Benefits in Victim Impact Statements' in Edna Erez and others (eds), *Therapeutic Jurisprudence and Victim Participation in Justice: International Perspectives* (Carolina Academic Press 2011).

[26] Erez and others, Ibid., 146.

[27] In the Justice Study, none of the lay participants said that they became involved in criminal justice in order to 'heal' from the traumatic effects of the incident. None indicated 'closure' as an objective that they sought (and see also, Bas Van Stokkom, 'Victims' Needs and Participation in Justice: Is There a Role for Vengeance?' (2013) 1 *Restorative Justice: An International Journal* 168–89).

[28] Doak (n 23) 295.

[29] Christine Englebrecht, 'Where Do I Stand? An Exploration of the Rules That Regulate Victim Participation in the Criminal Justice System' (2012) 7 *Victims and Offenders* 161–84.

[30] Kinga Tibori-Szabó and Megan Hirst, *Victim Participation in International Criminal Justice: Practitioners' Guide* (Asser Press 2017).

levels, he limits victim participation to the optional supply of expression, information and preference. The power-holders (though Edwards avoids the term) 'allow' or 'seek' these expressions and then they 'consider' them. Further, there is no gradation between consultation in the non-dispositive group, and control in the dispositive layer. They are singular and discrete moments. It is assumed that the ultimate aim of victim participation is to control the decision and exert authority as decision-maker. Edwards' starting assumption was that 'the victim is not in a position of inequality *vis a vis* the state'.[31] In his perspective, these are persons with power to negotiate and demand, and who have freedom to choose their level of engagement. He further assumed that the interests of the citizen-victim are one and the same as the interests of the state as delivered through criminal justice institutions.

Edwards' typology and the preceding sketch of participatory reforms sharply illuminate key points in the debate about citizen-victims' role in and relationship with criminal justice: who or what controls which decisions, when and in what circumstances. Yet this particular debate fails to attend to the complexities of citizen participation highlighted in the literature discussed in this chapter, and have also failed to engage with the density to citizen-victims' reasoning about involvement and participation. In the previous chapter these were revealed to include the uniqueness of being known and 'knowing'; as demonstrations of respect and recognition; as constituting dialogue between the individual and the entity; desires for full and 'proper' decision-making; and which recognized the power inherent in giving and receiving information (as well as being powerful in itself). The next section explores these nuances further. It asks whether voice is important and whether, through their influential voice, people wanted to control the outcome. Finally, I explore people's orientations towards participatory possibilities and how they reasoned their interest in them.

THE INFLUENTIAL VICTIM VOICE IN PARTICIPATION

In the Justice Study, the variables on voice clustered with peoples' preferred decision or outcome. For them, voice *influences*. There was a significant difference between the scale measuring influential voice with regard to the court, and the same scale with regard to police and

[31] Edwards contextualizing of the victim control proposition within certain supposed criminal justice codes in Islam is what Australians would call *dog whistling* ((n 14) 972 and 974–5).

prosecution. Participants also assessed their actual influence on police and prosecution as moderate and as weakly influential on the court. This finding that voice is differently influential could be disregarded except for its strong positive relationship to overall satisfaction, particularly in relation to prosecution and court. With regard to all three agencies, the stronger the influential victim voice, the more accepting are victims of outcomes reached by the entity. In support, a study of Dutch victims of crime found that 59 per cent would welcome the opportunity to submit a VIS, even if it did not have any impact on the sentence. However, if it were to have influence, this percentage increased to 84 per cent.[32]

Statistics like this only tell a small part of the story, however. They do not say how people thought about the nature of influence. For example, unprompted comments made by some interviewees in the Justice Study indicated they felt it would be 'improper' to have had influence on a decision-maker in their case. Analysis of participants' narrative therefore examines desires for decision control, the role of perceived expertise, perceptions of governance and norms, and evaluations about victim vulnerabilities.

Decision Control

If the influential victim voice was important, was there a desire for it to be dominant? Put more broadly, does the citizen participate in order to get what she wants? Do they aim for control? On this point, the lay participants were asked whether they agreed or disagreed that justice decision-makers (police, prosecution and judiciary) should have responsibility to decide 'in situations such as theirs'. A majority of people agreed with the statement: 88 per cent agreed that police have a responsibility to decide, 65 per cent thought so with regard to the prosecution, and 73 per cent with regard to the court. These findings are similar to other research.[33] Together the results suggest that people with a direct interest

---

[32] Discussed in Antony Pemberton and Sandra Reynaer, 'The Controversial Nature of Victim Participation: Therapeutic Benefits in Victim Impact Statements' in Edna Erez and others (eds), *Therapeutic Jurisprudence and Victim Participation in Justice: International Perspectives* (Carolina Academic Press 2011).

[33] Joanna Shapland, Jon Willmore and Peter Duff, *Victims in the Criminal Justice System* (Gower 1985); Jo-Anne Wemmers, *Victims in the Criminal Justice System* (Kugler Publications 1996); Jo-Anne Wemmers and Katie Cyr, 'Victims'

in a matter are open to 'decision by non-deliberative methods',[34] especially in a decision-making site where coercion is intrinsic if not always overt – for both civilian parties. From a dual identity as citizen-victim, the lay participants viewed constraint on their self-interest as expected and acceptable in the criminal justice space. Why and how?

Expertise, Experience, Function

When asking people why they constrained their self-interest, they reasoned in a number of ways. Strongest was the perspective that justice decision-makers were expert, trained and experienced. This expertise was both formal ('They're trained, qualified and educated and they are neutral', Polly) and lived ('Because they see different characters every day and it's their line of work and they are in the best position to make these types of decisions', Quinn). Similarly, Janelle agreed with decision-makers having responsibility 'because they know the laws better than anyone. If they think what he did was wrong then it should go ahead'. Moreover, it was 'their job', 'that's what they're there for' (Genevieve), and 'it's the police job to protect society' (Alex).

Governance

Next were wider contextual and social meanings given to the job of justice decision-makers. Svetlana emphasized collective review and responsibility in her observation that 'they are a whole group of people, not just one, who decide'. Not only was there a sense of 'if they don't [take responsibility] then who would'? (Teresa), but also 'you can't have ordinary people deciding these things. Imagine the chaos if they did' (Edward). Molly said something similar. Justice decision-makers were responsible, she said, 'otherwise you could turn around and lock up the neighbours. It is trust in the justice system'. Charlie's comment went wider to the public good focus of the justice decision-makers. They needed to be in control, he said, 'just because violence is a public crime and there are public policy concerns'.

Perspective on Restorative Justice: How Much Involvement are Victims Looking For?' (2004) 11 *International Review of Victimology* 259–74.

[34] Mansbridge and others (n 2) 68.

Normative Concerns

Reflections also related directly to the normative concerns that are constitutive of the justice concept – those of fairness, impartiality, and attention to evidence. Bailey said that the institutional responsibility of decision-making 'removes the emotional factor and allows for the most fair method of decision making'. Charlie and Imogene emphasized benefits to the parties. Charlie said they would know if the offender's 'career might be affected'. Imogene felt that 'it has to be a third party. It's the only way of protecting the person [the victim]'. Teresa reflected on the need for fairness to both parties when she said that: 'If the decision was to be made by me I wouldn't know what was reasonable or fair. I trust the system enough to know what to do, what is fair to both the parties.'

Part of the issue of fairness was that the decision-makers were seen as impartial, trained and as working within a larger frame of reference. 'They should do it for the community', was David's comment. Holly equated perceived impartiality of justice decision-makers with a dispassionate perspective. She said they were 'not emotionally involved in the situation [so] they can be objective about it. If it was left up to me, who would know?!' Others commented that decision-makers' access to more information and evidence strengthened their responsibility. As Xenia said, 'they're the ultimate decision-maker and have all the evidence in front of them'. Olivia concurred by saying, 'they are impartial and do this on the evidence'.

Victim Vulnerabilities

Finally, another strong convergence of reasoning was people's recognition of their own human frailties and that of others in a 'victim' position. Edward – even though he did not demonstrate this at all – commented that 'it would be crazy for victims to have this [responsibility to decide] because there'd be a lot of revenge and eye-for-eye stuff'. Domestic assault victims were very aware of the vulnerability and complexity inherent in their situation. Approving the police responsibility to decide in these circumstances, Imogene felt 'if the victim has [that] power then they can be influenced or persuaded or harassed or threatened to withdraw, therefore it's important that it is this way'. Furthermore, the prosecution's responsibility to decide to prosecute was vital because:

> It takes away the fear of being bullied and pressured and forced to drop the charge, which also takes away the fear of reprisal. I have no doubt that if it

> was me then I would have been subject to all amounts of pressure including a belting to get me to drop the charges.

As a victim, said Karla, 'it's easy for your mind to own some of the guilt or rationale on oneself' and in consequence to excuse or forgive the offending behaviour. 'But', she went on, 'in the light of day there's no excuse for violence. Those who are removed from the intense feelings of a relationship are in the best place to make decisions.'

For the minority who were more uncertain about police, prosecution or court having responsibility to make decisions in situations such as theirs, there was both recognition of the need for independent decision-makers combined with a desire for something more. Aimee, for example, had 'very mixed emotions' about justice authorities having decision-control. She said that 'on the one hand I felt really empowered. I got a lot of support and he was gone out of the house. But on the other hand I felt powerless and I was told there was nothing I could do'. Repeated most often on this issue was a refrain about being asked, being consulted, having views taken into account, and involving others; basically having 'some say' somewhere.

PROSPECTIVE PROCESS PREFERENCES AND THE INFLUENTIAL VICTIM VOICE

If this group of people brought multiple meanings to the idea of voice including that it be influential, but generally abjured control, how did they envisage the operationalizing of voice? To examine this question, the lay participants were asked their preferences for different resolution pathways. At Time 1 people were provided with options (in both visual and written formats) that were descriptions of real possibilities to the criminal justice process that was yet before them. The options were presented as points of judicial decision-making with a variety of participatory opportunities for the victim, including making a VIS and different restorative opportunities.[35] The latter was described as an occasion, with a trained facilitator, to discuss with the violent person what happened and what should happen next. At Time 2, after the case had finalized at court,

[35] At the time of the Justice Study, restorative opportunities in the ACT were only available after sentencing for adult criminal matters. However, pre-conviction options for a restorative encounter were put to the study participants. They were advised that these options were not actually available to them and that they were being asked in order to gain some idea of the level of interest.

people were asked if they would have liked a restorative opportunity if they had been offered it. If they answered yes, then they were asked at what stage in the process they would have liked this opportunity. Thus, the first voiced preference is prospective, and the second is retrospective. This section describes preferences only from those interviewed at Time 1 and Time 2 (N=26).

Time 1 – Prospective Justice Process Preferences

Looking ahead to the criminal justice process after police had charged the violent person and before the matter had been to court, two groups emerged in the analysis. A majority wanted formal justice resolution. These were all non-domestic assault victims and a majority of domestic assault victims. Of this formal grouping, six wanted the case to be decided at court with a guilty finding. They wanted the system to 'deal with it'. After a court finding, two equal sub-groups emerged. Eight wanted to be involved through VIS and eight said they preferred a combination of participatory and restorative opportunities. A second group of four preferred informal justice resolution. These were all domestic assault victims (see Table 8.2).

Reasoning prospective process preferences

A majority wanted formal judicial adjudication and 15 per cent preferred an informal justice process. But how did people understand and consider these participatory opportunities? What did these mean for their idea of an influential voice?

The four women in the group who expressed a preference for diversion away from the formal justice system following the police intervention wished to remain in the relationship with the person who had assaulted them. However, this was not a simple connection. Xenia felt that diversion was 'attractive because it recognises the situation may have changed from the emotion fuelled night' of the original incident. Her husband's 'rehabilitation has already started; the desired effect of the arrest has started'. She thought that 'a mediator would help us talk about where to go from here'. However, she also qualified her interest by saying that 'if he hadn't hit rock bottom and bounced back I might have a different opinion'. Roslyn's views about the process were also contingent. She had had a previous domestic assault case before the courts with the same partner. She had been troubled by the delays in the process and the consequences in her relationship. With this second incident, she preferred:

avoiding the justice system but being able to work out the dilemma that's got us to this point. The others [formal process options] are unattractive because they all involve long timeframes. If you can work it out with a facilitator, then the time would be considerably lessened.

Table 8.2 Time 1 preferred justice process (N=26)

Process options			Non-DV N=5	DV N=21	Total N=26
Informal justice process preference	Diversion (4=15 per cent)	Admission, divert and mediate	0	3	3
		Admission, restorative opportunity, no formal sentence	0	1	1
Formal justice process preference	No/minimal participation (6=23 per cent)	Finding and sentence	1	5	6
	Participation, no restorative opportunity (8=31 per cent)	Finding, VIS and sentence	3	5	8
	Participation and restorative opportunities (8=31 per cent)	Finding, restorative opportunity, no sentence	0	0	0
		Finding, restorative opportunity, court hears agreement, sentence	0	3	3
		Finding, sentence, restorative opportunity	0	1	1
		Finding, VIS, sentence, restorative opportunity	1	3	4

Source: A different version of Table 8.2 first appeared in Robyn Holder and Kathleen Daly, 'Sequencing Justice: A Longitudinal Study of Justice Goals of Domestic Violence Victims' (2017), *British Journal of Criminology*, OUP (online). Reproduced with permission.

Yvette was also interested in the possibility of working the issues through with her partner directly. She was adamant that 'in our situation I think it's wrong that people are making decisions on our behalf and not actually listening to us. All because it's got to go through "a process"!'

For the 22 who preferred a formal and adjudicated process, six people said they wanted no or minimal participatory interaction, and 16 were interested in a process with some participatory options. For the former six who were interested in the court making a finding meant there would be 'no question he is guilty' (Finn). Some expressly rejected contact and engagement with the violent person. Eliza didn't 'want to have to [deal with it]. I just don't want any contact'. Zola wanted 'it taken out of my hands' and for 'the people in the right positions to make the decisions'. Finoula didn't 'like the idea of the restorative justice'. She did not 'want to see' her ex-partner and didn't 'want anything to do with him'. Others emphasized the potential influence on the violent person of a formal court decision. David reasoned that 'people like [...] is just a "crim" so a face-to-face wouldn't do anything. He brags about being a crim. He'd play along to get a bit off his sentence'. Quinn emphasized that it was the potential impact of the public authority on the violent person that she was looking for. She said, 'the fact that I don't have to be around him and that it's done by someone who is seen to be "the law" so it sends the message to him that what he's done is not acceptable'. For these people, the formal decision by an authoritative decision-maker was of central importance.

Those interested in a VIS as a participatory opportunity after the adjudication felt that it was important for both the court and the violent person to hear about the impact of the offence on them. Edward wanted the harm done to him to be heard in addition to the case being dealt with efficiently. He said, 'the system costs a lot to us in the community so we don't want the case coming to and fro. I would like the accused person to know the effect on me'. Janelle did not want to face her ex-partner in court but she also wanted to 'tell him what it [the incident/abuse] has done and how it has made me feel'. The possibility of communication through a VIS in this manner was not simply about conveying the harm. Some saw it as an opportunity for dialogue with the decision-maker. Polly, for example, felt it was important that 'the judge hears what effects this [incident] has had on me'. She saw her potential participation as 'an opportunity to ask for what outcome I would like to see happen'. She went on to explain how the sequence of steps might work:

> For example, a 12-month suspended sentence if he breaks A, B, C, etc. Then the judge decides the sentence preferably so maybe it could be doing some good and gives a chance to make matters right. Hopefully by paper! I want to

> hear what he has to say and admits to and then I can respond and tell the judge how I feel and be able to respond and then the judge decide what is fair.

Both Alice and Nada similarly wanted the VIS to influence the decision-maker. Alice said that 'what level of impact it has made on my life now and at the time should be dealt with accordingly – which should aid their sentence'. 'They need to hear the whole history' said Nada. The magistrate 'really needs to hear from the victim to make a proper decision. There is a lot lost between what happens and reading something off a paper. If they can read a VIS and ask questions it would be good'. On the other hand, Bailey, who expressed a first preference for the court to hear his VIS and to then sentence, was more ambivalent about his input. He said:

> My preference is that I don't want to feel like … I want to feel like my impact has been heard but I don't want to feel like I'm sentencing. I don't think it is right for my personal feelings to be part of this. It is a conflict of interest. I do see the benefit of restorative justice after all of this in sorting out bad feelings and help clear the air and make sure there is nothing further there.

Of the third who expressed an interest in a hybrid mix of participatory and restorative opportunities, these were also preferred after the authoritative finding of guilt. People reasoned that culpability was then clear. For Karla, it was important that her ex-partner was 'actively taking responsibility for his actions and being part of deciding what should happen in front of me'. This would be, she said, 'quite healing for me'. She wanted the court to make a finding, then to have a restorative opportunity, and then for the court to hear the agreement and to sentence. She commented that her ex-partner had 'hatred and blame' for her and she wanted 'that responsibility to shift. The feeling of his consent to the sentence feels important. The judge can impose it but he can still not own it'. This interaction between private interests and public authority was also part of Olivia's reasoning. She preferred the same process as Karla and wanted her ex-partner to be 'found guilty and then [have] the chance to come together to talk about the impacts on me but also to work together about how to make things different in the future'. The opportunity would enable her 'to highlight the services that could help [him]. These could be agreed and then come back to the court'. In this step-by-step manner Olivia felt that she and her ex-partner would both be 'able to be heard and be heard at the sentence where our ideas are taken into account at sentence. Both [would] have a chance to influence the sentence. But if you can't then the judge would make the final sentence'.

Others emphasized that the determination of culpability also brought clarity on the wrongdoing. Winona said she preferred her assailant 'to be found guilty and then have a face-to-face. Then he can be ashamed of what he did'. Aimee reasoned that 'if there was the finding from an authority and then the mandatory phase of examining what happened and working out steps [then] it doesn't happen again'. Finn expressed something similar. 'The attractive thing,' he said was 'the judge deciding first, hears the impact and then there's the opportunity for face-to-face where there is no question he is guilty. There's no chance for crossed lines during court proceedings.' Imogene reasoned her preference for a finding, a VIS, the sentence and then a restorative opportunity by saying, 'I like the mesh between justice and mercy, between acceptance of responsibility combined with finger-waving deterrence "don't do it again"'. Views such as these almost reflect formal sentencing objectives.

In summary, the lay participants reasoned their prospective process preferences drawing on influences that were similar to their reasons for mobilizing the law. That is, possible resolution pathways were informed by situational, social, interpersonal, civic and juridicial concerns (Table 5.1 and Table 8.3).

RETROSPECTIVE REFLECTION ON PARTICIPATORY OPPORTUNITIES

Time 2 – Retrospective Justice Process Preferences

At their second interview at Time 2 everyone's case had finished at court. On this occasion participants were asked if they would have liked a restorative opportunity had it been offered. Compared to the first interview in which eight said that they would have taken the opportunity, more said they would have liked to do so at their Time 2 interview (N=15, 58 per cent). Most were domestic assault victims (N=13). Of these, eight agreed that they would 'definitely' have taken the opportunity with a further five (plus two non-domestic assault victims) indicating that 'maybe' they would have liked the opportunity. Overall, five people were unsure if they would have taken up the opportunity if it had been offered, and six said that they were not interested.

Table 8.3 Summary of prospective process preferences and reasons (Time 1)

Process preferences	Reasons
Diversion	Commitment to relationship Work through issues themselves Avoid time of justice process Wrong for others to make decisions on others' lives Rehabilitation started after arrest Help from mediator
No/minimal participation	Public authority impact on violent person Definite finding by authority – wrongfulness, clarity Just 'deal with it' – no contact, system to do it, no stress Make things worse
Participation, no restorative opportunity	Get help for violent person Get on with own life Violent person to hear impact in 'safe' space Find answers Avoid cost to community of on-going process Impact and 'whole story' to aid sentencer Dialogue with sentencer
Participation and restorative opportunities	Find guilt first – no 'crossed lines' 'Mesh of justice and mercy' Violent person to hear impact Feel part of process Violent person take active responsibility, then be part of deciding what to do Violent person to 'own' outcome Care for violent person – give information on sources of help Work out together and sentence to hear from each; work out prevention together

Analysing the 15 victims further, there were different views about when in the criminal justice process they would have been interested to participate in a restorative opportunity. Of those who preferred it coming *after* the court finding two were non-domestic assault victims and six were domestic assault victims. After a guilty finding, Finn said there would be 'no error for him arguing the fact'. Seven domestic assault victims said that they would have preferred a restorative opportunity *before* a finding. Yvette maintained this preference from her first interview. It should, she said, take place 'towards the beginning … because in the early days you are in shock but it would make a better understanding for all involved and it might give another idea other than prosecuting – maybe counselling'. She, along with two others, wanted to continue her relationship with the violent person. However, most of the domestic assault victims who would have liked a restorative opportunity had it been offered, did not want the relationship to continue.

Whether they were interested in the restorative opportunity coming before or after the guilty finding, the participants mentioned possible outcomes such as getting answers, understanding, closure, forgiveness, getting things in the open and that the violent person might realize the impacts of his behaviour and might understand his wrongdoing. For the non-domestic assault victims, the idea of a restorative opportunity appeared to provide a means of getting answers and satisfying their curiosity about why someone would have hit them. Edward said, 'I'm curious to know why. Was it entertainment for these guys?' Finn was curious 'to see his reaction and my reaction'. For domestic assault victims, there was also an interest in getting answers. Roslyn, Teresa and Polly 'wanted to know why'. Polly said, 'it ate away [at me]. It was really because it was just so aggressive.' Other of the domestic assault victims indicated that a restorative opportunity might have had an effect on the violent person.

While none mentioned an interest in apology, the participants wanted to convey the harm done to them, the consequences to others, and the wrongfulness of the violence. They expressed hope that the offender might learn or that there might be a difference develop to the relationship. Holly said a restorative opportunity might have helped 'to get everything out in the open and to sort of understand each other a bit better, why he needed to do his drink and drugs all the time. And for me to get it off my chest'. Genevieve said she would 'have liked to have gotten him to admit what he was doing was wrong or to see if he could even admit this'. Karla thought the opportunity might make her ex-partner 'realise how the violence made me feel'. Imogene would definitely have taken up a restorative opportunity had it been offered in order 'to try to get him to understand that there are consequences to others'. Deanna was interested in the way an interactive process might work for 'understanding' and that 'it would have helped give closure'. She had written to her ex-partner to forgive him for the assault but had not received a response. Deanna did not think he was 'taking it in a positive manner'.

Some felt that a restorative opportunity offered scope for more informed decision-making for themselves as principal parties as well as for authorities. Roslyn said she definitely would have taken the opportunity 'right at the outset'. She reasoned that decision-makers 'would have had information about me and about why it [the abuse] was an issue for me. We're only now talking about it and it should have happened earlier to make peace if wanted'. Olivia was also definitely interested in an early opportunity 'with a mediator'. She and her ex-partner had not had, she felt, 'an opportunity to discuss the issues, why it had happened and what the law was. He could see it wasn't me. It would be negotiation and acknowledged'.

For those 11 people who were unsure or not interested in a restorative opportunity – both domestic and non-domestic assault victims – there was a preference for keeping or extending the distance between themselves and the violent person. Alex was assaulted by a neighbour and said, 'there was no real relationship between us [so] there is nothing to "salvage" through that [restorative] conference'. He did not 'want to be involved in an on-going process. I just want [my neighbour] to get the help he obviously needs and I can get on with my life'. Nada also recognized the distance between herself and her ex-partner. She 'needed to be as removed as possible from the situation. He was such in a bad state that anything I would have done would have inflamed [him]'. For some of the domestic assault victims, concern about their safety underlay their caution about a possible restorative interaction. Winona didn't 'really have anything to say to him' and thought she would 'be a bit scared he would lash out at me again'. Ursula, who continued to live with her husband, was nonetheless cautious. He remained, she said, 'a bit unpredictable'. They had talked together when he was in hospital, but outside those confines she 'felt a bit unsure, unsafe'. Others who were unsure or not interested in a restorative opportunity commented that the violent person would not have been genuine or would have been manipulative, blaming or threatening in a restorative interaction. David, assaulted by a neighbour, said that the assailant 'was happy about what he did. There'd be no point. He was just smiling all the way through'. Lorraine said her ex-partner was 'very good at putting on a front especially when it comes to guilt. He's a very good actor'. Svetlana just said, 'no'. Compared to those who saw some potential in a restorative opportunity, these participants were concerned about their own safety and saw little evidence about readiness to change on the part of the violent person.

People's positive interest in participation in the justice process at Time 2 is discussed here primarily through their perspective on restorative opportunities as part of formal decision-making. They perceived the level of involvement they chose as entirely legitimate and reasonable. They saw their influencing voice as conveying information, impact and consequences both to the violent person and to the public authority. Participation as a set of practices carried multiple ideas and was clearly intended to enhance the justice process and not to derail or divert it.

Moreover, the lay participants recognized the unique character of the decision-making spaces in which they were engaged. They understood and accepted constraint on their role as necessary and even welcome.

REFLECTING ON JUSTICE FOLLOWING PARTICIPATION

Time 3 – Retrospective Reflection on Justice

The Time 3 interviews took place six to eight months after the case had finished at court. Of the 26 interviewed twice, 19 remained to be interviewed on a third and final occasion. Of these, five were non-domestic assault victims and 14 were domestic assault victims. Their original motivation in mobilizing the law had been largely realized: 84 per cent said that they felt safe and, of domestic assault victims, 57 per cent said that there had been no further violence. A majority (58 per cent) agreed with the statement that 'the justice system intervention has had an impact in stopping the violence against me' (of domestic assault victims the figure was 64 per cent).

At the end of this particular criminal justice journey the idea of justice emerged humbled and somewhat hobbled in its institutional form. When asked if they felt involved enough in the case during the criminal process: 58 per cent said they were, 42 per cent said they were not and 16 per cent were unsure. Just over half (53 per cent) agreed that 'justice had been done', 37 per cent did not agree and 11 per cent were unsure. In Finn's view, 'it would be a good thing if [justice] works. I know why the statue is blind. It doesn't have favouritism one way or another, victim or criminal. I don't know if that's a good thing. I know it's a way to get society to function'. From Teresa's perspective the idea of justice was 'so broad and there are so many areas of grey … the law applies to different cases in different ways even though the laws are the same'. This slipperiness to the nature of justice left Janelle 'not really sure' and Nada 'a little confused'. Some people struggled to contain its meaning: 'to me justice … you say the word and you know almost what it means', said Edward. Holly also felt that 'it's hard to explain. Justice would be to protect the victim and to try and help the person who did it fix themselves up, to rehabilitate them'. David was sure 'it's not like the movies or TV. It's based on money and circumstances'.

At the same time, the idea of justice as a multi-criterion subject was sustained. Thinking on the question harder, Edward said justice meant:

> there's an action and a reaction. Something that's fair and equitable. Something that helps get the victim back together and to feel protected and safe to go back into society. And for the perpetrator – a bit of a wake-up call that you can't perform like that.

Aimee's reflections emphasized justice working in multiple ways over time. She said:

> I think it's being confronted, that I am made aware that the perpetrator has been made to confront in a court of law the seriousness of his actions in a time frame that doesn't infringe on my rights and is compelled to continue to assess the consequences of these actions over 12 months or so that's suitable to the gravity of the crime. And that there are change behaviour techniques interwoven into that follow-up.

Svetlana reflected that she had 'learned everyone has a different idea [of justice] and everyone interprets it so differently it's ironic'. There is a way in which her comment captures the way both justice and participation are demanding of citizens. Both ask people to consider possibilities other than their own and to step up to something more – even something higher – without presuming eventual agreement or consensus.

PARTICIPATION AND SEQUENCING

Interviewed on three occasions the lay participants in the Justice Study expressed multiple justice goals that were directed three ways: towards themselves as the victim, to the offender and to their community of others. Yet the multiple goals expressed at Time 1 raised questions of which comes first and how they could be realized. The social dilemma created within the space and ideation of justice asks for 'selfish' individual objectives to be accommodated in addition to a 'joint payoff' for a wider good.[36] However, a way through the social dilemma was illuminated through the prospective longitudinal research methodology of the study. The process preferences expressed at the beginning and at the end of the criminal process and the reasoning associated with these show how sequencing can work.

---

[36] David Schroeder and others, 'Justice within Social Dilemmas' (2003) 7 *Personality and Social Psychology Review* 374. An earlier study examining the role of voice in conflict resolution procedures found that, controlling for other factors, participants prefer procedures that offer the most voice (Robert Folger and others, 'Elaborating Procedural Fairness: Justice Becomes Both Simpler and More Complex' (1996) 22 *Personality and Social Psychology Bulletin* 435–41).

Given the opportunity to speak on more than one occasion over time and participants described multi-faceted goals. These combined procedural and substantive elements. While there was consistency to victims' justice goals, different ones came to the fore at different time points or were given different emphases at the three interview points. In particular, at both the beginning and end of the justice process and expressed at Time 1 and Time 2, there was consistent priority placed on offender accountability. This objective worked as a core motivation to mobilize the law and as a primary threshold goal for the court. Offender accountability also worked as a process point. Participants' prospective preference for a resolution pathway was for a formal decision-making process in which the criminal court could find the violent person guilty (is brought to account). Their retrospective preference showed a higher interest in the possibility of a restorative opportunity and that this, in the main, could take place after the formal guilty finding by a court. That is, the offender be brought to account and then discursively engaged in accepting responsibility (is held to account). Participants' interest in composite sentencing options grounded their concerns for the objects of their justice trilogy. At Time 3, offender accountability comprised a thread to overall justice judgments about the function, purpose and performance of criminal justice.

Looking more closely at the sequencing of participatory preferences, it was *after* attaining formal accountability through a guilty verdict or finding that people felt able to contemplate more interest in different configurations of opportunities. In the Justice Study these were giving a VIS and/or some restorative engagement. In reality of course, these are not the only ways victims can participate in criminal justice. Reporting the incident to police and giving witness testimony are two others. But for some of the study participants the opportunities offered additional ways to communicate with the violent person and/or to public authorities. On the former, the opportunity to communicate, as an example, the impact of the violence contributed to an individual's justice goal of specific deterrence. On the latter, participants saw their interaction as informing or assisting the court to arrive at decisions that were appropriate, responsive, equitable and holistic to both parties and to the wider community. Still others expressed their interest in interactive opportunities as an engagement with both the violent person and the public authority. This triangulation of interaction was focused on that institution most associated with the idea of justice by ordinary people: the court. People's goals communicated private and public interests for which they gave reasons that were both instrumental and ethical.

Within the temporal and procedural space of the court, it is the sequencing of steps in the process that facilitates this sequencing of justice objectives. Sequencing enables the ordering of justice objectives or priorities. Citizen-victim participation in justice is not, therefore, a singular moment; but neither is it easily contained. Their interest is clearly in the give and take of information and reflection in a decision-making flow. The possibility of greater participation expressed *after* the trauma and shock of victimization and *after* formal adjudication provides important information. Not only is the formal criminal justice system valued for its authority to interrupt and stand against the violence, but it then demarcates a boundary for possible future dialogue.

This account therefore argues that, arriving at an *idea* and a *sense* of justice that is deep, broad and rich, requires interaction and dialogue. Amartya Sen argues that,

> understanding the demands of justice is no more of a solitarist exercise than any other human discipline … not only are dialogue and communication part of the subject matter of the theory of justice … it is also the case that the nature, robustness and reach of the theories proposed themselves depend on contributions from discussion and discourse.[37]

The architecture of criminal justice that is placed around the resolution of a violent event does not necessarily oblige that a particular objective is prioritized over another. What is required is enabling different multiple objectives to be articulated, and then accommodating these in a step-by-step manner. It is simply not necessary to pose multiple objectives and different actors as in perpetual and irreconcilable conflict.

CONCLUDING DISCUSSION

In centring the victim on their status as a *citizen first*, what has been illuminated in this discussion about their voice and participation? Most obviously, there are all the activities that institutions assume without much acknowledgment: reporting, attending, meeting, and being available for authorities. But what else is added to the vocabulary of citizenship? Definitely there is speaking up and being involved where voice and being heard constitute a form of civic practice. But there are other contributions to this unique democratic practice that are more socially and politically situated. That is, adding specificity to certain

37 Sen (n 1) 88–9.

social and legal norms, playing a part in public discourse about the nature of the common good, participating in re-calibration of inter-connectedness, and advancing inclusive justice to notice a few. In the wider public policy context of citizen participation these practices of citizenship are prized. Through their involvement in criminal justice, citizen-victims are able to convey complex messages about what happened, why it happened, the after-effects and implications, and what they seek for the future for themselves, the offender and for others. Their various interests – as social group members, users, consumers, taxpayers, and as witness and victim – can be accommodated under the citizen mantle. They do not have to choose or be forced to choose. Similarly, they are not required to perform a particular representation of how a victim of violence should appear.

This chapter has shown that participatory justice is a *series* of processes and interactions in which matters of importance to the victim, the violent person and the community at large unfold. Viewed in this light, the justice process comes more clearly into view as a (potentially) deliberative one involving citizens and justice decision-makers. The idea of citizen *power* that Arnstein equates with citizen participation we then see not as power *over* but power *to*. Citizens here are not passive and external, but as people with agency, intimately connected to achieving a just outcome in a just process. That is, as people whose voice is influential in settling matters of importance to them in their community. Justice in its institutional manifestation becomes a creative space for citizens to engage with each other and with authorities, and to deliberate what is fair and just.

In this context, influence means influence and not control. Citizen-victims' interest is in an interactive and communicative dialogue with decision-makers in which features of both their victim status and their citizen identities are respected. Their reasoning and reflections recognize the particular nature of the decision-making spaces and the multiple civic values (fairness, equality, efficiency) that inhabit these. They accept constraint on their self-interest which, in this unique public domain, is not abnegation of self. In the 'distinctive enterprise of living together' self-constraint requires recognition, adjustment and the likelihood of incomplete resolutions.[38] This version of inclusion is demanding of citizens. Interviewing people three times in the Justice Study over the course of the criminal process revealed a shift from them expressing (as

[38] Anthony Duff, 'Towards a Theory of Criminal Law?' (2010) 84(1) *Aristotelian Society Supplementary Volume* 1, 5.

any of us might) a general opinion about the 'idea of justice', to thinking hard about it. They had to. Justice as a deliberative and participatory process asks people what they really think and what they really think in this particular circumstance. Asking about their reasoning opens the deliberative space further. This is hard work on people and work that takes time. But it is work which nurtures judgment and decision in citizens.[39] Their justice *interests* are expansive multi-criterion and multi-dimensional concerns that connect to a trilogy of interests. What they bring from their private world is codetermined with public concerns.

In claiming that justice is not a solitarist exercise, John Dryzek says that Sen has 'made democracy central' to justice. In this democratic evocation, citizens' voices are multi-faceted. They are constituted as being influential, and as saying something about their identities and their connections and disconnections to the social world. Their involvement rests on the 'core principle' that those 'affected' – those with a direct interest in a matter – ought to be involved.[40] The voices of citizen-victims are made manifest in the criminal justice process *because* of this democratic principle.

---

[39] Benjamin Barber, *Strong Democracy: Participatory Politics for a New Age* (U Cal P 1984).

[40] John Dryzek, 'The Deliberative Democrat's Idea of Justice' (2013) 12 *European Journal of Political Theory* 329, 330, 334.

9. After the democratic turn

> You need to have time to think. It can't be a heat of the moment but also not too long that it's forgotten. (Bailey, 2011)

> Understanding the demands of justice is no more of a solitarist exercise than any other human discipline ... . (Sen, 2009, 88–89)

In this book I have surfaced more complex conversations about justice than people as victims are usually allowed. I used a number of different lenses through which to read their ideas about justice; ideas sharpened at moments of conflict and within a criminal justice process. The lenses have filtered ancient and contemporary thought through more vernacular frames, and have illuminated concerns demanding the attention of justice. Seeing through the eyes of citizen-victims has revealed justice as a means of critical evaluation, a standard of assessment, an inclusive structure, as a communal construct, and as an improbable horizon. Working towards justice was, for those in this study, frustrating, agitating, puzzling and demanding. That they were prepared to be involved in a process intended to achieve justice is a core feature that enlivened this book.

It is well known that people who are victimized by violence and who engage with the criminal justice system usually find the experience unsatisfactory and bruising. On this point, scholars, legal officials, victim advocates and even the general public can agree. What flows from this recognition diverges widely. Some want to abandon formal criminal justice, some argue to graft ameliorative processes to the larger framework, and some in institutional elites maintain orthodox continuity. Underpinning these disparate visions are much larger debates about the values and reasoning that people ascribe to actions, about cooperation or conflict models of society, the role of criminal law in social and political systems, and the nature and extent of state authority over peoples. Threaded through it all are questions about the involvement of ordinary people in formal decision-making on matters in which they are directly affected. In this concluding chapter I draw on these deep debates to indicate the significance of this book.

It was the critical insights afforded by Amartya Sen's idea and analysis of justice in the real world that enabled me to refigure and reconceptualize what had become a confused and somewhat toxic clash about victims and criminal justice. But I extended Sen's framework by drawing on other ideas regarding direct interests in deliberation, and on democracy and difference. In this concluding chapter, I briefly summarize the findings of the Justice Study and then consider their implications for theory, law and policy. In closing, I contemplate future lines of inquiry that arise from the tensions inherent in deliberating injustice.

REVISITING THE BEGINNING

Having commenced the Justice Study worrying over the procedural treatment of people who were victims of violence, their voices stilled me to listen more closely to what they were saying about the nature of justice itself. In many ways their bewilderment in encountering a system that was both familiar and foreign mirrored my own confusion about its justifying arguments. Talking with the 33 people who were the bedrock to the research encouraged me to go below the surface in search of what was really at stake. Returning to speak with many of them over several months showed how potent is the Gramscian assertion that ordinary people are philosophers of their everyday lives. It was this journey of reflection that pointed me towards justice as deliberation.

Ultimately, the book amplifies these voices from below – in all their diversity and complexity – in a place where power-holders circumscribe who may speak, when and how. Being heard, however, is more than a platitude. This is the challenge that citizen-victims acting to shape their individual and communal lives make of justice institutions in a democracy. I argue for the capacity and the right of the citizen to speak frankly and with dignity,[1] and accepting that no one is all good or always innocent. I imagine acknowledgement of citizen-victims as members of a political community where collective and individual interests can be accommodated; and where plurality and contestation may work towards that accommodation but not oblige it. I understand that some injustices in actual lives may not be amenable to the comprehensive outcome that Sen theorizes. I expect it is a particular challenge for criminal justice systems

[1] That dignity is absolutely central to individual evaluations of their interaction with authorities is a point made eloquently by Lucie White in 'Subordination, Rhetorical Survival Skills, and Sunday Shoes: Notes on the Hearing of Mrs G' (1990) 38 *Buffalo Law Review* 1–58.

to be open to the indeterminate. Nonetheless, I emphasize the obligation of the state (here through its justice institutions) to ensure conditions for the active participation of citizens in matters in which they have a direct stake; but also because it should and must check its own power. I join emphatically with Iris Young in prioritizing inclusion as a fundamental ideal of democratic citizenship and decision-making in a democratic society.

Recognizing the citizen status of the victim enabled this democratic turn. Through this lens, criminal justice is reframed as a civic institution that is – or should be – deferential to the people it serves. Introducing the *demos* to criminal justice, however, does bring inconvenience, uncertainty, contradiction and ambiguity. They are unruly and difficult to contain. All of these are things that the modernist project of institutional justice (represented in this book by public prosecutors) seeks to replace with consistency, regularity and stability. The narrowing and concentration of power that public prosecution has accrued, with token formal checks, is a manifestation of 'de-democratisation'[2] from older, more participatory roots. Challenging this trend certainly raises a counter-argument about populist justice. Acknowledging the (entirely predictable) manner in which media and politicians conjure menacing majorities or oppressive opinion does not detract from the main point, however. Inflammatory representations of victim, victimhood and visions of public order mask authentic complexities. It obscures many publics with an abstract singular public. Perhaps worst of all, it confuses direct affected interest with majoritarian clamour.

THE ARGUMENT IN BRIEF – JUST INTERESTS

Justice emerges from injustice and as means and a measure to address it. Justice acts as an imaginary that opens and orders action(s) but does not drive it. In the public space designated for matters that seek justice, people victimized by violence speak in an expanded frame that is inhabited by three key areas of concern – victim, offender and their community of others. These relational and communal concerns reveal private and public interests as constitutive and co-determining.

To these three domains, the victim – posed as a citizen first – brings multiple goals that follow offender accountability, and which are grounded in reasoning that reflects private and public interests. The

[2] Charles Tilley, *Democracy* (CUP 2007) 59.

citizen-victim draws on public policy narratives about ending violence and places their personal desire to be safe within that frame. They bring with them a further public policy outlook that justice institutions will do their jobs, be fair and efficacious. Yet their expectations are uncertain. In reasoning their motivations, goals and expectations in the different decision-making moments of the criminal justice process, citizen-victims comment through moral commitments *and* contemplate what might occur in the future. The conceptions of justice that influenced victim goals were normative and spoke of duty and of accountability.

Behind flat statements of satisfaction or dissatisfaction with justice lie a number of dimensions that constitute an integrated justice judgment. These reveal the premium placed on fair outcome, fair and respectful treatment of victim and of the offender, and for an influential victim voice. Conceptions of justice that were context sensitive and contingent operated to calibrate these judgments. In a further iteration of the interactive nature of private and public, citizen-victims indicate preferences for a range of participatory opportunities while deferring to public authorities as decision-makers. These opportunities denote occasions when citizenship becomes demanding. That is, where a person's everyday opinion on what is just must evolve to actual expressions with real consequence for all concerned. In these circumstances, principles of fairness, equality, respect and recognition underpin citizen-victims' views about participation.

As a set of findings, none settles argument about what the constituency of victims of violence want, nor identifies the correct emphasis to place on proper treatment or substantive outcome. Law is neither wholly certain nor a simple solution in this argument. Instead, the significance of the book lies in part on laying out the complexity of justice in real lives, and showing that the different philosophical approaches to justice do not only reside in libraries. I am aware that the ways in which I have examined justice in this book should arguably be separated – that is, justice as normative value, justice as judgment, justice as standard, and justice as institution. However, in real lives in a real and complex process, such separations slip. People confronted with radical particularity must step up to give opinion, respond to options, puzzle, think, reason, manage emotional states, and deliberate what justice means to them and to those around them. They do not want a single thing; they want a lot of things. We cannot arrive at a sense of deep justice through one moment.

VICTIMS, LAW AND JUSTICE REVISITED

This brief snapshot of the main arguments arises from five areas of detail in the Justice Study: institutional depictions of justice; of victims as 'ordinary people' in a particular location; the diverse goals articulated over three time points to the ultimate goal of achieving justice; experiences of police, prosecution and court; and peoples' preferences for different participatory opportunities.

Mapping Institutional Justice

The institutional logics to criminal justice dominate public discussion about the place of victims. These logics conceal where power resides in criminal justice and, at the same time, drive how it works. Posed as commonplace administrators on the one hand and as exercising sovereign prerogative on the other, public prosecutors exemplify the institutional logic of the state in criminal justice. Theirs is an extraordinarily powerful role. Yet I could not spend a couple of hours in deep discussion on a subject about which they are passionate, and not also see good people. Good people putting their intellect, compassion and expertise to work. As good people they could not, however, say the unsayable – that individual members of the public are sacrificed to this work.

I am conscious of the irony in using the reflections of this elite group, good people though they are, in a depersonalized single narrative form. In the public realm it is usually they who have individual identity and substance. Through the interviews with ex-Directors, and ex- and serving senior prosecutors, I showed how their selective telling of certain historical transitions has silenced a more complex account of the evolution and invocation of criminal law and criminal justice. That is, one in which private citizens authored their own story of prosecution, messy and partial as it undoubtedly was. While the institutional birth of public prosecution is very recent, prosecutors nonetheless have attached themselves to an extended master narrative that maps to a civilizing trajectory. They project a discourse of benign competence, inevitability and naturalness. To this image of the benevolent mandarin, prosecutors add the language of high principle. The assertion of independence connects them to visions of integrity. The claim to represent community diverts scrutiny of them; just as custodianship of public interest suggests democratic authenticity. Essential to what is in essence an authoritarian discourse is seemingly opposing depictions of a public that is vulnerable and in need of protection, and a public that is vengeful. The benign prosecutor stands central to the management of both/either.

It is through the claim to *be* the entity representing public *with* the mandate to determine who and what among the publics are legitimated, *plus* definitional authority on what constitutes the interests of that public that the unique ideological power of prosecution achieves pre-eminence. As discourse it compels universal acceptance. As ideology it masks hegemony. As hegemony it makes itself felt in the day-to-day exercise of unfettered discretion. But does this practice of discretion always work to the interest of institutional power? Discretion is, after all, responsiveness to case circumstance. It takes place within a gap in the rules where the public prosecutor, representing the state and its own idea of common good, may appear merciful or may disadvantage individual members of the public.[3] It masks the fact that prosecution decision-making is absolute and essentially without review. The rights-bearing citizen-victim is simply impossible to recognize, whereas there is no doubt that the accused has rights. For prosecutors, the idea of justice became simply a calculation of risk and benefit. Ironically, institutional constraint meant that their reflections on justice were less resonant with the philosophical ideal than were those of lay people.

However, the gap in which prosecutor and citizen-victim interact and where discretion plays out is richly textured. Considerable diversity of characterization and experience inhabit prosecutors' anecdotes about their work with victims and offenders. That which is posed as rigidly formal is actually riven with informality. In their day-to-day practice prosecutors experience the generic and abstract figure of the public to be deeply marked by private tragedies and transgressions. Legal formality requires a particular modelling of these private affairs of citizens but it cannot change their essential informal nature. Pierre Bourdieu's suggestion that the distinction between public and private is over-determined therefore works two ways. He illuminates those, such as the prosecutors, who benefit from boundary setting. But he also invites us to look the other way, to notice the constitutive nature of public and private as it emerges in the public realm of criminal justice.

Ordinary People and Citizens

Looking down from above – as prosecutors do – people who are victims come from a private elsewhere and enter a public somewhere. Essentially,

---

[3] The alleged offender and the victim, both being citizens, are disadvantaged if a prosecution proceeds or if it does not. Sometimes the disadvantage to each is similar and sometimes not. It may be argued that proceeding to prosecute is more likely in the victim's interests. However, this is a contestable proposition.

the individual becomes a tool for their larger project. Rather than articulate this, splintered pictures of the victim fill the public space.

In various realms – of the legal official, academia and wider society – these victim splinters are rendered as pathetic or punitive in others' media and political wars. Stepping away from this noise takes effort. The borrowed terms of 'ordinary people' and 'citizen' enabled a view of people as more than their transitional victim status. I wanted to follow Amartya Sen's urging that a theory of justice must account for actual lives in the real world. In the first iteration as 'ordinary', the latent structure of people's values, attitudes and beliefs showed them embedded within a social world that was both various and regular. As ordinary people, the participants had varied lives and histories, and different engagements with the civic world. They are part of a larger mass. By connecting people to this mass I made a pronounced distinction between them and power-holders such as public prosecutors. With this distinction in place, naming them next as *citizen* married social status with political status. As a definitional concept, describing victims as 'citizens first' opened a larger space in which the lay participants could talk about their ideas of justice.

At the second and third interviews with victims, the intensity of the incident and police intervention was subsumed by a different tone of comment about prosecution and court. I was struck by how consistently people would acknowledge that officials have a job to do, and then go on to ask for something more individual to their circumstance. They wanted account taken of their questions, requirements, requests and reasons. At the same time, they were acutely aware of the public function and duties of the various institutions. As citizens do, they thought of the particular *and* the general – a characteristic that is deep in ideas of justice.

In terms of their personal values, beliefs and attitudes about criminal justice the lay participants in the Justice Study were not so different to the wider Australian population. They felt a strong commitment to the moral obligation of the law even though some had mixed histories with legal and welfare authorities. However, they were significantly more muted in their confidence in criminal justice. In this too they were similar to other Australians. When faced with decisions in circumstances in which their agency was circumscribed, these latent features were influential. But their beliefs were also unstable. If people expected the criminal justice system to be fair, they also expected fairness to be discharged unevenly and differentially. Other elements contributing to individual decision-making to mobilize the law after the violence were an emotional, cognitive and contextual mix generated by the incident and its aftermath plus various interactions with significant others and with authorities. Through these influences, men and women were informed by reasoning that was relational and communal, and that linked to public policy appeals that violence was wrong and not to be tolerated. This wider orientation showed that 'thinking like a citizen' did not oblige people to discard their own interests. The idea of justice may act to engage people's 'ethical identity' in a unique and pivotal manner.[4]

People constructed their idea of justice from different standpoints. As disinterested citizen, they saw criminal justice through its potent symbols, and in an assessment of its efficacy, as acknowledgment of its multiple governance functions, and finally in evaluation of its performance of certain norms that are core to the wider ideal. Untangling this imaginary showed justice to have concrete manifestations, performances and idealizations. In this latter form, the ideal elements of justice – fairness, equality, respect for all, and neutrality – are clearly compelling to lay people. However, they are also viewed as contingent and ambiguous in the real world.

Exploring Justice Goals

If the justice imaginary is unstable, then mobilizing law is made with a hesitant step. Law is one among a number of options after violence and its mobilization is discretionary. It is a structural opportunity infused with drawbacks as much as with possibilities. To this opportunity the citizen-victim brings multiple goals. Asking people what they wanted and why at different points in the justice process and at different times revealed how the idea of justice lived and moved.

The emotional and physical after-effects of violence were significant, although different in intensity and degree among the lay participants. Between the first and second interviews, victims' feelings of anger and fear towards the person who had used the violence lessened. However, there was no change in the ascription of intentionality to that person. Having been motivated to seek justice through the experience of injustice, people's sense of a wrong done did not diminish over time. The desire for the wrong to be *brought to account* and for persons to be *held to account* was strong for the citizen-victim. Reasoning here was deontological in character. I conclude that offender accountability is a unifying threshold condition for justice and one that is sustained over the course of multiple encounters with different justice entities.

---

[4] Nathan Harris, 'Shame, Ethical Identity and Conformity: Lessons from Research on the Psychology of Social Influence' in Susanne Karstedt and others (eds), *Emotions, Crime and Justice* (Hart Publishing 2011).

But if accountability is a starting point for the realization of justice, is it also an end? On this point the idea of justice shifted to thinking about consequence. Here the lay participants articulated diverse reasons for seeking justice. These were instrumental and non-instrumental, personal and public. They were consistent in the abstract as well as the concrete. Their goals were directed towards three domains: the victim; the offender; and their community of others. This trilogy of interests represented different objects of value to which the good of justice was to be directed. Taken together, these interests, sub-goals and reasons constitute what Sen calls 'plural grounding' for justice. Associating the idea of justice to each in the trilogy triggered expansive thinking. In asking about justice, people necessarily thought of others.

This point then complicates the proposition that achieving justice for the victim is getting what they want, or getting their outcome preference. If getting a favourable outcome is something that is personally beneficial, then can this work with the different objects to which justice is directed? Part of the answer to this puzzle is Sen's argument that the plural grounds for justice can be 'partially ordered'. Interviewing people three times in a prospective longitudinal panel showed their multiple goals to be sequenced. They did not change as much as unfold and deepen. The priorities of one person are different to those of another and for different reasons. However as a group, the lay participants wanted the court to arrive at composite sentences that were protective, rehabilitative and that drew on the authority of the court. They prioritized principles of rehabilitation, specific deterrence and victim protection. As a group they drew on reasons that were private as well as reasons that were communal. Yet each sequenced or ordered all of these features differently.

Plurality, ordering and sequencing illuminated a further puzzle. The lay participants were asked questions about getting the outcome they wanted, whether they were satisfied with the outcome, and whether justice was done. There was complexity and contradiction in just about every person's responses. People even said that the sentence (as one manifestation of outcome) was 'about right' when it was not what they wanted. Clearly contrary positions appear to survive. In puzzling this complexity, what was revealing in people's reflections at their final interview was a sense of incomplete resolution. That is, that the interests of the offender and the community were accounted for in the justice deliberation, but not those of the victim. As ordinary citizens, people carry, interpret and manage their own and others' ideas about justice as a multi-directional conception. Their commentary is informationally rich and infused with relational and emotional content which responds to shifts in context and emphasis. Reasoning their motivations and goals showed people thinking from moral commitments and as consequentialists. There is an oscillation that works between these two modes of thinking about justice that is particularly noticeable in interactions where people are provided with a number of interactive occasions and a number of probes.

Experiencing Justice

But justice is not only imagined, it is also experienced. This experience is usually measured as satisfaction or dissatisfaction. What lies behind these assessments are procedural and substantive elements that interacted strongly in an integrated conception of justice. Moreover, over the three interviews, people's justice judgments were context sensitive as well as malleable and fluid. Rather than ascribe 'single motives or simple frames' at singular moments to human behaviour, people are 'both flexible and complex' in their thinking about justice.

However, the procedural and substantive approaches helped to unpack understanding what ordinary people say is fair and just. These constructions were active, dynamic and interactive within criminal justice and within people's wider social context. The interactions with authorities were moments during which ideas about justice could be experienced and enacted, and which then flowed into the next interface. Satisfaction with police was significantly higher than satisfaction with prosecution, court and with the justice system overall. However, different dimensions, consistent with the literature, underlay assessments. These criteria of outcome acceptance, the quality of interpersonal treatment, an influential victim voice, and respect for offenders' rights showed the experience of justice was multi-layered. These components fluctuate in importance but all were present in assessments about the three justice agencies. For all three justice agencies, the strongest positive correlation with overall satisfaction was with outcome acceptance and the quality of the interpersonal treatment. But the elements also linked strongly with each other in differing ways. Outcome acceptance and interpersonal treatment correlated strongly together; and the influential victim voice connected strongly with outcome acceptance for all three agencies. While the elements can be separated, they are not separate. Rather, they form supple dimensions.

Moreover, these different dimensions were nuanced in highly contextualized and particularized reflection from lay participants. The emphases people placed on the quality of their interpersonal treatment embraced recognition of their unique standing and circumstances, as well as respect for their personhood. Respect and recognition were demonstrated through the manner in which information was or was not provided by authorities.

Citizen-victims experienced information as a power resource. They also understood interaction with authorities as dialogue. The strong expectation for fairness in criminal justice that people had articulated at their first interview emerged on later occasions in how they experienced equitable and fair treatment of themselves as well as of the violent person.

Justice as the attainment of outcome was experienced in a number of ways. The reflections people offered went to the trilogy of interests they articulated at the commencement of their engagement with authorities. At the same time, these considerations sharpened at the second interview to focus primarily on the nature, appropriateness and impact of the sentence on the violent person, and the consequences to themselves and others. In an echo of their initial citizen evaluations about justice, at their third and final interview people pondered the extent to which the outcome calibrated with the normative and governance functions of justice. Perhaps inevitably, the resolutions they experienced were partial and incomplete.

Participating in Justice

The nature and reach of citizen-victims' voice underpinned justice judgments. The lay participants assessed their voice as moderately influential with police and prosecution and weakly influential with the criminal court. As a composite scale, the influential victim voice showed strong and significant positive correlation between overall satisfaction with prosecution and with court.

People's narratives signalled voice to be a unique set of practices and not only as expression. They indicated that being heard was to be recognized as someone with distinctive and important insight into particular circumstances. To be heard was about influence that was meaningful; to be heard by authorities was a way of connecting 'the victim' to their different publics. To be heard was to have and to experience an influential voice embodied in the dual status of citizen-victim. Notwithstanding the stress placed on the *influence* of voice, people did not wish to supplant or dominate decision-makers. They deferred to their expert status, to the experience and to the distinctive roles of authorities. In deferring they also referred to values constitutive of justice: fairness, impartiality and attention to evidence. They understood constraint in a unique public space.

These demanding expectations of justice that the longitudinal interviews revealed also raised questions about how these could be met and were actually met. At their Time 1 interview, the majority of citizen-victims indicated a preference for a formal resolution process and for the criminal court to make a guilty verdict. This particular decision is of course central to their desire for offender accountability. A majority also preferred that this formal process include some participatory opportunities. Of those who did indicate an interest in these as opportunities, whether expressive or restorative or both, it was predominately for something *after* the court finding and *after* the formal sentence. Interest in these opportunities was grounded in desires for the decision-maker as well as the offender to listen, to hear and to understand issues that referenced private and public concerns.

At their Time 2 interview (after the case had finalized) more people were prepared to consider a restorative opportunity *had it been offered.* Central to this interest was a desire to find answers, and to interact with both the offender and with the decision-maker. Through interaction, people felt they would have been able to convey messages about the harm, the wrongfulness, the consequences, and what was hoped for in the future. Restorative justice theorists emphasize these messages as healing and as flowing between victim and offender. However, only one person mentioned healing, few were interested in apology and their interest in interaction triangulated between victim, offender and the public authority. Nonetheless, to the idea of sequencing justice goals, can be added sequenced steps towards achieving justice.

At the end of their justice journey, only a third of those participants interviewed on all three occasions expressed overall satisfaction with the handling of the case by the justice system. In their reflections on what the idea of justice now meant to them they pondered its slippery nature. At the same time, their remarks affirmed the terms' expansive capacity. That is, they spoke again of the different objects of value that come within justice's realm, the many criteria embedded within it, and its ability to accommodate the ordering and sequencing of priorities.

AFTER THE DEMOCRATIC TURN

So where does the democratic turn to this book take debate about victims and justice? First, it must be recognized that people who become victims of violence exist as *citizens* in a social space and as members of a political community before, during and after their engagements with criminal justice authorities. The political character of citizen status then argues for a more humble set of institutions, and for attention to the nature and meaning of the claims that citizens make. Here the standing of persons is not a legal construct. Moreover, it says that to exclude affected persons with a direct interest in a matter from its resolution is profoundly anti-democratic.[5]

From this point comes a second one, that *citizens* have a range of interests in how justice is seen and done. Their justice interests look to different objects of value, and integrate a number of dimensions. When they interact on an individual basis with justice institutions their personal interests surface but do not eradicate continuing attentiveness to public values and concerns. Thus private and public are not – as both orthodox and restorative justice advocates claim – in essential and irreconcilable conflict.[6] Rather, they are constitutive and co-determining. In interpreting what is a wrong, one does not exist without the other. In accepting complex accountabilities, what is public and who is private are not abstractions.

Third, bringing in these affected and affective voices will necessarily make transparent multiple meanings to the idea of justice and different principles for arriving at justice. This plurality and difference are not only part and parcel of contemporary democracy, but are arguably necessary to it. So it seems absurd to have to state that people who are victims are as diverse as people who offend. Thus, just as institutions of representative democracy must constantly adjust and respond to many communities and overlapping concerns, so too must justice institutions serve diversity.[7] These institutions may be essential to the architecture of a democratic system, but engagement with its *demos* is essential to the legitimacy of justice in a wider sense. This is less an argument for court community engagement programmes (for example) and more one for routine inclusion of those of the *demos* who are directly affected in particular cases.

Emerging from these three points is recognition that space designed with particular characteristics – here actually *spaces* to achieve justice for and on behalf of the political community – can work to demand more of citizens. While some deliberative democrats may look for disinterested

---

[5] Archon Fung, 'The Principle of Affected Interests and Inclusion in Democratic governance' in Jack Nagel and Rogers Smith (eds), *Representation: Elections and Beyond* (U Penn P 2013); Jane Mansbridge and others, 'The Place of Self-Interest and the Role of Power in Deliberative Democracy' (2010) 18 *The Journal of Political Philosophy* 64–100.

[6] This is an argument made by traditionalists as well as abolitionists (Matt Matravers, 'The Victim, the State and Civil Society' in Anthony Bottoms and Julian Roberts (eds), *Hearing the Victim: Adversarial Justice, Crime Victims and the State* (Willan 2010); Heather Strang, *Repair or Revenge: Victims and Restorative Justice* (Clarendon Press 2002)).

[7] Archon Fung, 'Continuous Institutional Innovation and the Pragmatic Conception of Democracy' (2012) 44 *Polity* 609–24.

publics or non-partisan discussants, it is directly affected citizens who bring issues of personal and public concern to the door of criminal justice. Some quite obviously walk away and leave it to authorities to deal with. Most would like information about what is to be done, and many ask for more involvement. These spaces ask for a unique practice of citizenship – reporting, giving information, responding to query, being available, asking questions, being interviewed, giving evidence, offering impact and so on. Presently the institutions simply take these actions. As an opportunity, however, it is rich with potential; potential to recast the process as a deliberative system.[8] The possibility does not require dramatic change. Justice professionals should ask individuals what justice means to them (and to those around them), what values they think might inhabit a just process and just outcome, and what outcomes they might wish to see for the trilogy of victim, offender and community. For the many good people who work within and alongside criminal justice, the proposition may seem an impossible luxury. But the fact is that these interactions already take place. The spaces in which professionals work can be made to do more by asking individuals for reasoning about their preferences and encouraging thinking and discussion that is broad and deep, collective and individual. It is hard work, but work that nurtures judgment and decision. It argues making deliberation work for justice. It argues that achieving justice is not just a decision.

Justice practitioners may wearily roll their eyes at these suggestions and turn to the next case file. But how can a prosecutor balance different concerns within the public interest if these are not all made transparent and each actively considered? The public prosecutor should retain overall responsibility to pursue and protect the public interest. But they do not own the victim any more than they own the accused person. Each of these civilian parties, as well as the prosecutor, share interests in the fair administration of justice but what this looks like in detail is likely to be different. One civilian party has access to legal representation to ensure these detailed interests are protected but the other does not. Various domestic and international legal systems have found ways to respond to this gap. The issue now for common law adversarial systems is how to design a victim advocate role. Currently these professionals are diverse and scattered with different disciplinary foci. They must use their greater exposure to the citizen-victim through the course of the latter's engagement with various justice entities to both open out their client's justice

---

[8] John Parkinson and Jane Mansbridge (eds), *Deliberative Systems* (CUP 2012).

reasoning but also to ensure decision-makers hear it and take account of it. If they seek representation and rights for people as victims and witnesses within criminal justice then victim advocates must bring justice back in to their work with victims.

In combination, these arguments imagine criminal justice as a space for an ethical citizen. Crucially, however, a fifth point necessarily must recognize that not everything can be resolved or is reconcilable after violence and from the experience of injustice.[9] While the emphasis on participation in justice of affected persons recognizes a human capacity for reflexivity, it does not assume or require forgiveness, healing, restoration or even agreement. Inclusive deliberation is not a guarantee of an agreed shared outcome (if this is one idea of justice). It is certainly also no assurance of 'satisfaction'. Participation is simply based on rights of more profound origin than a legal nod.

Finally, if the democratic turn I make to debate about victims is demanding of them as citizens, it is also (perhaps most importantly) demanding of authorities. On this point there is no gesturing to courtesy or reliance on good people. This point demands that authorities recognize and discharge their duties to people – *both* victims and offenders – as rights-bearing citizens. Lest this assertion suggest subservience, the space actually demands active engagement with ethical practice by justice professionals; in particular, for authorities to guard against their own power and their own convenience. The citizen-victims in the Justice Study articulated goals for themselves as well as for others. When matters came to court, however, personal goals often fell away. How easy it is for time-poor justice practitioners to let victim-oriented concerns disappear into the shadows of the law. An ethical practice of justice would accept obligation to each in the justice trilogy; would make sure each is articulated and acted upon.

THE PLACE AND POLITICS OF JUSTICE

In closing I return to ponder Jonathon Simon's remarks that people who were victims of crime and who sought recognition from and involvement with the justice system were anti-democratic. It was this inference that turned me to consider whether democratic theory had anything to say to justice. It seemed to me that Simon assumed people as victims did not or could not demonstrate 'solidarity and responsibility' within criminal

---

[9] Iris Marion Young, *Justice and the Politics of Difference* (Princeton UP 1990); Chantal Mouffe, *On the Political* (Routledge 2005).

justice. This obligation is surely a shared one. I hope anyway that I have been able to show a little of how 'solidarity and responsibility' can be enacted in spaces where people are afforded equal respect and concern.

Hitherto, the victim's exclusion from criminal justice has not been recognized as a democratic deficit. Indeed the very notion of democratic practices has been excluded. The orthodox space of contemporary criminal justice allows only strictly circumscribed roles and recitals to victims – and also to offenders. Criminal justice evokes different fears, expectations and imagery where experts rule. It is a powerful presence in our democratic society more than it is actually present in ordinary people's lives. It provides a window through which to see mundane even squalid pictures of human interaction. It is a platform on which different performances are enacted – those drawing on the flourish of high principle and lofty language, and those depicting skirmish and dissonance.

The justice system highlights the social divisions, conflicts and entitlements that give rise to the commission of crime. It draws attention to ways in which the system regulates these divisions and acts to punish transgression. This way of thinking about the political in justice – its social control function – is recognized. Obscured from our understanding of the justice system as political is the exclusion of affected citizens – victims as well as offenders – from a direct and dignified role. The legal justification for this marginalization has masked what is in effect a profoundly anti-democratic rationale. Underneath the high rhetoric about public interest and representing community is simply utilitarian logic. This is a project that human rights law and activism has yet to discover. What is at stake is not only fair and inclusive justice, but deep democracy.

Appendix: Justice Study methodology*

The Justice Study methodology consisted of:

- lay and legal populations;
- a longitudinal prospective panel of lay participants;
- quantitative survey with repeat measures and scales;
- qualitative interviewing;
- discourse mapping and analysis.

The Lay Sample of Citizen-Victims

The lay sample comprised persons who had been victims of violence and who were in contact with support services. The selection criteria for the sample were that:

- people were aged 18 years and over;
- people were primary victims in that they had directly experienced the conduct from which the criminal charge arose;
- the incident included some element of violence; and
- the incident from which the charge arose was committed in the Australian Capital Territory (ACT) and hence would be resolved in the ACT courts.

The number of lay participants comprising the longitudinal panel commenced with N=33 and ended with N=19 (Table A.1), and their characteristics were diverse (Table A.2).

* Aspects of the methods of the Justice Study were first published in Robyn Holder, 'Untangling the meanings of justice: a longitudinal mixed methods study' (2016), *Journal of Mixed Methods Research,* (online), a Sage journal. Reproduced with permission.

Table A.1 Numbers and percentage of lay interviews at three stages

Interview	Total (%)
TIME 1	33 (100)
TIME 2	26 (79)
TIME 3	19 (58)

Table A.2 Demographic characteristics of lay participants (N=33)

Demographics	Domestic assault (female) N=27	Non-domestic assault (male) N=6	Total N=33 (%)[1]
Australian born	23	6	29 (88)
English only spoken	19	5	24 (73)
Aboriginal	0	0	0
Disability	1	2	3 (9)
Children at home	19	2	21 (64)
Home rental	13	5	18 (55)
Employment status			
Full-time	11	2	13 (39)
Part-time	6	2	8 (24)
Other	10	2	12 (36)
Occupation			
Professional, managerial	9	3	12 (36)
Clerical, sales, service	4	1	5 (15)
Tradesperson, labourer, transport, factory	2	2	4 (12)
Missing	12	0	12 (36)
Level of education			
Tertiary	9	2	12 (33)
Secondary	16	3	19 (57)
Other	1	1	2 (6)
Gross annual income			
Under $25k	10	3	13 (39)
$25–45k	4	1	5 (15)
$45–100k	11	2	13 (39)
$100–250k	1	0	1 (3)
Missing	1	0	1 (3)

Note: [1] Percentages rounded up or down to the nearest percentage point.

The prospective interview schedule commenced after police had charged an alleged offender. Table A.3 displays this as procedural point 1 (Time 1). The next two procedural points, Time 2 and Time 3, comprised a combination of both retrospective and prospective questions.

Table A.3 Justice study design: procedural interview points and outcome for each

Interview	Procedural interview point	Substantive outcome
Time 1	After police had charged an accused person with an offence and prior to a court hearing	The police arrest and charge decision
Time 2	After the finalization of the matter at court	The decision to prosecute or not, and on what charges
		The court verdict and sentence (if any)
Time 3	Approximately six to eight months after finalization	Overall justice done

Survey/Interview Design

The Time 1 survey comprised 82 questions, generating 273 variables plus qualitative narrative. Parts dealt with the incident, after effects and the offender; others with the police response, and prospective preferences. A final section asked about civic and social values. Factor analysis of assessment of justice items was used to reduce the data and to identify clusters. Scales relating to various aspects of people's civic identity and orientation were created as:

a) disinterested justice assessment scales
b) social value scales
c) personal and offender assessments
d) specific justice assessment scales and repeat measures (Table A.4).

The Time 2 instrument was in four parts. Part I dealt with overall feeling about justice and safety; Part II dealt with prosecution; Part III with the court; and Part IV about other support. The Time 3 instrument consisted of some closed questions but was predominately open and semi-structured.

Table A.4 Items comprising the justice assessment scales (and repeat measures) (N=33)

Scale	Variables	Reliability Score[A]	Mean inter-item correlation
Outcome acceptance	Agree with decision Accept decision Honest explanation for decision Understand decision Decision fair Decision expected	0.9	0.78
Quality of interpersonal treatment[D]	I was treated with respect I was treated with dignity Fair treatment of me Respect my rights[B] Helpful[B] Treated as victim[B]	0.9	0.6
Influential voice	Opportunity to express views Able to influence decision Views considered before decision Decision deserved Decision wanted	0.84	0.52
Respect offender rights[D]	Treated the violent person with respect Respect offender rights[B]	0.83	0.71

Notes: [A] Cronbach's alpha (rounded).
[B] Reverse scored item.
[D] Variables comprising these scales in the second survey were scored on a six-point Likert scale where 6 = not applicable. The 6 score was treated as a missing value and recoded using the mean of 1 to 5 for each variable.

Bibliography

Adams JS, 'Inequity in Social Exchange' (1965) 2 *Advances in Experimental Social Psychology* 267–99.

Albiston C, 'Legal Consciousness and Workplace Rights', in B Fleury-Steiner and LB Neilson (eds), *The New Civil Rights Research: A Constitutive Approach* (Ashgate 2006) 55–76.

Allen J, S Edmonds, A Patterson and D Smith, 'Policing and the Criminal Justice System – Public Confidence and Perceptions: Findings from the 2004/2005 British Crime Survey Research Study No.07/06' (Home Office 2006).

Anderson J, K Richards and K Willis, *Evaluation of the ACT Sexual Assault Reform Program (SARP): Final Report* Technical and Background Paper No.51 (AIC 2013).

Arnstein S, 'A Ladder of Citizen Participation' (1969) 35 *Journal of the American Institute of Planners* 216–24.

Ashworth A, 'Developments in the Public Prosecutor's Office in England and Wales' (2000) 8 *European Journal of Crime, Criminal Law and Criminal Justice* 257–82.

Ashworth A, *Sentencing and Criminal Justice* (5th ed, Cambridge University Press 2010).

Ashworth A and M Redmayne, *The Criminal Process* (4th ed, Oxford University Press 2010).

Australian Bar Association, *Barristers' Conduct Rules* (ABA November 2010).

Australian Bureau of Statistics, *Women's Safety Survey* Cat 4128.0 (ABS 1996).

Australian Bureau of Statistics, *Crime and Safety, Australia* Cat 4509.0 (ABS April 2005).

Australian Bureau of Statistics, *Crime Victimisation*, Australia 2011–12 Cat 4530.0 (ABS 2013).

Australian Bureau of Statistics, *Criminal Courts 2011–12* Cat 4513.0 (ABS 2013).

Ayres I and J Braithwaite, *Responsive Regulation: Transcending the Deregulation Debate* (Oxford University Press 1992).

Bagaric M, *Punishment and Sentencing: A Rational Approach* (Cavendish Publishing 2001).

Bandura A, *Social Learning Theory* (Prentice-Hall 1977).

Barata P, 'Abused Women's Perspectives on the Criminal Justice System's Response to Domestic Violence' (2007) 31 *Psychology of Women Quarterly* 202–15.

Barber B, *Strong Democracy: Participatory Politics for a New Age* (University of California Press 1984).

Barzilai G, *Communities and Law: Politics and Cultures of Legal Identities* (University of Michigan Press 2003).

Baumeister RF, A Stillwell and SR Wotman, 'Victim and Perpetrator Accounts of Interpersonal Conflict: Autobiographical Narratives about Anger' (1990) 59(5) *Journal of Personality and Social Psychology* 994–1005.

Baumer E and J Lauritsen, 'Reporting Crime to the Police, 1973–2005: a Multivariate Analysis of Long-term Trends in the National Crime Survey (NCS) and National Crime Victimization Survey (NCVS)' (2010) 48 *Criminology* 131–85.

Beattie JM, *Crime and the Courts in England 1660–1800* (Lightening Source 2008).

Bell M, S Perez, L Goodman and M Dutton, 'Battered Women's Perceptions of Civil and Criminal Court Helpfulness: The Role of Court Outcome and Process' (2011) 17 *Violence Against Women* 71–88.

Beloof D, 'The Third Wave of Crime Victims' Rights: Standing, Remedy, and Review' (2005) 2 *Brigham Young University Law Review* 255–370.

Beloof D, P Cassell and S Twist, *Victims in Criminal Procedure* (3rd ed, Carolina Academic Press 2017).

Benhabib S and D Cornell (eds), *Feminism as Critique* (University of Minnesota Press 1987).

Beresford P, 'User Involvement in Research and Evaluation: Liberation or Regulation' (2002) 1 *Social Policy and Society* 95–105.

Berlin I, *The Crooked Timber of Humanity* (Princeton University Press 1990).

Black D, 'The Mobilization of Law' (1973) 2 *The Journal of Legal Studies* 125–49.

Black D, *Towards a General Theory of Social Control* (Academic Press 1984).

Black D and A Reiss, 'Patterns of Behavior in Police and Citizen Transactions' (1967) 2 *Studies in Crime and Law Enforcement in Major Metropolitan Areas* 1–139.

Blackstone A, C Uggen and H McLaughlin, 'Legal Consciousness and Responses to Sexual Harassment' (2009) 43 *Law and Society Review* 631–68.

Blau P, 'Justice in Social Exchange' (1964) 34 *Sociological Inquiry* 193–206.

Blumenthal S, 'Of Mandarins, Legal Consciousness and the Cultural Turn in American Legal History' (2012) 37 *Law and Social Inquiry* 167–86.

Blumer H, *Symbolic Interactionism: Perspective and Method* (University of California Press 1969).

Bochel C, H Bochel, P Somerville and C Worley, 'Marginalised or Enabled Voices? "User Participation" in Policy and Practice' (2008) 7 *Social Policy and Society* 201–10.

Booth T, '"Cooling Out" Victims of Crime: Managing Victim Participation in the Sentencing Process in a Superior Sentencing Court' (2012) 45 *Australian and New Zealand Journal of Criminology* 214–30.

Bosniak L, 'Citizenship Denationalized' (2000) 7 *Indiana Journal of Global Legal Studies* 447–509.

Bourdieu P, 'The Force of Law: Towards a Sociology of the Juridicial Field' (1987) 38 *The Hastings Law Journal* 814–53.

Bradford B, 'Voice, Neutrality and Respect: Use of Victim Support Services, Procedural Fairness and Confidence in the Criminal Justice System' (2011) 11 *Criminology and Criminal Justice* 345–66.

Braithwaite J, *Crime, Shame and Reintegration* (Cambridge University Press 1989).

Braithwaite J, 'Crime in a Convict Republic' (2001) 64 *The Modern Law Review* 11–50.

Braithwaite J and R Nickson, 'Timing Truth, Reconciliation, and Justice after War' (2012) 11 *Ohio State Journal on Dispute Resolution* 443–76.

Braithwaite J and P Pettit, *Not Just Deserts: A Republican Theory of Criminal Justice* (Clarendon Press 1990).

Braithwaite V, *The Community Hopes, Fears and Actions Survey: Goals and Measures* Working Paper No.2 (Centre for Tax System Integrity The Australian National University 2001).

Braithwaite V, *Defiance in Taxation and Governance: Resisting and Dismissing Authority in a Democracy* (Edward Elgar Publishing 2009).

Braithwaite V, 'Security and Harmony Value Orientations and their Roles in Attitude Formation and Change' (2009) 20 *Psychological Inquiry* 162–7.

Brake W, *Shaping History: Ordinary People in European Politics, 1500–1700* (University of California Press 1998).

Brandl SG and F Horvath, 'Crime-Victim Evaluation of Police Investigative Performance' (1991) 19 *Journal of Criminal Justice* 293–305.

Bright S and C Bakalis, 'Anti-Social Behaviour: Local Authority Responsibility and the Voice of the Victim' (2003) 62 *The Cambridge Law Journal* 305–34.

Brockner J and B Wiesenfeld, 'An Integrative Framework for Explaining Reactions to Decisions: Interactive Effects of Outcomes and Procedures' (1996) 120 *Psychological Bulletin* 189–208.

Brockner J, G Ackerman, J Greenberg, MJ Gelfand, AM Francesco, ZX Chen, K Leung, G Bierbrauer, C Gomez, BL Kirkman and D Shapiro, 'Culture and Procedural Justice: The Influence of Power Distance on Reactions to Voice' (2000) 37 *Journal of Experimental Social Psychology* 300–315.

Bronitt S and B McSherry, *Principles of Criminal Law* (2nd ed, Thomson Lawbook Company 2005).

Bumiller K, *The Civil Rights Society: The Social Construction of Victims* (Johns Hopkins University Press 1998).

Burcar V and M Åkerström, 'Negotiating a Victim Identity: Young Men as Victims of Violence' (2009) 10 *Journal of Scandinavian Studies in Criminology and Crime Prevention* 37–54.

Buzawa E and C Buzawa, *Domestic Violence: The Criminal Justice Response* (Sage 2003).

Cahn E and J Cahn, 'Power to the People or the Profession? The Public Interest in Public Interest Law' (1970) 79 *Yale Law Journal* 1005–48.

Cairns D, *Advocacy and the Making of the Adversarial Criminal Trial, 1800–1865* (Clarendon Press 1998).

Campbell T, *Justice* (Palgrave Macmillan 2001).

Carcach C, 'Reporting Crime to the Police' (1997) 68 *Trends and Issues* (Australian Institute of Criminology).

Cardenas J, 'The Crime Victim in the Prosecutorial Process' (1986) 9 *Harvard Journal of Law and Public Policy* 358–98.

Carlsmith K, 'The Roles of Retribution and Utility in Determining Punishment' (2006) 42 *Journal of Experimental Social Psychology* 437–51.

Carlsmith K, J Darley and P Robinson, 'Why do we Punish? Deterrence and Just Deserts as Motives for Punishment' (2002) 83 *Journal of Personality and Social Psychology* 284–99.

Carr S, 'Participation, Power, Conflict and Change: Theorising Dynamics of Service User Participation in the Social Care System of England and Wales' (2007) 27 *Critical Social Policy* 266–76.

Cassell P, 'In Defense of Victim Impact Statements' (2008) 6 *Ohio State Journal of Criminal Law* 611–48.

Christie N, 'Conflicts as Property' (1977) 17 *British Journal of Criminology* 1–15.

Christie N, 'The Ideal Victim' in E Fattah (ed), *From Crime Policy to Victim Policy: Reorienting the Justice System* (Macmillan 1986) 17–30.

Clare J and F Morgan, 'Factors Affecting Perceived Criminality: Evidence from Victims of Assault' (2009) *Trends and Issues in Crime and Justice* (Australian Institute of Criminology).

Clayton S and S Opotow, 'Justice and Identity: Changing Perspectives on What is Fair' (2003) 7 *Personality and Social Psychology Review* 298–310.

Cook B, F David and A Grant, *Victims' Needs, Victims' Rights: Policies and Programs for Victims of Crime in Australia* Research and Public Policy Series No.19 (Australian Institute of Criminology 1999).

Cornell D, *The Imaginary Domain: Abortion, Pornography, and Sexual Harassment* (Routledge 1995).

Corns C, 'Police Summary Prosecutions in Australia and New Zealand: Some Comparisons' (2000) 19 *University of Tasmania Law Review* 280–310.

Cornwall A, 'Unpacking "Participation": Models, Meanings and Practices' (2008) 43 *Community Development Journal* 269–83.

Cotterrell R, *The Politics of Jurisprudence: A Critical Introduction to Legal Philosophy* (Butterworths 1989).

Cotterrell R, *Law, Culture and Society: Legal Ideas in the Mirror of Social Theory* (Ashgate Publishing 2006).

Couldry N, *Inside Culture: Re-imagining the Method of Cultural Studies* (Sage 2000).

Council of Europe, *The Role of the Public Prosecution in the Criminal Justice System* Recommendation Rec(2000)19, 4 <https://rm.coe.int/16804be55a> accessed 10 October 2017.

Cowdery N, 'Challenges to Prosecutorial Discretion' (2013) 39 *Commonwealth Law Bulletin* 17–20.

Coy M and L Kelly, *Islands in the Stream* (Trust for London 2011).

Crawford A (ed), *International and Comparative Criminal Justice and Urban Governance* (Cambridge University Press 2011).

Crenshaw K, 'Mapping the Margins: Intersectionality, Identity Politics, and Violence Against Women of Color' (1991) 43 *Stanford Law Review* 1241–99.

Crespi F, *Social Action and Power* (Blackwell 1992).

Cropanzo R and M Ambrose, 'Procedural and Distributive Justice are More Similar Than You Think: A Monistic Perspective and a Research Agenda' in J Greenberg and R Cropanzano (eds), *Advances in Organizational Justice* (Stanford University Press 2001) 119–51.

Cussen T and M Lyneham, 'ACT Family Violence Intervention Program Review' Technical and Background Papers No.52 (Australian Institute of Criminology 2012).

Dahl R, *Democracy and its Critics* (Yale University Press 1989).

Dai M, J Frank and I Sun, 'Procedural Justice During Police-Citizen Encounters: The Effects of Process-Based Policing on Citizen Compliance and Demeanor' (2011) 39 *Journal of Criminal Justice* 159–68.

Daly K, 'Mind the Gap: Restorative Justice in Theory and Practice' in A Von Hirsch (ed), *Restorative Justice and Criminal Justice: Competing or Reconcilable Paradigms?* (Hart Publishing 2003) 219–36.

Daly K and B Bouhours, *Conventional and Innovative Justice Responses to Sexual Violence* (Australian Institute of Family Studies 2011).

Darley J and D Gromet, 'The Psychology of Punishment: Intuition and Reason' in R Bobocel, A Kay, M Zanna and J Olson (eds), *The Psychology of Justice and Legitimacy: The Ontario Symposium* 11th Vol (Taylor and Francis 2010) 229–50.

Darley J and T Pittman, 'The Psychology of Compensatory and Retributive Justice' (2003) 7 *Personality and Social Psychology Review* 324–36.

Davis R and C Mulford, 'Victim Rights and New Remedies: Finally Getting Victims their Due' (2008) 24 *Journal of Contemporary Criminal Justice* 198–208.

D'Cruze S, *Everyday Violence in Britain, 1850–1950: Gender and Class* (Longman 2000).

De Brouwer A, 'What the International Criminal Court Has Achieved and Can Achieve for Victims/Survivors of Sexual Violence' (2009) *International Review of Victimology* 183–209.

De Certeau M, *The Practice of Everyday Life* (Rendall, S. trans) (University of California Press 1984).

Deetz S, *Democracy in an Age of Corporate Colonization: Developments in Communication and the Politics of Everyday Life* (State University of New York Press 1992).

Deutsch M, *Distributive Justice: A Social-Psychological Perspective* (Yale University Press 1985).

Devlin P, *The Criminal Prosecution in England* (Oxford University Press 1960).

Didion J, *The White Album* (Farrar, Straus and Giroux 1990).

Doak J, 'Victims' Rights in Criminal Trials: Prospects for Participation' (2005) 32 *Journal of Law and Society* 294–316.

Doak J, *Victims' Rights, Human Rights and Criminal Justice: Reconceiving the Role of Third Parties* (Hart Publishing 2008).

Doak J and D Mahoney, 'The Venegeful Victim? Assessing the Attitudes of Victims Participating in Restorative Youth Conferencing' (2006) 13 *International Review of Victimology* 157–77.

Dryzek J, *Discursive Democracy: Politics, Policy, and Political Science* (Cambridge University Press 1990).

Dryzek J, *Deliberative Democracy and Beyond: Liberals, Critics, Contestations* (Oxford University Press 2000).

Dryzek J, 'The Deliberative Democrat's Idea of Justice' (2013) 12 *European Journal of Political Theory* 329–46.

Duff RA, *Punishment, Communication, and Community* (Oxford University Press 2001).

Duff RA, 'Philosophy and "The Life of the Law"' (2009) 26 *Journal of Applied Philosophy* 245–58.

Duff RA, 'Towards a Theory of Criminal Law' (2010) 84(1) *Proceedings of the Aristotelian Society Supplementary Volume* 1–28.

Dzur A, 'Civic Implications of Restorative Justice Theory: Citizen Participation and Criminal Justice Policy' (2003) 36 *Policy Sciences* 279–306.

Dzur A, *Punishment, Participatory Democracy, and the Jury* (Oxford University Press 2012).

Edwards I, 'An Ambiguous Participant: The Crime Victim and Criminal Justice Decision-Making' (2004) 44 *British Journal of Criminology* 967–82.

Elias R, *Victims of the System: Crime Victims and Compensation in American Politics and Criminal Justice* (Transaction Books 1983).

Elliott I, S Thomas and J Ogloff, 'Procedural Justice in Contacts with the Police: The Perspective of Victims of Crime' (2012) 13 *Police Practice and Research: An International Journal* 437–49.

Emsley C, 'Crime and Punishment: 10 Years of Research' (2005) 9 *Crime, History and Societies* 1–21.

Englebrecht C, 'Where Do I Stand? An Exploration of the Rules That Regulate Victim Participation in the Criminal Justice System' (2012) 7 *Victims and Offenders* 161–84.

Equality and Human Rights Commission, *Human Rights in Action: Case Studies from Regulators, Inspectorates and Ombudsmen (RIOs)* (EHR 2014).

Erez E, 'Integrating Restorative Justice Principles in Adversarial Proceedings' in E Cape (ed), *Reconcilable Rights? Analysing the Tension between Victims and Defendants* (Legal Action Group 2004) 81–96.

Erez E, M Kilchling and J Wemmers (eds), *Therapeutic Jurisprudence and Victim Participation: International Perspectives* (Carolina Academic Press 2011).

Ewick P and S Silbey, 'Conformity, Contestation, and Resistance: An Account of Legal Consciousness' (1992) 26 *University of New England Law Review* 731–49.

Ewick P and S Silbey, *The Common Place of Law* (The University of Chicago Press 1998).

Ezendam H and F Wheldon, 'Recognition of Victims' Rights through EU Action: Latest Developments and Challenges' in F Mukwiza, A Pemberton and I Vanfraechem (eds), *Justice for Victims: Perspectives on Rights, Transition and Reconciliation* (Routledge 2014) 51–65.

Felson R, S Messner, A Hoskin and G Deane, 'Reasons for Reporting and Not Reporting Domestic Violence to the Police' (2002) 40 *Criminology* 617–48.

Felstiner W, R Abel and A Sarat, 'Emergence and Transformation of Disputes: Naming, Blaming, Claiming' (1981) 15 *Law and Society Review* 631–54.

Ferraro K, 'Policing Woman Battering' (1989) 36 *Social Problems* 61–74.

Findlay M, S Odgers and S Yeo, *Australian Criminal Justice* (4th ed, Oxford University Press 2010).

Fionda J, *Public Prosecutors and Discretion: A Comparative Study* (Clarendon Press 1995).

Fleury-Steiner R, D Bybee, C Sullivan, J Belknap and H Melton, 'Contextual Factors Impacting Battered Women's Intentions to Reuse the Criminal Legal System' (2006) 34 *Journal of Community Psychology* 327–42.

Flynn A, 'Bargaining with Justice: Victims, Plea Bargaining and the *Victims' Charter Act 2006* (VIC)' (2011) 37 *Monash Law Review* 73–96.

Folger R and R Cropanzano, 'Fairness Theory: Justice as Accountability' in J Greenberg and R Cropanzano (eds), *Advances in Organizational Justice* (Stanford University Press 2001) 1–55.

Folger R, R Cropanzano, TA Timmerman, JC Howes and D Mitchell, 'Elaborating Procedural Fairness: Justice Becomes both Simpler and More Complex' (1996) 22 *Personality and Social Psychology Bulletin* 435–41.

Ford D, 'Prosecution as a Victim Power Resource: A Note on Empowering Women in Violent Conjugal Relationships' (1991) 25 *Law and Society Review* 313–34.

Forst BF and JC Heron, 'The Criminal Justice Response to Victim Harm' in *Research in Brief* (US Department of Justice 1985).

Frederick B and D Stemen, *The Anatomy of Discretion: An Analysis of Prosecution Decision-Making* (Vera Institute of Justice 2012).

Fung A, 'Continuous Institutional Innovation and the Pragmatic Conception of Democracy' (2012) 44 *Polity* 609–24.

Fung A, 'The Principle of Affected Interests and Inclusion in Democratic Governance' in J Nagel and R Smith (eds), *Representation: Elections and Beyond* (University of Pennsylvania Press 2013) 236–68.

Galanter M, 'Justice in Many Rooms: Courts, Private Ordering, and Indigenous Law' (1981) 13 *Journal of Legal Pluralism* 1–47.

Garland D, *The Culture of Control: Crime and Social Order in Contemporary Society* (Oxford University Press 2001).

Geertz C, *Local Knowledge* (Basic Books 1983).

Genn H, *Paths to Justice: What People Do and Think about Going to Law* (Hart Publishing 1999).

Gergen K and M Gergen, 'Polyvocal Organizing: An Exploration' in C Steyaert and B Van Looy (eds), *Relational Practices, Participative Organizing*, Vol 7 (Emerald Group Publishing 2010) 261–73.

Gibbs N, 'The Nature of Law as an Interpretive Practice and Its Associated Modes of Inquiry' (2009) 29 *Legal Studies* 576–91.

Giddens A, *The Constitution of Society* (Polity Press 1984).

Gilligan C, *In a Different Voice: Psychological Theory and Women's Development* (Harvard University Press 1982).

Gilling D, 'Crime Control and Due Process in Confidence-Building Strategies: A Governmentality Perspective' (2010) 50 *British Journal of Criminology* 1136–54.

Godfrey B, 'Changing Prosecution Practices and their Impact on Crime Figures, 1857–1940' (2008) 48 *British Journal of Criminology* 171–89.

Godfrey B and G Dunstall (eds), *Crime and Empire – 1840–1940: Criminal Justice in Local and Global Context* (Willan 2005).

Goodey J, *Victims and Victimology: Research, Policy and Practice* (Pearson Education 2005).

Gordon R, 'Critical Legal Histories' (1984) 36 *Stanford Law Review* 57–125.

Gordon R, 'Critical Legal Histories Revisited: A Response' (2012) 37 *Law and Social Inquiry* 200–215.

Goudriaan H, J Lynch and P Nieuwbeerta, 'Reporting to the Police in Western Countries: A Theoretical Analysis of the Effects of Social Context' (2004) 21 *Justice Quarterly* 933–69.

Goudriaan H, K Wittebrood and P Nieuwbeerta, 'Neighbourhood Characteristics and Reporting Crime Effects of Social Cohesion, Confidence in Police Effectiveness and Socio-Economic Disadvantage' (2006) 46 *British Journal of Criminology* 719–42.

Gourash N, 'Help-Seeking: A Review of the Literature' (1978) 6 *American Journal of Community Psychology* 413–23.

Greenberg J and R Cropanzano (eds), *Advances in Organizational Justice* (Stanford University Press 2001).

Greenberg M and R Ruback, *After the Crime: Victim Decision-Making* (Plenum Press 1992).

Greenberg M, R Ruback and D Westcott, 'Decision Making by Crime Victims: A Multi-Method Approach' (1982) 17 *Law and Society Review* 47–84.

Greenhouse C, B Yngvesson and D Engel, *Law and Community in Three American Towns* (Cornell University Press 1994).

Gromet D and J Darley, 'Punishment and Beyond: Achieving Justice through the Satisfaction of Multiple Goals' (2009) 43 *Law and Society Review* 1–38.

Guest J, *Ordinary People* (Viking Press 1976).

Hadfield G, 'Framing the Choice between Cash and the Courthouse: Experiences with the 9/11 Victims Compensation Fund' (2008) 42 *Law and Society Review* 645–82.

Hall M, *Victims of Crime: Policy and Practice in Criminal Justice* (Willan 2009).

Hampton J, 'Retribution and the Liberal State' (1994) 5 *Journal of Contemporary Legal Issues* 117–44.

Harris JW, *Legal Philosophies* (2nd ed, Butterworths 1997).

Harris N, 'Shame, Ethical Identity and Conformity: Lessons from Research on the Psychology of Social Influence' in S Karstedt, I Loader and H Strang (eds) *Emotions, Crime and Justice* (Hart Publishing 2011) 193–209.

Hart T and C Rennison, 'Reporting Crime to the Police, 1992–2000' in *Special Report* (US Bureau of Justice Statistics 2003).

Hatfield E, W Walster and E Berscheid, *Equity: Theory and Research* (Allyn and Bacon 1978).

Hauenstein N, T McGonigle and S Flinder, 'A Meta-Analysis of the Relationship between Procedural Justice and Distributive Justice: Implications for Justice Research' (2001) 13 *Employee Responsibilities and Rights Journal* 39–56.

Hay D, 'Controlling the English Prosecutor' (1983) 21 *Osgoode Hall Law Journal* 165–86.

Hay D, 'The Criminal Prosecution in England and its Historians' (1984) 47 *The Modern Law Review* 1–29.

Hay D, 'Prosecution and Power: Malicious Prosecution in the English Courts, 1750–1850', in D Hay and F Snyder (eds), *Policing and Prosecution in Britain 1750–1850* (Oxford University Press 1989) 343–95.

Hay D, P Linebaugh, J Rule, EP Thompson and C Winslow, *Albion's Fatal Tree: Crime and Society in 18th Century England* (Pantheon Books 1975).

Hay D and F Snyder, *Policing and Prosecution in Britain 1750–1850* (Oxford University Press 1989).

Herman J, *Trauma and Recovery: The Aftermath of Violence – From Domestic Abuse to Political Terror* (Basic Books 1992).

Herman J, 'Justice from the Victim's Perspective' (2005) 11 *Violence Against Women* 571–602.

Hetherington T, *Prosecution and the Public Interest* (Pergamon Press 1989).

Hindelang M and M Gottfredson, 'The Victim's Decision not to Invoke the Criminal Justice Process' (1976) *Criminal Justice and the Victim* 57–78.

Hinds L and K Murphy, 'Public Satisfaction with Police: Using Procedural Justice to Improve Police Legitimacy' (2007) 40 *Australian and New Zealand Journal of Criminology* 27–42.

Hoffman E, 'Legal Consciousness and Dispute Resolution: Different Disputing Behaviour at Two Similar Taxicab Companies' (2003) 28 *Law and Social Inquiry* 691–718.

Hogg R and D Brown, *Rethinking Law and Order* (Pluto Press Sydney 1998).

Holder R, 'Police and Domestic Violence: An Analysis of Domestic Violence Incidents Attended by Police in the ACT and Subsequent Actions' (2007) *Research Paper No.4* Australian Domestic and Family Violence Clearinghouse.

Holder R, 'The Quality of Justice: Operation of the Victims of Crime Act 1994 in the Australian Capital Territory 1996–2007' (Victims of Crime Coordinator 2008).

Holder R, 'Satisfied? Exploring Victims' Justice Judgements' in D Wilson and S Ross (eds), *Crime, Victims and Policy: International Contexts, Local Experiences* (Palgrave Macmillan 2015) 184–213.

Holder R, 'Untangling the Meanings of Justice: A Longitudinal Mixed Methods Study' (2016) *Journal of Mixed Methods Research*, online DOI: 10.1177/1558689816653308.

Holder R, 'Seeing the State: Human Rights Violations of Victims of Crime and Abuse of Power' in L Weber, E Fishwick and M Marmo (eds) *The Routledge International Handbook of Criminology and Human Rights* (Routledge 2017) Ch. 39.

Holder R and J Caruana, 'Criminal Justice Intervention in Family Violence in the ACT 1998–2006' (VoCC 2006).

Holder R and K Daly, 'Sequencing Justice: A Longitudinal Study of Justice Goals of Domestic Violence Victims' (2017) *British Journal of Criminology* doi:10.1093/bjc/azx046.

Holder R and N Mayo, 'What Do Women Want? Prosecuting Family Violence in the ACT' (2003) 15 *Current Issues in Criminal Justice* 5–25.

Hoyle C, *Negotiating Domestic Violence* (Clarendon Press 1998).

Hughes R, *The Fatal Shore* (Vintage 2003).
Hunt A, 'Law, Community, and Everyday Life: Yngvesson's Virtuous Citizens and Disruptive Subjects' (1996) 21 *Law and Social Inquiry* 173–84.
Irvine R and J Stansbury, 'Citizen Participation in Decision-Making: Is it Worth the Effort?' (2004) 64 *Public Administration Review* 55–65.
Isin E, *Being Political: Genealogies of Citizenship* (University of Minnesota Press 2002).
Isin E, 'Citizenship in Flux: The Figure of the Activist Citizen' (2009) 29 *Subjectivity*, 367–88.
Isin EF and B Turner (eds), *Handbook of Citizenship Studies* (Sage Publications 2002).
Jansson K, British Crime Survey: Measuring Crime for 25 Years (2008).
Johnson D, *The Japanese Way of Justice: Prosecuting Crime in Japan* (Oxford University Press 2002).
Johnson H, 'Crime Victimisation in Australia: Results of the 2004 International Crime Victimisation Survey' (Australian Institute of Criminology 2005).
Jonzon E and F Lindblad, 'Disclosure, Reactions, and Social Support: Findings from a Sample of Adult Victims of Child Sexual Abuse' (2004) 9 *Child Maltreatment* 190–200.
Kaukinen C, 'The Help-Seeking Decisions of Violent-Crime Victims: An Examination of the Direct and Conditional Effects of Gender and the Victim-Offender Relationship' (2002) 17 *Journal of Interpersonal Violence* 432–56.
Kaukinen C, 'The Help-Seeking Strategies of Female Violent-Crime Victims: The Direct and Conditional Effects of Race and the Victim-Offender Relationship' (2004) 19 *Journal of Interpersonal Violence* 967–90.
Kearon T and B Godfrey, 'Setting the Scene: A Question of History', in S Walklate (ed), *Handbook of Victims and Victimology* (Willan Publishing 2007) 17–36.
Kelly DP, 'Victims' Perceptions of Criminal Justice' (1984) 11 *Pepperdine Law Review* 15–22.
Kelly L, *Surviving Sexual Violence* (Polity Press 1988).
Kershaw C, S Nicholas and A Walker, 'Crime in England and Wales 2007/08: Findings from the British Crime Survey and Police Recorded Crime' (Home Office 2008).
King P, *Crime, Justice, and Discretion in England 1740–1820* (Oxford University Press 2003).
Kirchengast T, *Victims and the Criminal Trial* (Palgrave Macmillan 2016).

Klug F, 'Human Rights and Victims' in E Cape (ed), *Reconcilable Rights? Analysing the Tension between Victims and Defendants* (Legal Action Group 2004) 111–24.

Kohlberg L, 'Moral Stages and Moralization: The Cognitive-Developmental Approach' (1976) *Moral Development and Behavior: Theory, Research, and Social Issues* 31–53.

Korsgaard C, *The Sources of Normativity* (Cambridge University Press 1996).

Korsgaard C, *The Constitution of Agency: Essays on Practical Reason and Moral Philosophy* (Oxford University Press 2008).

Korsgaard C, *Self-Constitution: Agency, Identity and Integrity* (Oxford University Press 2009).

Krehbiel P and R Cropanzano, 'Procedural Justice, Outcome Favourability and Emotion' (2000) 13 *Social Justice Research* 339–60.

Krone T, 'The Limits of Prosecution Authority' (2003) Regulatory Institutions Network The Australian National University 18.

Kymlicka W, 'Rawls on Teleology and Deontology' (1988) 17 *Philosophy and Public Affairs* 173–90.

Kymlicka W and W Norman, 'Return of the Citizen: A Survey of Recent Work on Citizenship Theory' (1994) 104 *Ethics* 352–81.

Lacey N and C Wells, *Reconstructing Criminal Law: Text and Materials* (2nd ed, Butterworths 1998).

Ladinsky J, 'The Traffic in Legal Services: Lawyer-Seeking Behavior and the Channeling of Clients' (1976) 11 *Law and Society Review* 207–23.

Langbein J, 'The Origins of Public Prosecution at Common Law' (1973) 17 *American Journal of Legal History* 313–35.

Langbein J, 'Albion's Fatal Flaws' (1983) 98 *The Past and Present Society* 96–120.

Langbein J, *The Origins of the Adversary Criminal Trial* (Oxford University Press 2003).

Langford I, 'Fair Trial: The History of an Idea' (2009) 8 *Journal of Human Rights* 37–52.

Law Reform Commission of Australia, *Sentencing of Federal Offenders*, Report No.15 (AGPS 1980).

Laxminarayan M, M Bosmans, R Porter and L Sosa, 'Victim Satisfaction with Criminal Justice: A Systematic Review' (2013) 8 *Victims and Offenders* 119–47.

Lempert R, 'Mobilizing Private Law: An Introductory Essay' (1976) 11 *Law and Society Review* 173–89.

Lerner M, 'The Justice Motive: Some Hypotheses as to its Origins and Forms' (1977) 45 *Journal of Personality* 1–52.

Lerner M, *The Belief in a Just World* (Springer US 1980).

Lerner M, 'The Justice Motive: Where Social Psychologists Found It, How They Lost It, and Why They May Not Find It Again' (2003) 7 *Personality and Social Psychology Review* 388–99.

Levenson L, 'Working Outside the Rules: The Undefined Responsibilities of Federal Prosecutors' (1999) 26 *Fordham Urban Law Journal* 553–71.

Levine J, L Resnick and T Higgins, 'Social Foundations of Cognition' (1993) 44 *Annual Review of Psychology* 585–612.

Lewis R, RP Dobash, RE Dobash and K Cavanagh, 'Protection, Prevention, Rehabilitation or Justice? Women's Use of the Law to Challenge Domestic Violence' (2000) 7 *International Review of Victimology* 179–205.

Liang B, L Goodman, P Tummala-Nurra and S Weintrub, 'A Theoretical Framework for Understanding Help-Seeking Processes among Survivors of Intimate Partner Violence' (2005) 36 *American Journal of Community Psychology* 71–84.

Lievore D, 'No Longer Silent: A Study of Women's Help-Seeking Decisions and Service Responses to Sexual Assault' (Australian Institute of Criminology 2005).

Lind EA, 'Fairness Heuristic Theory: Justice Judgments as Pivotal Cognitions in Organizational Relations' in J Greenberg and R Cropanzano (eds), *Advances in Organizational Justice* (Stanford University Press 2001) 56–88.

Lind EA and T Tyler, *The Social Psychology of Procedural Justice* (Plenum Press 1988).

Livingstone S, P Lunt and L Miller, 'Citizens, Consumers and the Citizen-Consumer: Articulating the Citizen Interest in Media and Communications Regulation' (2007) 1 *Discourse and Communication* 63–89.

Loader I, 'Policing, Recognition, and Belonging' (2006) 605 *The ANNALS of the American Academy of Political and Social Science* 202–21.

MacCoun R, 'Voice, Control, and Belonging: The Double-Edged Sword of Procedural Fairness' (2005) 1 *Annual Review of Law and Social Science* 171–201.

Macedo S (ed), *Deliberative Politics: Essays on Democracy and Disagreement* (Oxford University Press 1999).

MacIntyre A, *After Virtue* (2nd ed, Duckworth 1984).

Mackenzie G, C Spiranovic, K Warner, N Stobbs, K Gelb, D Indermaur, L Roberts, R Broadhurst and T Bouhours, 'Sentencing and Public Confidence: Results from a National Australian Survey on Public Opinions Towards Sentencing' (2012) 45 *Australian and New Zealand Journal of Criminology* 45–65.

Maguire M and T Bennett, *Burglary in a Dwelling: The Offence, the Offender, and the Victim* (Heinemann 1982).

Malsch M, *Democracy in the Courts: Lay Participation in European Criminal Justice Systems* (Routledge 2009).

Mani R, *Beyond Retribution: Seeking Justice in the Shadows of War* (Polity Press 2004).

Manikis M, 'Navigating Through an Obstacle Course: The Complaints Mechanism for Victims of Crime in England and Wales' (2012) 12 *Criminology and Criminal Justice* 149–73.

Manikis M, 'Imagining the Future of Victims' Rights in Canada: A Comparative Perspective' (2015) 13 *Ohio State Journal of Criminal Law* 163–86.

Mansbridge J, J Bohman, S Chambers, D Estlund, A Føllesdal, A Fung, C Lafont, B Manin and JL Martí, 'The Place of Self-Interest and the Role of Power in Deliberative Democracy' (2010) 18 *The Journal of Political Philosophy* 64–100.

Mansbridge J, J Bohman, S Chambers, T Christiano, A Fung, J Parkinson, DF Thompson and ME Warren, 'A Systemic Approach to Deliberative Democracy' in J Parkinson and J Mansbridge (eds), *Deliberative Systems* (Cambridge University Press 2012) 1–26.

Marcus P and V Waye, 'Australia and the United States: Two Common Criminal Justice Systems Uncommonly at Odds' (2004) 12 *Tulane Journal of International and Comparative Law* 27–116.

Marks RJ, 'Some Research Perspectives for Looking at Legal Need and Legal Services Delivery Systems: Old Forms or New' (1976) 11 *Law and Society Review* 191–205.

Marshall A, 'Injustice Frames, Legality, and the Everyday Construction of Sexual Harassment' (2003) 28 *Law and Social Inquiry* 659–89.

Marshall A and S Barclay, 'In Their Own Words: How Ordinary People Construct the Legal World' (2003) 28 *Law and Social Inquiry* 617–28.

Martin G, '"Ordinary People Only": Knowledge, Representativeness, and the Publics of Public Participation in Healthcare' (2008) 30 *Sociology of Health & Illness* 35–54.

Matravers M, 'The Victim, the State, and Civil Society' in A Bottoms and J Roberts (eds), *Hearing the Victim: Adversarial Justice, Crime Victims and the State* (Willan 2010) 1–16.

Matsuda M, 'Looking to the Bottom: Critical Legal Studies and Reparations' (1987) 22 *Harvard Civil Rights-Civil Liberties Law Review* 323–99.

Mayhew P and J Reilly, 'Victims' Experiences and Needs: Findings from the New Zealand Crime and Safety Survey 2006' (New Zealand Ministry of Justice 2008).

McAdams RH, 'A Focal Point Theory of Expressive Law' (2000) 86 *Virginia Law Review* 1649–729.
McBarnet D, 'Magistrates' Courts and the Ideology of Justice' (1981) 8 *British Journal of Law and Society* 181–97.
McBarnet D, 'Victim in the Witness Box – Confronting Victimology's Stereotype' (1983) 7 *Contemporary Crises* 293–303.
McCann M, *Rights at Work: Pay Equity Reform and the Politics of Legal Mobilization* (University of Chicago Press 1994).
McFarlane J, P Willson, D Lemmey and A Malecha, 'Women Filing Assault Charges on an Intimate Partner' (2000) 6 *Violence Against Women* 396–408.
McGonigle Lehy B, *Procedural Justice? Victim Participation in International Criminal Proceedings* (Intersentia 2011).
McGregor K, L Renshaw and H Andrevski, *ACT Victims of Crime Referral Project: Final Report* Technical and Background Paper No.55 (Australian Institute of Criminology 2013).
McLaughlin H, 'What's in a Name: "client", "patient", "customer", "consumer", "expert by experience", "service user" – what's next?' (2009) 39 *British Journal of Social Work* 1101–17.
Mendus S, 'The Importance of Love in Rawls' Theory of Justice' (1999) 29 *British Journal of Political Science* 57–75.
Menkel-Meadow C, 'From Legal Disputes to Conflict Resolution and Human Problem-Solving: Legal Dispute Resolution in a Multidisciplinary Context' (2004) 54 *Journal of Legal Education* 7–29.
Merry S, *Getting Justice and Getting Even: Legal Consciousness among Working-Class Americans* (The University of Chicago Press 1990).
Meuser M and U Nagel, 'The Expert Interview and Changes in Knowledge Production' in A Bogner, B Littig and W Menz (eds), *Interviewing Experts* (Palgrave Macmillan 2009) 17–42.
Meyers D, 'Two Victim Paradigms and the Problem of "Impure" Victims' (2011) *Humanity* 255–75.
Mezey N, 'Out of the Ordinary: Law, Power, Culture, and the Commonplace' (2001) 26 *Law and Social Inquiry* 145–67.
Mikula G, 'On the Experience of Injustice' (1993) 4 *European Review of Social Psychology* 223–44.
Mikula G, 'Testing an Attribution-of-Blame Model of Judgments of Injustice' (2003) 33 *European Journal of Social Psychology* 793–811.
Mikula G, K Scherer and U Athenstaedt, 'The Role of Injustice in the Elicitation of Differential Emotional Reactions' (1998) 24 *Personality & Social Psychology Bulletin* 769–83.
Mikula G and K Schlamberger, 'What People Think About an Unjust Event: Toward a Better Understanding of the Phenomenology of

Experiences of Injustice' (1985) 15 *European Journal of Social Psychology* 37–49.
Miller D and N Vidmar, 'The Social Psychology of Punishment Reactions' in M Lerner and S Lerner (eds), *The Justice Motive in Social Behaviour* (Academic Press 1981) 145–72.
Miller R and A Sarat, 'Grievances, Claims, and Disputes: Assessing the Adversary Culture' (1981) 15 *Law and Society Review* 525–66.
Mills L, 'Killing Her Softly: Intimate Abuse and the Violence of State Intervention' (1999) 113 *Harvard Law Review* 550–613.
Montada L and M Lerner (eds), *Responses to Victimization and Belief in a Just World* (Plenum Press 1998).
Morenoff J, R Sampson and S Raudenbush, 'Neighborhood Inequality, Collective Efficacy, and the Spatial Dynamics of Urban Violence' (2001) 39 *Criminology* 517–58.
Morgan B and K Yeung, *An Introduction to Law and Regulation: Text and Materials* (Cambridge University Press 2007).
Morgan J and L Zedner, *Child Victims: Crime, Impact and Criminal Justice* (Oxford University Press 1992).
Moriarty L and RA Jerin (eds), *Current Issues in Victimology Research* (Carolina Academic Press 2007).
Mouffe C, 'Citizenship and Political Identity' (1992) 61 *October* 28–32.
Mouffe C, *On the Political* (Routledge 2005).
Mouzos J and T Makkai, 'Women's Experiences of Male Violence: Findings from the Australian Component of the International Violence Against Women Survey (IVAWS)' (Australian Institute of Criminology 2004).
Mulhall S and A Swift, *Liberals and Communitarians* (Wiley 1996).
Mullen C, D Hughes and P Vincent-Jones, 'The Democratic Potential of Public Participation: Healthcare Governance in England' (2011) 20 *Social and Legal Studies* 21–38.
Murphy K, 'Public Satisfaction with Police: The Importance of Procedural Justice and Police Performance in Police-Citizen Encounters' (2009) 42 *Australian and New Zealand Journal of Criminology* 159–78.
Murphy K, B Murphy and M Mearns, 'The 2007 Public Safety and Security in Australia Survey: Survey Methodology and Preliminary Findings Working Paper No.16' (Alfred Deakin Research Institute 2010a).
Murphy K, B Murphy and M Mearns, The 2009 Public Safety and Security in Australia Survey: Survey Methodology and Preliminary Findings Working Paper No.17 (Alfred Deakin Research Institute 2010b).

Myjer E, B Hancock and N Cowdery (eds), *Human Rights Manual for Prosecutors* (Wolf Legal Publishers 2009).

Nader L (ed), *Law in Culture and Society* (University of California Press 1969).

Neal D, *The Rule of Law in a Penal Colony: Law and Power in Early New South Wales* (Cambridge University Press 1991).

Nespor J, 'Morphologies of Inquiry: The Uses and Spaces of Paradigm Proliferation' (2006) 19 *International Journal of Qualitative Studies in Education* 115–28.

New Zealand Ministry of Justice, Examining the Prosecution Systems of England and Wales, Canada, Australia and Scotland: a background document to the Review of Public Prosecution Services in New Zealand (NZ Ministry of Justice 2011).

Newburn T and E Stanko, 'When Men are Victims: The Failure of Victimology' in T Newburn and E Stanko (eds), *Just Men Doing Business: Men, Masculinities and Crime* (Routledge 1994) 153–65.

Nielsen L, 'Situating Legal Consciousness: Experiences and Attitudes of Ordinary Citizens About Law and Street Harassment' (2000) 34 *Law and Society Review* 1055–90.

Novisky M and R Peralta, 'When Women Tell: Intimate Partner Violence and the Factors Related to Police Notification' (2015) 21 *Violence Against Women* 65–86.

O'Neill O, *Bounds of Justice* (Cambridge University Press 2000).

Orth U, L Montada and A Maercker, 'Feelings of Revenge, Retaliation Motive, and Posttraumatic Stress Reactions in Crime Victims' (2006) 21 *Journal of Interpersonal Violence* 229–43.

Parkinson J and J Mansbridge (eds), *Deliberative Systems* (Cambridge University Press 2012).

Pateman C, *Participation and Democratic Theory* (Cambridge University Press 1970).

Pattie C, P Seyd and P Whiteley, *Citizenship in Britain: Values, Participation and Democracy* (Cambridge University Press 2004).

Pemberton A and S Reynaers, 'The Controversial Nature of Victim Participation: Therapeutic Benefits in Victim Impact Statements' in E Erez, M Kitchling and JA Wemmers (eds), *Therapeutic Jurisprudence and Victim Participation in Justice: International Perspectives* (Carolina Academic Press 2011).

Pescosolido B, 'Beyond Rational Choice: The Social Dynamics of How People Seek Help' (1992) 97 *American Journal of Sociology* 1096–138.

Piaget J, *The Child's Conception of the World* (Rowman and Littlefield 1929).

Piven F, *Challenging Authority: How Ordinary People Change America* (Roman and Littlefield Publishers 2006).

Plater D, 'The Development of the Prosecutor's Role in England and Australia with Respect to its Duty of Disclosure: Partisan Advocate or Minister of Justice?' (2006) 25 *University of Tasmania Law Review* 111–55.

Plater D, 'The Changing Role of the Modern Prosecutor: Has the Notion of "Minister of Justice" Outlived its Usefulness?' PhD Thesis (University of Tasmania 2011) <http://eprints.utas.edu.au/10743/2/David_Plater_whole.pdf> accessed 8 October 2017.

Plater D and L Line, 'Has the "Silver Thread" of the Criminal Law Lost its Lustre? The Modern Prosecutor as a Minister of Justice' (2012) 31 *University of Tasmania Law Review* 55–95.

Postow BC, 'Ethical Relativism and the Ideal Observer' (1978) 39(1) *Philosophy and Phenomenological Research* 120–21.

Rand MR, 'Criminal Victimization, 2008' in *Bureau of Justice Statistics Bulletin* (US Department of Justice 2009).

Rawls J, *A Theory of Justice* (Belknap Harvard 1971).

Rawls J, *Justice as Fairness: A Restatement* (Belknap Harvard 2001).

Roach K, *Due Process and Victims' Rights: The New Law and Politics of Criminal Justice* (University of Toronto Press 1999).

Roberts J, 'Public Confidence in Criminal Justice in Canada: A Comparative and Contextual Analysis' (2007) 49 *Canadian Journal of Criminology and Criminal Justice* 153–84.

Roberts J and E Erez, 'Communication in Sentencing: Exploring the Expressive Function of Victim Impact Statements' (2004) 10 *International Review of Victimology* 223–44.

Roberts L and D Indermaur, 'What Australians Think About Crime and Justice: Results from the 2007 Survey of Social Attitudes', Research and Public Policy Series 101 (Australian Institute of Criminology 2009).

Robinson A and M Stroshine, 'The Importance of Expectation Fulfilment on Domestic Violence Victims' Satisfaction with the Police in the UK' (2005) 28 *Policing: An International Journal of Police Strategies & Management* 301–20.

Robinson P, 'Why does the Criminal Law Care what the Layperson Thinks is Just? Coercive Versus Normative Crime Control' (2000) 86 *Virginia Law Review* 1839–69.

Rock P, *After Homicide: Practical and Political Responses to Bereavement* (Oxford University Press 1998).

Rock P, 'Victims, Prosecutors and the State in Nineteenth Century England and Wales' (2004) 4 *Criminal Justice* 331–54.

Rock P, *Constructing Victims' Rights: The Home Office, New Labour, and Victims* (Oxford University Press 2004).
Rock P, 'Aspects of the Social Construction of Crime Victims in Australia' (2006) 1 *Victims and Offenders* 289–321.
Rock P, 'New Labour Policies for Victims' (2007) 67 *Criminal Justice Matters* 38–9.
Rodgers K, 'Wife Assault: The Findings of a National Survey', *Juristat Service Bulletin* March (Statistics Canada 1994).
Ross M and D Miller (eds), *The Justice Motive in Everyday Life* (Cambridge University Press 2002).
Ruback R, M Greenberg and D Westcott, 'Social Influence and Crime-Victim Decision Making' (1984) 40 *Journal of Social Issues* 51–76.
Rubenstein K, 'Citizenship and the Centenary: Inclusion and Exclusion in 20th Century Australia' (2000) 24 *Melbourne University Law Review* 576–608.
Sadurski W, *Giving Desert its Due: Social Justice and Legal Theory* (Reidel Publishing Company 1985).
Sampson RJ, SW Raudenbush and F Earls, 'Neighborhoods and Violent Crime: A Multilevel Study of Collective Efficacy' (1997) 277 *Science* 918–24.
Samuels G, 'Review of the New South Wales Director of Public Prosecutions' Policy and Guidelines for Charge Bargaining and Tendering of Agreed Facts' (NSW Attorney General's Department 2002).
Sandel M, *Liberalism and the Limits of Justice* (Cambridge University Press 1982).
Sandel M, 'The Procedural Republic and the Unencumbered Self' (1984) 2 *Political Theory* 81–96.
Sandel M, *Justice: What's the Right Thing to Do* (Farrar, Straus and Giroux 2009).
Sanders A (ed), *Prosecution in Common Law Jurisdictions* (Dartmouth Publishing Group 1996).
Sarat A, 'Law is all over: Power, Resistance, and the Legal Consciousness of the Welfare Poor' (1990) 2 *Yale Journal of Law and the Humanities* 343–79.
Sarat A, 'Vengeance, Victims and the Identities of Law' (1997) 6 *Social and Legal Studies* 163–89.
Sarat A and C Clarke, 'Beyond Discretion: Prosecution and the Logic of Sovereignty, and the Limits of Law' (2008) 33 *Law and Social Inquiry* 387–416.
Sarat A, M Constable, D Engel, V Hans and S Lawrence (eds), *Crossing Boundaries: Traditions and Transformations in Law and Society Research* (Northwestern University Press 1998).

Sarat A and TR Kearns (eds), *Law in Everyday Life* (The University of Michigan Press 1993).

Sarat A and TR Kearns (eds), *Justice and Injustice in Law and Legal Theory* (University of Michigan Press 1996).

Sarat A and TR Kearns (eds), *Law in the Domains of Culture* (The University of Michigan Press 1998).

Scanlon T, *What We Owe to Each Other* (Harvard University Press 1998).

Sced M, Public Satisfaction with Police Contact – Part II: Self-Initiated Contacts (Australasian Centre for Policing Research 2004).

Scheingold S, *The Politics of Rights: Lawyers, Public Policy, and Political Change* (2nd ed, University of Michigan Press 2004).

Scherer K (ed), *Justice: Interdisciplinary Perspectives* (Cambridge University Press 1992).

Schroeder D, J Steel, A Woodell and A Bembenek, 'Justice within Social Dilemmas' (2003) 7 *Personality and Social Psychology Review* 374–87.

Schwartz D, *Culture and Power: The Sociology of Pierre Bourdieu* (University of Chicago Press 1997).

Scott J, R Matland, P Michelbach and B Bornstein, 'Just Deserts: An Experimental Study of Distributive Justice Norms' (2001) 45 *American Journal of Political Science* 749–67.

Sebba L, *Third Parties: Victims and the Criminal Justice System* (Ohio State University Press 1996).

Sen A, *The Idea of Justice* (The Belknap Press of Harvard University Press 2009).

Shapland J, 'Victims, the Criminal Justice System and Compensation' (1984) 24 *The British Journal of Criminology* 131–49.

Shapland J (ed), *Justice, Community and Civil Society: A Contested Terrain* (Willan Publishing 2008).

Shapland J, J Willmore and P Duff, *Victims in the Criminal Justice System* (Gower Publishing 1985).

Shklar J, *The Faces of Injustice* (Yale University Press 1990).

Silbey S, 'After Legal Consciousness' (2005) 1 *Annual Review of Law and Society* 323–68.

Simon J, *Governing Through Crime: How the War on Crime Transformed American Democracy and Created a Culture of Fear* (Oxford University Press 2007).

Skitka L, 'Of Different Minds: An Accessible Identity Model of Justice Reasoning' (2003) 7 *Personality and Social Psychology Review* 286–97.

Skitka L, 'Exploring the "Lost and Found" of Justice Theory and Research' (2009) 22 *Social Justice Research* 98–116.

Skitka L, N Aramovich, B Lytle and E Sargis, 'Knitting Together an Elephant: An Integrative Approach to Understanding the Psychology of Justice Reasoning' in R Bobocel, A Kay, M Zanna and J Olson (eds), *The Psychology of Justice and Legitimacy: The Ontario Symposium* 11th Vol. (Taylor and Francis 2010) 1–26.

Skitka L, J Winquist and S Hutchinson, 'Are Outcome Fairness and Outcome Favorability Distinguishable Psychological Constructs? A Meta-Analytical Review' (2003) 16 *Social Justice Research* 309–41.

Sklansky D, 'The Problems with Prosecutors' (2017) 14 *Annual Review of Criminology* 2.1-2.19, doi.org/10.1146/annurev-criminol-032317-092440.

Skogan W, 'Citizen Reporting of Crime: Some National Panel Data' (1976) 13 *Criminology* 535–49.

Skogan W, 'Reporting Crimes to the Police: The Status of World Research' (1984) 21 *Journal of Research in Crime and Delinquency* 113–37.

Smith D, 'Public Confidence in the Criminal Justice System: Findings from the British Crime Survey 2002/03 to 2007/08' Research Series 16/10 (Ministry of Justice 2010).

Snare F, 'Misfortune and Injustice: On Being Disadvantaged' (1986) 16 *Canadian Journal of Philosophy* 39–61.

Stanko E, *Intimate Intrusions: Women's Experiences of Male Violence* (Routledge and Kegan Paul 1985).

Stanko E, *Everyday Violence: How Women and Men Experience Sexual and Physical Danger* (HarperCollins 1990).

Stenning P, *Appearing for the Crown: A Legal and Historical Review of Criminal Prosecutorial Authority in Canada* (Brown Legal Publications 1986).

Stenning P, *The Modern Prosecution Process in New Zealand* (Victoria University Press 2008).

Stover E, *The Witnesses: War Crimes and the Promise of Justice in The Hague* (University of Pennsylvania Press 2011).

Strang H, *Repair or Revenge: Victims and Restorative Justice* (Clarendon Press 2002).

Swift A, *Political Philosophy: A Beginners' Guide for Students and Politicians* (3rd ed, Polity Press 2014).

Tapley J, 'From "Good Citizen" to "Deserving Client": The Relationship between Victims of Violent Crime and the State Using Citizenship as The Conceptualising Tool' PhD thesis (University of Southampton 2003).

Temkin J and B Krahé, *Sexual Assault and the Justice Gap: A Question of Attitude* (Hart Publishing 2008).

Terdiman R, 'The Force of Law: Translator's Introduction' (1987) 38 *Hastings Law Journal* 805–13.

Tetlock PE, PS Visser, R Singh, M Polfroni, A Scott, SB Elson, P Mazzocco and P Rescober, 'People as Intuitive Prosecutors: The Impact of Social Control Goals on Attributions of Responsibility' (2006) 43 *Journal of Experimental Social Psychology* 195–209.

Thibaut J and L Walker, *Procedural Justice: A Psychological Analysis* (Lawrence Erlbaum Associates Publishers 1975).

Thompson EP, *Whigs and Hunters: The Origin of the Black Act* (Pantheon Books 1975).

Thumim N, 'Mediated Self-Representations: "Ordinary people" in "Communities"' in S Herbrechter and M Higgins (eds), *Returning (to) Communities: Theory, Culture and Political Practice of the Communal* (Rodopi B.V 2006) 255–74.

Tibori-Szabó K and M Hirst, *Victim Participation in International Criminal Justice: Practitioners' Guide* (Asser Press 2017).

Tilley C, *Democracy* (Cambridge University Press 2007).

Turner J, *A Theory of Social Interaction* (Stanford University Press 1988).

Tyler T, *Why People Obey the Law* (Princeton University Press 1990/ 2006).

Tyler T, 'A Psychological Perspective on the Legitimacy of Institutions and Authorities' in J Jost and B Major (eds), *The Psychology of Legitimacy: Emerging Perspectives on Ideology, Justice and Intergroup Relations* (Cambridge University Press 2001) 416–36.

Tyler T and S Blader, 'The Group Engagement Model: Procedural Justice, Social Identity, and Cooperative Behavior' (2003) 7 *Personality and Social Psychology Review* 349–61.

Tyler T, R Boeckmann, H Smith and H Yuen, *Social Justice in a Diverse Society* (Westview Press 1997).

Tyler T and Y Huo, *Trust in the Law: Encouraging Public Cooperation with the Police and Courts* (Russell Sage Foundation 2002).

Umbreit M, R Coates and B Kalanj, *Victim Meets Offender: The Impact of Restorative Justice and Mediation* (Criminal Justice Press 1994).

Van den Bos K and EA Lind, 'The Psychology of Own Versus Others' Treatment: Self-oriented and Other-oriented Effects on Perceptions of Procedural Justice' (2001) *Personality and Social Psychology Bulletin* 1324–33.

Van den Bos K, R Vermunt and H Wilke, 'Procedural and Distributive Justice: What is Fair Depends More on What Comes First Than on What Comes Next' (1997) 72 *Journal of Personality and Social Psychology* 95–104.

Van Dijk J, J Van Kesteren and P Smit, 'Criminal Victimisation in International Perspective: Key Findings from the 2004–2005 ICVS and EU ICS' (WODC 2007).
Van Kesteren J, P Mayhew and P Nieuwbeerta, 'Criminal Victimisation in Seventeen Industrialized Countries: Key Findings from the 2000 International Crime Victims Survey' (WODC 2000).
Van Stokkom B, 'Victims' Needs and Participation in Justice: Is There a Role for Vengeance?' (2013) 1 *Restorative Justice: An International Journal* 168–89.
Vidmar N and R Schuller, 'Individual Differences and the Pursuit of Legal Rights' (1987) 11 *Law and Human Behaviour* 299–317.
Wacks R, *Philosophy of Law: A Very Short Introduction* (Oxford University Press 2006).
Walby S and J Allen, 'Domestic Violence, Sexual Assault and Stalking: Findings from the British Crime Survey Home Office Research Study 276' (Home Office 2004).
Walklate S, *Imagining the Victim of Crime* (Open University Press 2007).
Walklate S (ed), *Handbook of Victims and Victimology* (Willan Publishing 2007).
Walster E, W Walster and E Berscheid, *Equity Theory and Research* (Allyn and Bacon 1978).
Walzer M, *Spheres of Justice: A Defense of Pluralism and Equality* (Basic Books 1983).
Waye V and P Marcus, 'Australia and the United States: Two Common Criminal Justice Systems Uncommonly at Odds' (2009) 18 *Tulane Journal of International and Comparative Law* 335–401.
Weitekamp E and H-J Kerner (eds), *Restorative Justice: Theoretical Foundations* (2nd ed, Taylor and Francis 2011).
Wells W, 'Type of Contact and Evaluations of Police Officers: The Effects of Procedural Justice across Three Types of Police-Citizen Contacts' (2007) 35 *Journal of Criminal Justice* 612–21.
Wemmers J, *Victims in the Criminal Justice System* (Kugler Publications 1996).
Wemmers J, 'The Meaning of Justice for Victims' in S Shoham, P Knepper and M Kett (eds) *International Handbook of Victimology* (CRC Press 2010) 27–43.
Wemmers J and K Cyr, 'Victims' Perspective on Restorative Justice: How Much Involvement are Victims Looking For?' (2004) 11 *International Review of Victimology* 259–74.
Wemmers J and K Cyr, 'What Fairness Means to Crime Victims: A Social Psychological Perspective on Victim-Offender Mediation' (2006) 2 *Applied Psychology in Criminal Justice*, 102–28.

White C, *Bridging Divides in Transitional Justice: The Extraordinary Chambers in the Courts of Cambodia* (Intersentia 2017).
White L, 'Subordination, Rhetorical Survival Skills, and Sunday Shoes: Notes on the Hearing of Mrs G' (1990) 38 *Buffalo Law Review* 1–58.
Whitehead E, 'Witness Satisfaction: Findings from the Witness Satisfaction Survey 2000' Home Office Research Study 230 (Home Office 2001).
Williams R, *Keywords: A Vocabulary of Culture and Society* (Routledge 1976/2011).
Williams R, *Marxism and Literature* (Oxford University Press 1977).
Willis T and F Gibbons, 'Commentary: Using Psychological Theory in Help-Seeking Research' (2009) 16 *Clinical Psychology: Science and Practice* 440–44.
Wong K, 'Black's Theory on the Behaviour of Law Revisited' (1995) 23 *International Journal of the Sociology of Law* 189–232.
Woods G, *A History of Criminal Law in New South Wales: The Colonial Period 1788–1900* (The Federation Press 2002).
Yngvesson B, *Virtuous Citizens, Disruptive Subjects: Order and Complaint in a New England Court* (Routledge 1993).
Young A, *Imagining Crime: Textual Outlaws and Criminal Conversations* (Sage 1996).
Young IM, 'Impartiality and the Civic Public' in S Benhabib and D Cornell (eds), *Feminism as Critique* (University of Minnesota Press 1987) 57–76.
Young IM, *Justice and the Politics of Difference* (Princeton University Press 1990).
Young IM, *Inclusion and Democracy* (Oxford University Press 2000).
Young R and A Sanders, 'The Ethics of Prosecution Lawyers' (2004) 7 *Legal Ethics* 190–209.
Zehr H, *Changing Lenses: A New Focus for Criminal Justice* (Herald Press 1990).
Zelditch M, 'Theories of Legitimacy' in J Jost and B Major (eds), *The Psychology of Legitimacy: Emerging Perspectives on Ideology, Justice and Intergroup Relations* (Cambridge University Press 2001) 33–53.
Zemans F, 'Framework for Analysis of Legal Mobilization: A Decision-Making Model' (1982) 7 *Law and Social Inquiry* 989–1071.
Zemans F, 'Legal Mobilization: The Neglected Role of the Law in the Political System' (1983) 77 *The American Political Science Review* 690–703.

Index